TWO-YEAR COLLEGE WRITING STUDIES

TWO-YEAR COLLEGE WRITING STUDIES

Rationale and Praxis for Just Teaching

EDITED BY
DARIN JENSEN AND BRETT GRIFFITHS

UTAH STATE UNIVERSITY PRESS
Logan

© 2023 by University Press of Colorado

Published by Utah State University Press
An imprint of University Press of Colorado
1580 North Logan Street, Suite 660
PMB 39883
Denver, Colorado 80203-1942

All rights reserved

 The University Press of Colorado is a proud member of the Association of University Presses.

The University Press of Colorado is a cooperative publishing enterprise supported, in part, by Adams State University, Colorado State University, Fort Lewis College, Metropolitan State University of Denver, University of Alaska Fairbanks, University of Colorado, University of Denver, University of Northern Colorado, University of Wyoming, Utah State University, and Western Colorado University.

ISBN: 978-1-64642-467-2 (hardcover)
ISBN: 978-1-64642-468-9 (paperback)
ISBN: 978-1-64642-469-6 (ebook)
https://doi.org/10.7330/9781646424696

Library of Congress Cataloging-in-Publication Data

Names: Jensen, Darin Lee, editor. | Griffiths, Brett M., 1973– editor.
Title: Two-year college writing studies : rationale and praxis for just teaching / edited by Darin Jensen and Brett Griffiths.
Description: Logan : Utah State University Press, [2023] | Includes bibliographical references and index.
Identifiers: LCCN 2023023169 (print) | LCCN 2023023170 (ebook) | ISBN 9781646424672 (hardcover) | ISBN 9781646424689 (paperback) | ISBN 9781646424696 (ebook)
Subjects: LCSH: English language—Rhetoric—Study and teaching (Higher) | Report writing—Study and teaching (Higher) | Community colleges. | Junior colleges.
Classification: LCC PE1404 .T96 2023 (print) | LCC PE1404 (ebook) | DDC 808/.0420711—dc23/eng/20230819
LC record available at https://lccn.loc.gov/2023023169
LC ebook record available at https://lccn.loc.gov/2023023170

Cover photo: "Something Good," by Dr. Charissa Che

CONTENTS

Foreword
  Mark Reynolds   vii

Acknowledgments   xi

1. Introduction: Sign o' the Times
    Brett Griffiths and Darin Jensen   3

2. A Social Justice Institution
    Patrick Sullivan   27

3. Identity Agents in the Two-Year College Classroom
    Bernice Olivas   47

4. Translating Habits of Persistence: Supporting Generation 1 Learners in the Community College
    Emily K. Suh   61

5. "I've Never Been a Good Writer": Disrupting Raciolinguistically Marginalized Students' Negative Writerly Self-Image
    Jamila M. Kareem   79

6. Institutional Thinking from Thirdspace: A Case Study of Interactional Inquiry into 2YC Student Learning Outcomes
    Rhonda Grego   102

7. "The Painful Eagerness of Unfed Hope": Equity-Centered Writing Assessment
    Kirsten Higgins, Anthony Warnke, and Jake Frye   129

8. Strategic Organizing: Scaling Up Two-Year College Teacher-Scholar-Activism
    Joanne Baird Giordano and Holly Hassel   145

    Afterword: Considering the Conversation
    Darin Jensen and Brett Griffiths   162

    Index   175
    About the Authors   187

FOREWORD

Mark Reynolds

When I began teaching in a two-year college in 1968, fresh from a graduate teaching assistantship and MA graduate program, like most of my colleagues at the time and for years afterwards, I was eager and excited but unknowingly unprepared to teach mostly composition to a diverse student population of mainly first-generation college students. Naïve as I was, I expected students like those I had just left at the university, especially since the textbooks for my four Composition 101 classes were the same ones I had used at the university. I prepared a similar syllabus and marched forth the first day to meet four large writing classes ranging from twenty-eight to thirty-one students. After introductory remarks in each class, I asked the students for a writing sample—a page explaining their expectations and goals for their first year at the college. When I read those papers later that afternoon, it didn't take long for me to realize that not only was the syllabus inappropriate but so were the textbooks—a rhetoric, a collection of expository essays, and a grammar handbook—and that I'd have to rethink everything and immediately seek advice from colleagues who already had a couple of years' experience at the college.

Fortunately, those colleagues were helpful, because in those days the few publications available about composition were not. Luckily for me and my colleagues, a new professional group had emerged nationally in the form of NCTE two-year college regional organizations, which held annual conferences in different areas of the country, including my Southeast. A few years later, a new national journal, *Teaching English in the Two-Year College* (*TETYC*) was created at East Carolina University. It began to publish pedagogical articles, providing a significant resource for those teaching in two-year institutions. For those of us who availed ourselves of them, those two early support systems, along with colleagues, sustained us, helped nurture us, and above all, let us know we did not labor alone. Soon, the new field of rhetoric and composition blossomed and produced considerable literature, journals, and books, and multiple conferences and workshops around the country. The problem, of course, was that the focus was on university-level students, scholarship, and research. We two-year faculty had to extrapolate from those new resources, adapt, modify, and outright reject much that was irrelevant to our situations.

I was fortunate, however, in 1975, to discover a new graduate program especially established at Carnegie Mellon University to train two-year college English faculty. It was one of the first such programs in the country, but like most at the time, short-lived (1975–1983), yet of great value for those lucky enough to participate. Other than a scattering of similar programs and some doctor of arts programs, appropriate professional development and help for teaching in the nation's two-year colleges remained dismally limited.

In those early decades of two-year college growth, much training of necessity was self-initiated and self-directed and full of trial and error. Faculty who were interested, dedicated, motivated, or desperate relied for help with teaching writing on journal articles in *TETYC*, the *Journal of Basic Writing*, *The Writing Center Journal*, *Technical Writing Teacher*, and occasional articles in "university journals" by scholars like Peter Elbow on freewriting, Nancy Sommers on revision, and Ed White on writing assessment. We also turned, with rarity, to books, notably from Mina Shaughnessy on basic writing and Mike Rose on open-access education.

With the "university journals" and the large numbers of books on composition and rhetoric regularly published from the 1970s on, we always had to be judicious in our choices and were almost always forced to adapt the material to our own students and institutions, whether it dealt with reader-response theory, tagmemics, literacy narratives, storying, heuristics, or rhetorical analysis. Not until the 1990s did significant books begin to appear exclusively about work in two-year English studies. Even so, limited numbers of books about two-year English get published, and *TETYC* remains the only journal exclusively dedicated to two-year college English pedagogy, scholarship, and research.

That is why it is both exciting and important to have this present volume that focuses solely on the teaching of writing in two-year colleges. It also helpfully provides in its introduction and conclusion important assessments of the current state of two-year college English and an account of some of the biggest problems currently facing two-year faculties: the lack of appropriate graduate training, the overuse of and inappropriate working conditions of adjunct faculties, and the almost total neglect of two-year college research in writing studies.

Importantly, many of the essays that follow in this collection offer new insights by mining contemporary thinking in such important areas as critical race theory and identity theory and applying those theories to two-year college writing classrooms. Essays cover writing assessment and explore appropriate curriculum for two-year students. The collection's second chapter by Patrick Sullivan hopefully reminds us that two-year college history grew out of the Truman Commission's late 1940s mandate to shore up democracy by providing affordable education for all through the nation's two-year colleges. This chapter stands in contrast to the final chapter, a significant discussion about the dangers of neoliberal policies that resulted in the dismantling of the University of Wisconsin's system of two-year campuses, recounted by two faculty members who lived that disgraceful and damaging political nightmare. Never has it been more important to remember the promising ideal promoted by the Truman Commission as we continue to strive for social equity and justice across all the nation's institutions and in our daily lives.

As it should be, two-year faculties can read in this collection studies and analyses conducted by those with experience in two-year college classrooms. They do not have to slog through university research reports trying to determine whether those reports have anything of value that can be adapted to fit their unique working and teaching situation. Two-year professionals can take from these essays valuable material for their daily work and become energized to continue the campaign for appropriate studies and analyses of two-year college work and their recognition by all of English studies.

It should never have taken nearly two decades for another book to be published about teaching and researching writing in the nation's two-year colleges, especially since, as two-year scholars have been pointing out for years and this book reasserts, the majority of teaching writing in college occurs in two-year institutions. The excellent essays in this volume serve as models for the kinds of discussions two-year faculties need to support their professional development. These examples should inspire other volumes as two-year professionals diligently work to assure two-year colleges a proper and respected place at higher education's table and to fill the void in appropriate two-year college writing scholarship.

ACKNOWLEDGMENTS

We began writing this book in another era—before COVID-19—working at different institutions than the ones where we work now. We envisioned this project as a way of giving back to the authors and colleagues who have so generously nurtured us in this field. Reviewers of the pre-COVID-19 draft of this manuscript offered rich critique and generative inquiries for our consideration just as the world began to shutter its doors and reinvent our ways of being and knowing, of teaching and learning with one another, in person and online. We owe a debt of gratitude to those reviewers for pushing us to dig deeper into what it means to write a book on two-year college writing studies and to the many colleagues who talked through this book idea with us at conferences, in hallways, or in chat rooms.

We owe an immense debt of gratitude to the authors in this anthology who revised and reinvented their chapters as the world around us seemed to shut down, reconfigure, and reemerge, all while they continued to mentor and support their students, colleagues, and institutions through this time with resilience and—yes—through fatigue. Thank you for your patience, your willingness to push your own questions, and your willingness to continue working with us to bring this book out on the other side. We have learned so much from you—and we continue to do so. We believe this book is only possible because of your shared perspectives and experiences. We know readers will continue to reap these benefits for some time in the future. Thank you.

Finally, we would like to thank our families (Sara, Lindsey, Ian, Max and Sebastian, Aaron, and Raphael) for their support of our unusual—and we believe essential—obsessions.

TWO-YEAR COLLEGE WRITING STUDIES

1
INTRODUCTION
Sign o' the Times

Brett Griffiths and Darin Jensen

NECESSARY IS NOT ENOUGH: TROUBLING COMMUNITY COLLEGE WRITING STUDIES

We brought together this collection during the years 2019–2021: a strange and terrible moment in history, a potential fulcrum for critical corrections in education. We were teaching, tutoring, advising, and administering programs from mostly remote and hybrid environments—meeting with students via web-conferencing tools, communicating largely through texts, chats, videos; voicing our challenges, concerns, encouragements to stacks of small black boxes and the occasional face, smile, colleague, friend, nod of a student on a screen that looked eerily like the opening to the *Brady Bunch*. When we met our students in person, half of our faces—that is to say, most of our emotions—were hidden behind masks, shields, and plexiglass dividers. We felt, in some ways, more removed from our students than we had ever been. In other ways, however, we were closer to our students' lives; their homes and families were opened, more visible, their living rooms and kitchens overflowing into the provisional spaces where we hosted our COVID-19 classrooms, writing centers, and office hours.

At the margins of our classroom screens and learning-management systems, a consistent feed of violence streamed live: Black citizens were insulted, attacked, and murdered through sanctioned and unsanctioned violence by the state, Asians and Asian Americans were attacked, spit on, cut, and murdered. A coalition of insurgents made up of white supremacists, Christian Nationalists, and chaos opportunists caused the buckling of Washington, DC, a global symbol—however flawed or romantic—of the ideals of deliberative intellectualism and aspirational humanism. The pandemic has cost more than 1,100,000 lives in the United States alone and has revealed even more clearly the ways our society is inequitable and often hostile. Without any irony, we feel the prescience of

https://doi.org/10.7330/9781646424696.c001

whoever first said truth is stranger than fiction. Quite literally, rhetoric is on trial in the US—and our students, the students of two-year colleges, are squatting at McDonalds and in our college parking lots to access reliable wi-fi to access a sliver of the uplift promised them by mythologies of American exceptionalism. Neither of us as editors, nor any of the writers here, likely imagined—no matter how dire we thought our situation was—that we would live and teach in our current dystopia.

In the chapters that follow, writers detail the ways their teaching and research efforts seek to unseat the pernicious reproduction of racist and classist institutional structures and to decrease the struggles for being and identity our students face every day in their pursuit of an education and an even playing field. Our writers describe the deliberative dialogues they engage on their campuses and with their disciplinary peers to recognize the role of rhetoric and composition in the social uplift of students enrolled in two-year colleges, students who disproportionately represent minoritized, disabled, first-generation, and/or otherwise underrepresented people in the enrollment histories of our higher education in the US (American Association of Community Colleges 2022). They describe their efforts to collaborate and adapt to top-down reform initiatives, to advocate for the very best teaching and assessment approaches to support and sustain their students. Ultimately, the authors of the final chapter in this book describe the systematic and politically motivated dismantling of the two-year college system in Wisconsin, where efforts to "reform education" led to the dramatic divorce of rural citizens from educational opportunities available in urban areas. Their case study echoes a mass disenfranchisement of students from academic transfer paths that emphasize learning and critical thinking to outcomes-driven education imperatives that prioritize completion and credentialing (i.e., Arum and Roska 2011; Johnson 2013).

It is not an aberration that the murder of George Floyd drove many of us out of our homes to defend the lives of our neighbors. Nor was it an aberration to when Right-wing radicals assaulted the capital and seat of our democracy. These moments are not new; they are more of the same—the US wrestling with the legacy of our democratic and our white-supremacist social contracts (Mills 2014). Those of us who work in two-year colleges know this because it has been playing out in our classrooms, in our institutions, and in the education policies that have shaped our work since the day our work began. It is present in the policy and economic rifts between our institutions and the neighboring universities down the road, and we hear it in the deafening silence and patronage of our colleagues at those universities who advocate for equity but frequently dismiss the day-to-day work at open-access colleges aimed at bringing it about. We know our pleas to administrators, to our colleagues in the field, to our professors and mentors in graduate school have gone largely unheard. For, even as disciplinary leaders call on us to "get uncomfortable" (Inoue 2019), to fight the racism and systemic injustices our country's educational systems reproduce through us, two-year colleges and the work they do generally go unnamed—or, perhaps worse, are raised solely to champion workforce development or bemoan low graduation rates (see, e.g., Jacobs and Worth 2019; Juszkiewicz 2017; McPhail 2011; Yarnall, Tennant, and Stites 2016). That is to say, half the instruction of the field and a disproportionate percentage of minority students are overlooked, elided, ignored, or pigeonholed even in these pleas. Our students continue to go unnamed, unseen, and labeled as unprepared, unacademic, and "not college material"—at least for the university down the street or up on the hill. As we pass the twentieth anniversary of John Lovas's (2002) clarion warning from 2002, "You cannot represent a field if you ignore half of it. You cannot generalize about composition if you don't know half of the work being done" (276), we argue twenty years is too long. We cannot trouble this concern enough. We know our own mentors, advisors, and colleagues often see our work as "less than" the work of four-year institutions or "outside the purview" of graduate mentoring and education. We know serving and advocating for those most underserved in our education system is not appealing when it happens every day, when it doesn't check a box for a tenure application at a research institution. Still, we struggle to understand how those advocating for equity in our field can visibly ignore two-year college professionals and activists. We struggle to understand how elite members of our field can marshal calls for equity and inclusion, all while unaware of or unperturbed by the teaching and learning environments of the two-year college. We think this lack of awareness and interest can only be possible in a world where the public disciplinary discourse has grown disparate from and desensitized to the professional reality of more than half its members.

NOT "JUST TEACHING": DISCIPLINARITY AND PROFESSION IN TWO-YEAR COLLEGE WRITING STUDIES

To interrogate the disconnect between disciplinary hallmarks and professional realities, we must disentangle the notions of disciplinary knowledge and professional identity. The field of writing studies continues to relegate two-year college writing instructors to the margins of the intellectual and educational field of writing studies—as consumers and recipients of the discipline, rather than as knowledge creators and scholarship shapers. As Louise Wetherbee Phelps and John M. Ackerman (2010) describe, "A disciplinary identity is necessary for [the scholarly and educational work] to be taken seriously within the meritocracies of higher education and to help sustain the working identities of practitioners, scholars, teachers, and administrators across the United States" (181). They argue that a key indicator of the existence of a discipline is the presence of its study in advanced education, meaning graduate school. Despite calls to develop graduate level programs that emphasize instructional methods that work in two-year college settings (Jensen 2017; Knodt 2005), few graduate programs name teaching at two-year colleges as a subject of study. In fact, Jensen (2017) and others have found that students in writing studies programs in elite research institutions are actively dissuaded from pursuing teaching positions in two-year colleges or situating their research at two-year colleges. While certainly more than a decade of attention paid to two-year colleges, including funding incentives to develop curricular interventions in two-year colleges, has helped bring greater awareness to these locations as sites for valuable research, our own field of writing studies continues to operate as if a veil separates the discipline of composition studies from the institutions where half the work of first-year college-level writing is taught.

If we apply Phelps and Ackerman's (2010) definitional lens for determining disciplinarity, then we can describe the profession of two-year college writing studies as aspirational and incomplete—well established enough to have decades of peer-reviewed scholarship and participation in scholarly activities, such as regional and national conferences, but missing from the sustained attention graduate education provides and, thus, the professionalization in institutional norms and methods of professional regulation (including but not limited to scholarly engagement, faculty collaborative mentoring, and professional service). In fact, we suspect the false dichotomy of "researcher versus teacher"—one teacher-scholar and teacher-scholar-activist movements have aimed to disrupt (Andelora 2005, 2013; Toth, Sullivan, and Calhoon-Dillahunt 2019)—reinforces the fallacy that two-year college writing instructors "just teach." In this way, "just teaching" most often means working outside of a research setting, regardless of what research, assessment, or advocacy the faculty member who "just teaches" does, thereby suppressing membership and ownership over disciplinary and professional conversations—both by ourselves and by our four-year colleagues. This lack of professionalization may explain why scholars and teacher-scholar-activists have noticed the apparent disengagement of so many two-year college writing instructors from their institutions and their professional communities (Suh and Jensen 2020; Toth and Sullivan 2016).

However, the just-teaching mythology is incomplete and misleading. Responding to the fastest changing demographics in higher education, we argue that two-year college instructors have a greater responsibility to follow pedagogical developments in the scholarship, that they have the right to be compensated for the labor engagement requires, and that their experience adapting their teaching approaches to support the diverse needs of a rapidly expanding student population constitutes a reason scholars at elite research institutions should be paying *more* attention. If the term *discipline* refers to the scope and depth of knowledge about a particular field, then we could conclude the discipline of two-year college writing studies is robust. Yet, if we apply Magali Sarfatti Larson's (2012) definition of profession in the postindustrial world—being recognized, having, sustaining, and regulating the dissemination and application of expert knowledge, to having control over the strategies and practices of one's disciplinary knowledge—then we can only conclude that our professional status is incomplete and provisional. Our status fluctuates with the foci of the media, the tides of educational policy, and the state and millage funding that determines our budgets. These pressures, compounded by structural variations in institutional organizations between two-year colleges and their four-year peers, profoundly undermine our work—and thus the learning of our students. As a result, even those two-year college writing instructors who are deeply engaged with their discipline and professions are often positioned poorly to affect discipline-oriented changes in their departments and at their institutions (Griffiths 2017; Griffiths and Jensen 2019; Toth, Griffiths, and Thirolf 2013).

Further, a general lack of knowledge about these institutional differences poorly prepares new graduates to effect change once they begin to work within a two-year college structure. Few graduate programs offer curricula addressing the unique political and educational histories of two-year college instruction or the pedagogical philosophies and strategies recommended for teaching in these contexts. Graduate work in composition studies alone insufficiently prepares instructors to teach at two-year colleges, in part because the administrative structures at two-year colleges are radically different from those at four-year institutions, with faculty positioned similarly to K–12 instructors (Griffiths 2015; Griffiths 2017; Griffiths 2020). More, for instructors whose only teaching experiences have been at four-year institutions, it is difficult to anticipate these differences alongside the diversity in student experiences, goals, and needs of students at two-year colleges—not only those tied to academic goals but those tied to the transportation, sustenance, and safety necessary to achieve those goals (Goldrick-Rab 2018; Nazmi et al. 2019; Nikolaus et al. 2020; Phillips, McDaniel, and Croft 2018), requiring increased flexibility and creativity from instructors (Griffiths and Toth 2017). To wit, practical strategies for teaching writing successfully to a student group that includes overlapping identities of students with unstable housing and insufficient access to food, forced immigrants, academic high achievers, underprepared students, domestic-violence survivors, new veterans, and minoritized students is rarely discussed in graduate programs, even if the concept of equity and individualized teaching is celebrated in abstraction.

Confounding this silence in the field, some graduate programs actively discourage students from working in two-year colleges (Jensen 2017). The notion of developing explicit graduate instruction in two-year college writing studies has existed since the very origins of the discipline of composition studies (Jensen 2019; Jensen and Toth 2017; Knodt 2005; Toth and Jensen 2017). However, as of 2022 few such programs or specializations exist (e.g., DePaul, San Francisco State University). When graduate programs fail to prepare students to teach developmental writing, students with disabilities, first-generation students, working poor, and students of color, they necessarily harm the millions of students at community colleges. Further, when they send these poorly prepared graduate students (Klausman 2018, 2019), they create poorly professionalized instructors, most of whom end up being contingent labor. The contingent labor crisis and the fossilization of two-year college English instructors who do not recognize the need to professionalize themselves (Suh and Jensen 2020; Toth and Sullivan 2016) represents our second major barrier: resistance from graduate institutions. A close analysis of the professionalization of graduate students in composition and rhetoric programs suggests our teaching discipline thrives as a twin at the margins of graduate learning. Graduate students often balance their studies and teaching while moonlighting as instructors at area colleges. They learn to navigate the complex shuffle of course preparation, grading, learning, and living that is the lifelong schedule of contingent instructors. This work, however, is neither visible nor valued within graduate conversations intended to prepare such students to take up the pedagogies and praxis of writing studies in our field.

This invisibility is inherent in the very design of our composition programs, which thrive on and perpetuate educational inequities within our departments. Graduate programs in English invite robust cohorts of students into their folds each fall, dependent upon them to teach ubiquitous writing-course requirements less expensively than full-time faculty instructors could in exchange for educational funding. However, while many such graduate students are introduced to the field of composition studies and to teaching in this way, university structures cannot sustain the movement of these students into research-intensive faculty positions. The structures that privilege research over teaching implicitly devalue the very education and experiences students take up by participating in the funding system and perpetuate a quasi-pyramid scheme for higher education, reinforcing a false research/teaching binary before students have become fully integrated into the graduate education community.

Unsurprisingly, first-generation graduate students, especially women (see, e.g., Drew et al. 2003; Schell 1998) and BIPOC, are disproportionately impacted by this move, seeking to be a part of the university community and often having little knowledge of the political workings of publication and tenure that invisibly separate those students seen as valuable from those seen as expendable. This hidden curriculum maintains an inequitable and tacitly classed and raced power structure that reverberates in job placement and professional opportunities. Moreover, those students who take us at our word in composition studies—following in the footsteps of Patricia Bizzell, Mike Rose, Jaqueline Jones Royster, and Asao Inoue—find themselves (as some of the authors of this volume have found ourselves) shunned or undermined in our graduate programs for wanting to enact the equitable teaching ideologies our field both celebrates and prescribes. By choosing to teach in access-oriented colleges where such equity initiatives can benefit the most students, new graduates find themselves inundated with disparate pressures from state mandates, national policies, and institutional deprofessionalization, while simultaneously being marginalized by their university peer colleagues and graduate programs. This process narrows the positionality and power faculty have to enact equitable pedagogies within the systems where they teach, especially given the few resources available to reprofessionalize themselves or to respond to their new environment. In essence, we are positioned simultaneously as professional "twins" (sister organizations) and as children—a junior or quasi-professional status alongside our peers.

The reality is that many—if not most—two-year college English faculty are left to professionalize themselves (Suh and Jensen 2017). Professional organizations such as TYCA exist and serve a valuable function for two-year college professionals (Jensen et al. 2021). Unfortunately, though, many institutions do not fund conference travel or recognize scholarly participation—even when lack of funding eliminates an important source of professional development that directly correlates to student success. In most two-year colleges, there is no pressure or impetus from external forces (such as program recognition or auditing), meaning two-year colleges have no reason to support such work, leaning instead on homegrown professional development in teaching that, while sometimes effective, can be divorced from disciplinary knowledge and—most often—administered by people who have limited or zero experience teaching in the classroom. This situation results in incomplete professionalization at two sites. First, from the preparation available in graduate school continued engagement with the discipline for two-year college instructors is neither acknowledged nor modeled. Second, incomplete professionalization happens within two-year colleges, where this disengagement is reinforced (or sometimes enforced) by the funding structures and tenure models in which continued engagement is unavailable or tacitly discouraged by colleagues who view participation in professional memberships as time "away" from students and therefore a shirking of the real duties of teaching.

Many top-down policy changes exacerbate this incomplete professionalization by constricting, redirecting, or revising the teaching initiatives at two-year colleges in service of finite goals for instrumentalist education driven by neoliberal logic (Giroux 2010; Stenberg 2015; Sullivan 2017; Welch 2018). These logics offer public-facing critiques of education and mandate inward-facing policies that undermine civic education and social uplift. They devalue public educational outcomes—such as a healthy, literate, and critically engaged society—while celebrating educational consumerism, in which education is reduced to individual economic benefits, a transaction of credits for jobs (see, e.g., Giroux 2010; Sullivan 2017). As we conduct final reviews of this book, a new book in print identifies explicit connections between this economic narrowing and the cost of higher education (Bunch 2022). The structural powers that undergird these initiatives and actors have made it difficult for the professionals working in two-year colleges to uphold the values of the field and to teach in ways that are inclusive, empowering, and ethical while using research-based pedagogy. Our incomplete professionals are perpetually disenfranchised on three fronts: by the institutions who do not understand and value the work of composition studies, by departmental colleagues who are divorced or disconnected from disciplinary knowledge, and by disciplinary colleagues in composition studies in university and graduate programs who ignore or devalue the work two-year college faculty do because of where they do it. Meanwhile, the discipline of composition studies migrates further and further from first-year writing, all while publicly agitating for antiracist, revolutionary writing pedagogies even though the site of their work is not where the majority of first-year writing students are in attendance. Where better to place those pedagogies than at the community college? Who better to include in that agitation than the two-year college instructors who work with the most minoritized students in higher education? And yet, at every turn, the tradition of our discipline and the cultures of our institutions present barriers to our full adoption into these realms.

We must move beyond our current tiered model of the profession, in which professional status for two-year college instructors is provisional and the commitment of the field to our students depends on the whims of political fashion, in which a token chapter in a collection or the occasional article or special issue of a journal addresses the community college. For writing studies to take up democratic and inclusive pedagogies as its charge, the possibilities of two-year college instruction must be recognized as a central component of that work, not an accessory to it. Only by positioning writing instruction at two-year colleges at the center rather than the margins of the discipline, and by enabling *two-year college writing studies* as a discipline to emerge alongside the professionalization of its faculty, can two-year college faculty be positioned to construct, disseminate, and expand the teaching knowledge available to educators. Such a shift in our professionalizing structures are preconditions for activating sustainable frameworks of equity and access. This collection presents evidence for such a discipline and profession and follows in a line of persistent if periodic attempts to instantiate the disciplinary and professional identities of two-year college writing instructors.

Our discipline is engaged in a political turn, but to be effective in that work, we must be inclusive of work occurring in open-access, public two-year colleges. Our colleagues must recognize and include our work and must be willing to learn from the interventions in which we are engaging (Jensen 2019). We recognize that the writing studies and composition communities have made strides in this direction in recent years—launching the first national TYCA conference (Andelora 2018), publishing various special-issue volumes in scholarly journals focused on the work of two-year colleges (*WPA*, *JWA*, *Praxis*, to name a few). However, so long as the work of teacher-scholar-activists is relegated to special issues and to token chapters within the journals of our discipline—the framing dialogues of our field—we are, by definition, exceptions to the discipline, tokens, outliers. This provisional status contributes to our confounded political status and lack of professional autonomy. Moreover, it tacitly undermines the knowledge being made in these institutions—and thus the disciplinary identities we form—thereby contributing, we argue, to the reproduction and justification of disciplinary disengagement among our colleagues.

EXIGENCE OR EXPEDIENCY: THIS POLITICAL MOMENT

Two-year colleges have always occupied a precarious political and educational space. Two-year college teachers, students, and staff have navigated this space, one foot rooted in the rhetorics of social uplift and pedagogical equity, the other in the shifting economics of workplace readiness and educational efficiency. Within these spaces we find deeply ingrained litanies of cultural values, personal goals, and the mercurial availability of resources such as time, emotion, and funding. Students' lives are often complicated by economic violence—including home and food insufficiency, institutional racism and classism, family responsibilities, a near daily need to hustle and grind to make ends meet—and a rhetoric of hope, hope for a better life for themselves, for the opportunity to model for their children a pathway of work for reward, the American dream they desperately believe in despite the persistent barriers placed in their path by the very system that propagates the dream.

The two-year college is popular now. Every president from Bill Clinton forward has incorporated community colleges into their State of the Union addresses. The current first lady, Dr. Jill Biden, is a two-year college professor, albeit with a mixed record of advocacy on instructional labor. The renewed interest and political popularity of two-year colleges might seem auspicious if the driving force of such popularity did not diverge fundamentally from the historical mission and potential of the institutions themselves. In each instance, our nation's leaders have articulated an ever-narrower vision for community college education, one that increasingly rests leadership and expertise on industry over education, one that fundamentally undermines pedagogical knowledge and autonomy of instructors. A cursory analysis of the presidential State of the Union addresses over the years and across administrations showcases the progression of these ideals. On January 20, 2004, George W. Bush described community colleges as a path for "training workers for industries" (Bush 2004). On January 27, 2010, Barack Obama identified community colleges as "career paths" for working families (Obama 2010), and then on January 28, 2014, he articulated a tighter nesting of education and industry, explaining "connecting companies to community colleges can help design training to fill their specific needs" (Obama 2014). Left unmentioned in these speeches are general education, transfer, and community education—three parallel educational avenues that comprise the nexus of our strength and promise as democratic institutions and our potential for service and uplift: the multifaceted mission of our colleges. While these utterances clearly echo the economic boogiemen of their rhetorical audiences, they commit violence to the historical mission and integrity of low-cost, well-integrated, and locally situated higher education. Former president Donald Trump merely took the next logical step in his statement that he didn't know what a "community college is" and that they should be called "vocational schools" (Strauss, *Washington Post*, February 1, 2018). And even though President Joe Biden has outlined 302 billion dollars of expanded higher education funding, including free two-year college—a provision sacrificed in the most recent negotiations as of this writing—there is no mistaking that his language and rhetorical choices are neoliberal rather than humanistic. He noted that "twelve years of free education, long the standard in the United States, was no longer enough 'to compete with the rest of the world in the twenty-first century'" (Taylor and Berger 2021), suggesting a focus on economic readiness rather than critical or citizenship education.

These rifts echo a historical tension rooted in the founding of the first two-year colleges: the Armour Institute and Joliet Junior College, both in Illinois, intended to serve distinct educational missions—the first vocational and the other general, liberal education (Quigley and Bailey 2003). It is precisely this fundamental conflict that the Truman Commission described when first applying the now most widely used moniker "community college" in 1947. Observing the radical shifts in the fabric of the US community and social potentials after World War II—and mindful of the lessons from the same—the commission articulated the following recommendations: two-year colleges should be free, and the vocational and liberal education missions should be "well-integrated" to serve economic, social, and civic educational missions. It ominously noted that a failure to achieve, recognize, and expand such integration and equity would have dire consequences (President's Commission on Higher Education 1947). The commission warned,

> If the ladder of educational opportunity rises high at the doors of some youth and scarcely rises at all at the doors of others, while at the same time formal education is made a prerequisite to occupational and social advance, then education may become the means, not of eliminating race and class distinctions, but of deepening and solidifying them. (55)

More than seventy years later we are in the moment they foretold.

The multifaceted mission of the two-year college affords multiple tensions, and those tensions have formed the source of misunderstanding and naïve branding of the purposes of our colleges (Cohen and Brawer 2008). Alongside the mission to prepare students to contribute to "the economy," community colleges also have the mission to provide the first two years of undergraduate coursework (general education) to most of their students who intend to transfer to four-year institutions, as well as provide and facilitate community engagement and professional development that supports lifelong learning for their surrounding communities. Across the paths for each of these missions there is also slippage, both in how students understand the purpose of their college experience and the ways college staff interpret and apply those missions to individual students. Burton R. Clark (1960) first described "cooling out"—the managing of students' expectations by directing them to different educational goals deemed more attainable (a certificate rather than a degree)—as an ethical responsibility of college staff and leaders. Since that time, others have critiqued "cooling out" in terms of the ways two-year colleges divert and dilute students' educational goals, leading working-class students into predominantly working-class jobs (Brint and Karabel 1989).

Either way, retrospective analysis is clear: our most vulnerable students—after they graduate—are underemployed, graduating into the same economic conditions neoliberal rhetorics have promised to eradicate (Ireland 2015; Valadez 2000). Too often the quest for "a little education" reifies the status quo and replicates economic stratification. Like the hidden curriculum of work described by Jane Anyon (2013) and explored by Patrick Sullivan in this collection, the issue here is not that low-wage jobs are of lower value to our communities. The global pandemic of 2019–2021 has, if nothing else, proven how very essential (albeit undervalued) some of the lowest-wage jobs, such as cashiers, are for the survival and well-being of communities. The issue is that the hand that extends an offer for "social uplift" renders that uplift moot with the very same mechanism by which it purports to effect equity. Efforts to "cool out" students—no doubt intended to help students reach education goals with less frustration—too often exchange big generational dreams at exchange rates far too costly to pair alongside the US rhetoric of merit. More poetically stated, we take in students' hopes and return fists full of bread and some pocket change.

Against this political and historical landscape, it is tempting to ascribe intention to the agents of US industry and policy, to identify a targeted conspiracy to undermine the authority and effectiveness of instruction for the purpose of widening the income and opportunity gaps among most Americans and the uber rich. Viewed from this perspective, we observe the sleight of hand—one shell exchanged for another, over time—democratic, integrated education exchanged for neoliberal rhetorics advanced through the language and policies of completion, austerity, and adjunctification. However, taking such a perspective—however righteous we may perceive it—leads to a cynicism from which little can be built, expanded, or sustained. Our intentions are precisely the opposite—to amplify the voices of teacher-scholar-activists in this moment, to celebrate the value of a disciplinary narrative now coming of age, and to place breadcrumbs on the path for colleagues newly joining our community. This book and the conversations in which it participates are acts of defiant hope for our profession.

THE VISION OF OUR CONTRIBUTORS

The arrangement of chapters in this book follows a purposeful arc we hope will resonate with readers' experiences and provide a touchstone for thinking about the notion of two-year college writing studies in our institutions. Here we have aimed to set the historical context, the political landscape, and the multifaceted exigence for this work. In chapter 2, Sullivan revisits our histories: the histories of community colleges, generally—their civic, social, and economic purposes for uplift begun during the Truman presidency—and our history—the history of English faculty working within, against, and in spite of histories over time to fight for the rights of our students not only to learn but to be seen and heard and valued in a system that has so often classified them as excess. By implication, Sullivan calls out the kinds of education and opportunities we amplify or undermine when we make community colleges the object of study, prosperity, reform, or neglect. Sullivan highlights the ways the aspirations and ideals of the community college movement put into motion by President Truman's Commission on Higher Education conflict at a fundamental and practical level with the ways Anyon's (2013) "hidden curriculum" play out in the community colleges of today—where working-class students are encouraged to seek a degree or certificate to achieve working-class jobs that offer little stability, civic participation, or economic uplift. Sullivan explains that the College Redesign movement often fails to acknowledge the lived experiences of our students and the reality of the community college as a site of intellectual rigor and social nuance, a site with the potential to expand and adapt to serve more than twice the number of student enrollments since 1973 (Snyder 1993; "Undergraduate Enrollment" 2022).

Sullivan reminds us two-year colleges are living institutions where teachers and students live, strive, adapt, resist, and ride out the tides of US economic and educational highs and lows, and that we do so first as humans living and reacting to other humans in our quests to understand, engage, and find our place in the social, economic, and political apparatuses we have called into being to organize our lives. Class is a part of this living. Racism is woven into its very fabric. The overlapping and deeply seated mythologies of literacy and work are part of this living. And the remaking of this fabric—of these mythologies—will require intentional, uncomfortable, and steady work at remaking ourselves and our own teaching. Sullivan describes community colleges as civic institutions whose purpose and responsibility are to serve and protect education as an accessible public good, rather than a private economic transaction.

Important, his chapter sets a hopeful stage for the continued potential of open-access two-year colleges and explores how all of us can fight for democratic and ennobling education. Sullivan argues that current community colleges remain ideally poised to take up the mission of social justice assigned to them by the Truman Commission, even if they have not always done so. At a time of extreme unrest and higher than normal rates of burnout, Sullivan's call may seem a bit naïve or even nostalgic. It returns to the idealistic origins of our fields in composition and writing studies, those wide-eyed justice-oriented days when open-access and free colleges were opening new doors and courses, days that saw the genesis of basic writing and the work now viewed as foundational to our field—that of Shaughnessy, of Rose, of Sommers. If Sullivan's chapter rings nostalgic, if the story he tells hits just too on the nose, perhaps it is because it speaks of promises woven into the foundations of writing studies—promises yet unrealized.

Sullivan argues that the foundational work of composition studies and our larger field of writing studies remains unfinished so long as writers are socially, economically, and racially excluded from their educational pursuits. Marilyn Smith Layton's Work "Lives Worth Fighting For" describes the ways her students—our students—teach us about composition studies, about teaching, about writing, and about learning as an embedded social relationship. She argues these relationships are still at the heart of our work and that supporting writers who are identified as under- or other-prepared for college in the traditional ways remains essential, not marginal, work for our field.

In chapters 3, 4, and 5, Bernice Olivas, Emily Suh, and Jamila Kareem dive into the hallowed space of our most important work—the classroom and the conversations afforded within them. They posit a pedagogy that validates students' identities, positionalities, and the structural and circumstantial barriers in their lives, incorporating each of these into the daily interactions of their courses. The authors envision and enact responsive learning approaches. They explore the ways organization, content, and ideology afford or dismiss students and their experiences.

Bernice Olivas, a first-generation scholar who went from GED to PhD in a decade, offers an intersectional pedagogy that resists student-deficit ideologies in her chapter "Identity Agents in the Two-Year College Classroom." She points to curricular and pedagogical interventions that help students rhetorically reframe themselves as college learners—as beings with an academic identity. Her model attacks deficit thinking in writing instruction and especially in first-year writing at community colleges. She pushes against the traditional paradigm of looking at students' deficiencies or mindsets and puts the onus on teacher-scholars to implement intersectional "identity-conscious classroom strategies." In Olivas's scheme, writing instructors as identity agents, rather than gatekeepers, help students position themselves as members of the academy. Her work draws on interactional theories of identity and takes up theoretical notions from Brandt and Freire to explore and model the nuances of identity construction and positionality in two-year college writing instruction.

Olivas applies the sociological framework of identity control theory (ICT) to describe how individual discursive interactions with students help shape their perceptions of themselves as college students or outsiders. She describes ways teachers can bring greater intentionality to the individual interactions and microinteractions of course design. These strategies help college learners position themselves as agentive in adopting or rejecting elements of this identity in ways that build trust, foster a sense of belonging, and empower them to engage in their learning as insiders. By drawing on this established sociological framework, she advances our methodological approaches to better reflect and respond to the social and political contexts in which we teach. She envisions two-year college writing studies as part of literacy sponsorship, investing in welcoming all who enter. Her work presents what we see as an important way to engage students and make them successful in the classroom.

In the fourth chapter, Emily K. Suh focuses on the specific identities and learning needs of first-generation, new immigrant language learners in developmental writing classrooms. Bringing together three theoretical frameworks of cultural participation and learning—Bourdieu's symbolic capital, Norton's theory of investment, and Knowles's theory of andragogy, Suh identifies gaps between our teaching instincts and students' abilities. Suh highlights ways teaching professionals confuse students' abilities to navigate and overcome complex lived experiences (social capital) with their ability to navigate complex learning spaces (academic symbolic capital). Specifically, Suh provides two case-study analyses to identify gaps between social capital students gain through life experiences and the values instructors assign that capital in terms of symbolic capital for students' transition into US academic culture. In some ways distinct from the students outlined in Sullivan's chapter, Suh highlights ways students can perform the social norms and attitudes of the successful college student while adhering to misaligned or undercontextualized notions of academic performance and help seeking. She cautions that this kind of confusion among educational professionals can render invisible the actual needs of students new to our educational landscape.

In chapter 5, "'I've Never Been a Good Writer': Disrupting Raciolinguistically Marginalized Students' Negative Writerly Self-Images," Jamila Kareem argues for "applying students' self-perceptions about their bad writing to see their already adaptable repository of social-rhetorical linguistic practices as a viable college-ready asset." Like Suh and Olivas, Kareem describes ways she helps students apply their lived experiences directly to their learning and writing at the two-year college. To accomplish this work, she turns to tenets of critical race theory (CRT). Kareem defines CRT as a theory that critically examines and responds to "racist ideas and actions in the legal system and other policy-making contexts in society, including education." She concludes that the language differences we see in academic and civic life are constructed to privilege and reinforce the linguistic hegemonies and structures of the historically dominant and artificially homogenous "standard"—a predominantly white, middle-class, artificial language of politics, education, and power.

Kareem's critique isn't new, but her insightful analysis of existing scholarship and its application to composition studies and two-year college writing studies pushes teacher-scholar-activists to act in our classrooms and institutions, not just our theoretical conversations. She examines our field's embrace—conscious or not—of the middle-class white enterprise of composition. In an incisive critical examination of some of our field's most treasured documents and an examination of "A DEMAND for Black Linguistic Justice," Kareem makes a compelling case for how composition has failed students who bring other Englishes, especially raciolinguistic dialects, to our classrooms. It is an important analysis for two-year college writing studies because the two-year college is the site where most students of the global majority begin their educational journey.

Kareem goes on to detail instructional practices that disrupt students' negative raciolinguistic writerly self-images. She discusses her syllabus, mini units with explicit instruction in multiple raciolinguistic rhetorical traditions, and explicit instruction in Black and Latinx rhetorical traditions, as well as Eurocentric rhetorical traditions. Her revisioning of a first-year writing course to make this work visible and explicit is detailed, compelling, and, we argue, vital to the future of writing studies, especially writing studies in the two-year college. These four chapters offer a vision of how two-year college writing studies can engage in the work of aiding students in developing. Sullivan's work in the first chapter frames teacher-scholar-activists as doing the democratic work of two-year college students because our students have "lives worth fighting for." Olivas, Suh, and Kareem provide an on-the-ground view of how this work happens in the intersectional multiracial, multilingual two-year college of the twenty-first century. These chapters offer a pedagogical and theoretical primer for who we can be and the work we can do.

Chapters 6 and 7 widen the focus to programmatic decisions, interactions between staff members and departments, and exploring strategies for naming and validating the tensions within our English departments while also responsively attending to the disciplinary differences among us and the inherited inequities our students experience when trying to navigate our layered and sometimes conflicting pedagogies. These concerns—while wider in scope—are vital to student success and the democratic mission of the two-year college. In chapter 6, Rhonda Grego examines the use of thirdspace theory and her work in creating writing studios. Grego's chapter, "Institutional Memory at a Two-Year College: A Case Study of Interactional Inquiry into 2YC Student Learning Outcomes," is a fascinating look into the work of two-year college English studies. She relates a case study in which she and her English Department built a department that uses authentic assessment and that has refigured their professional and curricular identity.

Grego makes a persuasive argument about how assessment data and research help create department and institutional change. She explains that "evidence-based storytelling" helped institutional and disciplinary connections evolve. She and her department coupled this work with what professional publications had to offer in helping the department build "professional authority." Grego's narrative is of value because it differs so much from what our four-year colleagues and graduate students might experience. Her chronicling of working with an entrenched literature-based department and an administration engaged in the neoliberal logics of austerity is one that will be familiar to many two-year college professionals. The negotiation of institutional history and institutional power structures in the ways she describes is endemic to many community college English departments in the United States. She provides one of the clearest examples of working toward professional autonomy (Griffiths) and epistemic authority (Larson) we've seen.

Further, Grego addresses the labor structures of two-year colleges. She recounts how her own professional journey and her group's authentic assessment of student learning outcomes mapped onto a lack of professional development for both full- and part-time faculty. She writes that "opening up a third space for resisting the hegemonic scripts of erasure and articulating connections between student learning and two-year college faculty labor generated the rhetorical exigence for [her] department's progressively stronger connection to professional organizations and publications." The work she describes addresses the political and institutional needs of community college English faculty. It also demonstrates how two-year college English studies is structurally and pedagogically distinct from English studies at our four-year counterparts. Her call to look "inward to our own professional experience" and "outward to our institutional environment" is important and needed.

In chapter 7, Kirsten Higgins, Anthony Warnke, and Jake Frye examine assessment in "The Painful Eagerness of Unfed Hope: Equity-Centered Writing Assessment." Their work intersects with Grego's work in that it examines the assessment practices at their two-year college and how those practices measure up to our discipline's "values that center on questions of equity and inclusion." The authors look at student assessment and how that assessment is still tied to deficit models of education, arguing that outcomes assessment "objectifies by separating through its analytical operation and dehumanizes both its practitioners and its objects of study." The authors wonder how they can move from this broken paradigm of assessment that is often couched in the term "good enough." The authors ask how "assessment can be functionally reimagined to better serve our students?" They theorize a reimagination of assessment at the two-year college that can be described as holistic and authentic, as it "treats as whole and connected students' bodies, lives, and work" with the knowledge that the community and local context cannot be separated from this evaluation.

Higgens, Warnke, and Frye forward two "assessment dispositions" to accomplish this work: "disruption and rhetorical attunement." The authors place these moves within the tradition of critical reform and see the work as both pragmatic and paradigmatic. The authors provide three examples of this work, arguing for how this work creates space for a better model of assessment they believe adds value to the two-year college. Notably, they see this work as needing internal incentivization from faculty as part of their professional commitment and work that should concomitantly be externally incentivized by institutions' "material commitment." This model is compelling and demonstrates the context of and lived reality of assessment work in the two-year college.

Chapter 8, "Strategic Organizing: Scaling Up Two-Year College Teacher-Scholar-Activism" by Joanne Giordano and Holly Hassel, chronicles the work of two-year college English departments at Wisconsin colleges. Those departments don't exist anymore. Their curricular work—award-winning, research-based, and faculty driven—was undone just as two-year colleges in Wisconsin were undone by neoliberal fiat. The teacher-scholar-activist movement, elections, and unions are important precisely because they give us the ability to exist so we can build and implement research-based best-practices curriculum. "However," Hassel and Giordano write, "in the end, our [Wisconsin community college faculty] efforts were completely insufficient to combat the powerful political forces intent on reducing access to higher education for underprepared students and consolidating resources among the most selective institutions in the state system." The attack on two-year colleges and public education in Wisconsin is well documented, but this chapter goes into detail about the staggering consequences. The authors end their chapter with a call to national action for the two-year college English profession. This book echoes and amplifies that call.

TO OUR COLLEAGUES AT TWO-YEAR AND OPEN-ACCESS INSTITUTIONS

We hope this book serves as a beacon to our colleagues and would-be colleagues in the profession. To those who are new to working in two-year college environments, we say welcome. The work you do is essential, the cornerstone of writing studies, the work of preparing and supporting writers to find their voices and to stake claims to their rights and their experiences. This book is an invitation. We encourage professionals and graduate students to participate in the growing body of literature and activism that celebrates our work as teachers and as scholars, to explicitly recognize the lived experiences of your colleagues and of your students, to embrace the work of amplifying voices from our classrooms, from our institutions, and from our profession. We believe the good work of the voices in this book—in concert with the voices joining every day to take up professional and political activism for writing departments and programs in two-year colleges—can bring not only greater awareness but also direct and practical adaptations to the professional environment and practices of our profession, to our classrooms, to our departments, and to the labor practices that embody and disembody the profession.

Contained in this anthology are chapters, yes—essays, studies, narratives, and reflections—but they are also letters written from our current educational contexts to you, our colleagues across the professions of writing studies, as a way of recognizing the work you do—that we do together—and a way of constituting the future work of our discipline. This collection is a love letter to the two-year college as an ideal, one situated in this kairotic moment, its potential and problems. In his public address in 2018 in Kansas City, Jeff Andelora described the Two-Year College English Association's long relationship with CCCC as relationship status = complicated. We couldn't agree more. Taken as a whole, it is a letter of love, appreciation, and commitment to the teacher-scholar-activists who have come before us and who have guided our practice and professional lives. Finally, the collection is a love letter to a possible future predicated in the chapters that follow. But hope and love—like equity and education—are mere abstractions without the grounding of daily work and substantial relationships, without the productive and difficult dialogues of critique (Calhoon-Dillahunt et al. 2017). Two-year college writing professionals are neither new to the discipline nor operating in the marginal niches of the field (Calhoon-Dillahunt 2018; Giordano and Hassel 2019; Hassel and Giordano 2013; Lovas 2002; Reynolds 1994, 2005; Reynolds and Holladay-Hicks 2005). Our love and our work are old, persistently bent to the wheel, theorizing and practicing writing pedagogies in a context shaped in equal parts by the promise of and resistance to social justice in the US, in the spotlight and the shadows of our educational mission.

Love might seem like a strange word choice here. But we draw on Jim Corder's (1985) notion in "Argument as Emergence: Rhetoric as Love," in which he "insist[s] that argument—that rhetoric itself—must begin, proceed, and end in love" (28). This volume seeks to create a space that allows the most diverse of institutions, two-year colleges, and the transdisciplinary work of writing studies within them, to be examined so our practices and selves can serve our students and the institutions' democratic potential, can be a space where our "distinct and significant profession" is made more visible to ourselves and others, empowered to take up the work with which we have been charged in earnest.

REFERENCES

American Association of Community Colleges. 2022. "2022 Fast Facts." aacc.nche.edu/research-trends/fast-facts/.

Andelora, Jeff. 2005. "The Teacher/Scholar: Reconstructing Our Professional Identity in Two-Year Colleges." *Teaching English in the Two-Year College* 32 (3): 307.

Andelora, Jeffrey T. 2013. "Teacher/Scholar/Activist: A Response to Keith Kroll's 'The End of the Community College English Profession.'" *Teaching English in the Two-Year College* 40 (3): 302.

Andelora, Jeff. 2018. "An Invitation to the First National TYCA Conference." *Teaching English in the Two-Year College* 46 (2): 105–6.

Anyon, Jean. 2013. "Social Class, School Knowledge, and the Hidden Curriculum: Retheorizing Reproduction." In *Ideology, Curriculum, and the New Sociology of Education*, edited by Lois Weis, Cameron McCarthy, and Greg Dimitriadis, 37–45. Abingdon, UK: Routledge.

Arum, Richard, and Josipa Roksa. 2011. *Academically Adrift: Limited Learning on College Campuses*. Chicago: University of Chicago Press.

Brint, Steven, and Jerome Karabel. 1989. *The Diverted Dream: Community Colleges and the Promise of Educational Opportunity in America, 1900–1985*. Oxford: Oxford University Press.

Bunch, William. 2022. *After the Ivory Tower Falls: How College Broke the American Dream and Blew Up Our Politics—And How to Fix It*. New York: William Morrow.

Bush, George W. 2004. "President Bush's 2004 State of the Union Address." Washingtonpost.com, January 20, 2004. Accessed May 15, 2023. https://www.washingtonpost.com/wp-srv/politics/transcripts/bushtext_012004.html.

Calhoon-Dillahunt, Carolyn. 2018. "Returning to Our Roots: Creating the Conditions and Capacity for Change." *College Composition and Communication* 70 (2): 273–93.

Calhoon-Dillahunt, Carolyn, Darin L. Jensen, Sarah Z. Johnson, Howard Tinberg, and Christie Toth. 2017. "TYCA Guidelines for Preparing Teachers of English in the Two-Year College." *College English* 79 (6): 550–60.

Clark, Burton R. 1960. "The 'Cooling-Out' Function in Higher Education." *American Journal of Sociology* 65 (6): 569–76.

Cohen, Arthur, and Florence Brawer. 2008. *The American Community College*. San Francisco: Jossey-Bass.

Corder, Jim W. 1985. "Argument as Emergence, Rhetoric as Love." *Rhetoric Review* 4 (1): 16–32.

Drew, Chris, Matt Garrison, Steven Leek, Donna Strickland, Jen Talbot, and A. D. Waldron. 2003. "Affect, Labor, and the Graduate Teaching Assistant: Can Writing Programs Become 'Spaces of Hope'?" *Works and Days* 21 (1 and 2): 169–86.

"Undergraduate Enrollment in 2-Year Postsecondary Degree-Granting Institutions in the United States from 1970 to 2030, by Institution Type." 2022. Statista. Accessed September 18, 2022. https://www.statista.com/statistics/236467/enrollment-in-us-2-year-postsecondary-institutions-by-institution-type/.

Giordano, Joanne Baird, and Holly Hassel. 2019. "Intersections of Privilege and Access: Writing Programs, Disciplinary Knowledge, and the Shape of a Field." *WPA: Writing Program Administration* 43 (1): 33–54.

Giroux, Henry A. 2010. "Bare Pedagogy and the Scourge of Neoliberalism: Rethinking Higher Education as a Democratic Public Sphere." *Educational Forum* 74 (3): 184–96.

Goldrick-Rab, Sara. 2018. "Addressing Community College Completion Rates by Securing Students' Basic Needs." *New Directions for Community Colleges* 2018 (184): 7–16.

Griffiths, Brett M. 2015. "This Is My Profession: How Notions of Teaching Enable and Constrain Autonomy of Two-Year College Writing Instructors." PhD diss., University of Michigan–Ann Arbor.

Griffiths, Brett M. 2017. "Professional Autonomy and Teacher-Scholar-Activists in Two-Year Colleges: Preparing New Faculty to Think Institutionally." *Teaching English in the Two Year College* 45 (1): 47–68.

Griffiths, Brett M. 2020. "Reinventing the Spiel: The Context and Case for Interinstitutional Collaboration in an Era of Education Austerity." *WPA: Writing Program Administration* 43 (3): 88–106.

Griffiths, Brett, and Darin Jensen. 2019. "Conceptualizing a Model for English Faculty at Two-Year Colleges." *Pedagogy* 19 (2): 301–21.

Griffiths, Brett M., and Christina M. Toth. 2017. "Rethinking 'Class': Poverty, Pedagogy, and Two-Year College Writing Programs." In *Class in the Composition Classroom*, edited by Genesea M. Carter and William H. Thelin, 231–57. Logan: Utah State University Press.

Hassel, Holly, and Joanne Baird Giordano. 2013. "Occupy Writing Studies: Rethinking College Composition for the Needs of the Teaching Majority." *College Composition and Communication* 65 (1): 117–39.

Inoue, Asao B. 2019. "How Do We Language So People Stop Killing Each Other, or What Do We Do about White Language Supremacy." *College Composition and Communication* 71 (2): 352–69.

Ireland, S. Mei-Yen. 2015. "Fostering Success or Stratification? A Macroapproach to Understanding 'Success' in the Community College Context." *Community College Journal of Research and Practice* 39 (2): 150–62.

Jacobs, James, and Jennifer Worth. 2019. "The Evolving Mission of Workforce Development in the Community College." Community College Research Center Working Paper 107, Teachers College, Columbia University.

Jensen, Darin L. 2017. "Tilting at Windmills: Refiguring Graduate Education in English to Prepare Future Two-Year College Professionals." PhD diss., University of Nebraska–Lincoln.

Jensen, Darin L. 2019. "The Political Turn and the Two-Year College." In *Writing Democracy: The Political Turn in and beyond the Trump Era*, edited by Shannon Carter et al., 119–27. New York: Routledge Taylor & Francis Group.

Jensen, Darin L., Carolyn Calhoon-Dillahunt, Brett Griffiths, and Christie Toth. 2021. "Embracing the Democratic Promise: Transforming Two-Year Colleges and Writing Studies through Professional Engagement." *New Directions for Community Colleges* 2021 (194): 55–66. https://doi.org/10.1002/cc.20452.

Jensen, Darin L., and Christie Toth. 2017. "Unknown Knowns: The Past, Present, and Future of Graduate Preparation for Two-Year College English Faculty." *College English* 79 (6): 561–92.

Johnson, Kristine. 2013. "Why Students Don't Write: Educating in the Era of Credentialing: Academically Adrift: Limited Learning on College Campuses." *Conversations on Jesuit Higher Education* 43 (1): 9.

Juszkiewicz, Jolanta. 2017. "Trends in Community College Enrollment and Completion Data, 2017." American Association of Community Colleges Report. https://vtechworks.lib.vt.edu/handle/10919/86967.

Klausman, Jeffrey. 2018. "The Two-Year College Writing Program and Academic Freedom: Labor, Scholarship, and Compassion." *Teaching English in the Two-Year College* 45 (4): 385–405.

Klausman, Jeffrey. 2019. "That's an Ugly Quote: Some Thoughts on Fear, Identity, and Indirect Activism." Teacher-Scholar-Activist, February 27. https://teacher-scholar-activist.org/2019/02/27/thats-an-ugly-quote-some-thoughts-on-fear-identity-and-indirect-activism/.

Knodt, Ellen Andrews. 2005. "Graduate Programs for Two-Year-College Faculty: History and Future Directions." In *The Profession of English in the Two-Year College*, edited by Mark Reynolds and Sylvia Holladay-Hicks, 125–36. Portsmouth, NH: Boynton/Cook.

Lovas, John C. 2002. "All Good Writing Develops at the Edge of Risk." *College Composition and Communication* 54 (2): 264–88.

McPhail, Christine Johnson. 2011. "The Completion Agenda: A Call to Action. Summary Report from the November 10–11, 2010, Meeting of the American Association of Community Colleges Commissions and Board of Directors." Washington, DC: American Association of Community Colleges.

Mills, Charles W. 2014. "The Racial Contract." In *The Racial Contract*. Ithaca, NY: Cornell University Press.

Nazmi, Aydin, Suzanna Martinez, Ajani Byrd, Derrick Robinson, Stephanie Bianco, Jennifer Maguire, Rashida M. Crutchfield, Kelly Condron, and Lorrene Ritchie. 2019. "A Systematic Review of Food Insecurity among US Students in Higher Education." *Journal of Hunger and Environmental Nutrition* 14 (5): 725–40.

Nikolaus, Cassandra J., Ruopeng An, Brenna Ellison, and Sharon M. Nickols-Richardson. 2020. "Food Insecurity among College Students in the United States: A Scoping Review." *Advances in Nutrition* 11 (2): 327–48. https://doi.org/10.1093/advances/nmz111.

Obama, Barack. 2010. "Remarks by the President in State of the Union Address." Whitehouse.gov, January 27, 2010. https://obamawhitehouse.archives.gov/the-press-office/remarks-president-state-union-address.

Obama, Barack. 2014. "President Barack Obama's State of the Union Address." Whitehouse.gov. January 28, 2014. https://obamawhitehouse.archives.gov/the-press-office/2014/01/28/president-barack-obamas-state-union-address.

Phelps, Louise Wetherbee, and John M. Ackerman. 2010. "Making the Case for Disciplinarity in Rhetoric, Composition, and Writing Studies: The Visibility Project." *College Composition and Communication* 62 (1): 180–215.

Phillips, Erica, Anne McDaniel, and Alicia Croft. 2018. "Food Insecurity and Academic Disruption Among College Students." *Journal of Student Affairs Research and Practice*, 55 (1): 1–20.

President's Commission on Higher Education. 1947. *Higher Education for American Democracy*. New York: Harper & Brothers Publishers.

Quigley, Martin, and Thomas R. Bailey. 2003. *Community College Movement in Perspective: Teachers College Responds to the Truman Commission*. Lanham, MD: Scarecrow Press.

Reynolds, Mark. 1994. *Two-Year College English: Essays for a New Century*. Urbana, IL: National Council of Teachers of English.

Reynolds, Mark. 2005. "Two-Year College Teachers as Knowledge Makers." In *The Profession of English in the Two-Year College*, edited by Mark Reynolds and Sylvia Holladay-Hicks, 1–15. Portsmouth, NH: Boynton/Cook.

Reynolds, Mark, and Sylvia Holladay-Hicks, eds. 2005. *The Profession of English in the Two-Year College*. Portsmouth, NH: Boynton/Cook.

Sarfatti Larson, Magali. 2012. *The Rise of Professionalism: Monopolies of Competence and Sheltered Markets*. New Brunswick, NJ: Transaction Publishers.

Schell, Eileen E. 1998. *Gypsy Academics and Mother-Teachers: Gender, Contingent Labor, and Writing Instruction*. Portsmouth, NH: Boynton/Cook.

Stenberg, Shari J. 2015. *Repurposing Composition: Feminist Interventions for a Neoliberal Age*. Logan: Utah State University Press.

Snyder, Thomas D., ed. 1993. *120 Years of American Education: A Statistical Portrait*. Washington, DC: US Department of Education, Office of Educational Research and Improvement.

Suh, Emily, and Darin Jensen. 2017. "Building Professional Autonomy: A Way Forward in Hard Times." *Journal of Developmental Education* 41 (1): 28–29.

Suh, Emily, and Darin Jensen. 2020. "Examining Communities of Practice: Transdisciplinarity, Resilience, and Professional Identity." *Journal of Basic Writing* 39 (2): 33–59.

Sullivan, Patrick. 2017. *Economic Inequality, Neoliberalism, and the American Community College*. New York: Palgrave Macmillan.

Taylor, Adam, and Miriam Berger. 2021. "Biden's Plans to Expand Free Education May Be New for the US, but in Other Countries, They're the Norm." Trinity University, April 30. https://discover.trinitydc.edu/news/bidens-plans-to-expand-free-education-may-be-new-for-the-us-but-in-other-countries-theyre-the-norm/.

Toth, Christie M., Brett M. Griffiths, and Kathryn Thirolf. 2013. "'Distinct and Significant': Professional Identities of Two-Year College English Faculty." *College Composition and Communication* 65 (1): 90–116.

Toth, Christie, and Darin Jensen. 2017. "Responses to the TYCA Guidelines for Preparing Teachers of English in the Two-Year College." *Teaching English in the Two-Year College* 45 (1): 29.

Toth, Christie, and Patrick Sullivan. 2016. "Toward Local Teacher-Scholar Communities of Practice: Findings from a National TYCA Survey." *Teaching English in the Two-Year College* 43 (3): 247.

Toth, Christie, Patrick Sullivan, and Carolyn Calhoon-Dillahunt. 2019. "Two-Year College Teacher-Scholar-Activism: Reconstructing the Disciplinary Matrix of Writing Studies." *College Composition and Communication* 71 (1): 86–116.

Valadez, James R. 2000. "Searching for a Path Out of Poverty: Exploring the Achievement Ideology of a Rural Community College." *Adult Education Quarterly* 50 (3): 212–30.

Welch, Nancy. 2018. "'Everyone Should Have a Plan': A Neoliberal Primer for Writing Program Directors." *WPA: Writing Program Administration* 41 (2): 104–12.

Yarnall, Louise, Elizabeth Tennant, and Regie Stites. 2016. "A Framework for Evaluating Implementation of Community College Workforce Education Partnerships and Programs." *Community College Journal of Research and Practice* 40 (9): 750–66.

2
A SOCIAL JUSTICE INSTITUTION

Patrick Sullivan

One of the most hopeful, democratic, and revolutionary developments in the long, troubled history of education in the US is the establishment of a national system of local, affordable community colleges in the late 1960s and early 1970s. Before this system was built, higher education in the US was the exclusive domain of a privileged elite, rigidly segregated like the rest of nation by race, class, gender, and disability (hooks 2003; Hubrig 2022; Ladson-Billings 2006; Urban, Gaither, and Wagoner 2019). Power, identity, and positionality have played a central role in educational opportunity in the US for centuries (and perhaps always will, in one form or another). These issues have become key concerns for educators today across institutional boundaries, as the editors of this volume note. The open-admissions community college revolution, therefore, is an extraordinary moment in our history, disrupting hundreds of years of privilege and oppression. It was—and continues to be—an inspiring triumph for our democracy as well.

The impetus and vision for this extraordinary development came from the Truman Commission and its 1947 report, *Higher Education for American Democracy*. The title of this report suggests its ambition. The commission was appointed by Harry Truman and charged with mapping a course for US higher education and democracy following WWII. What is of historic significance about this document is the clarity the authors bring to their understanding of the role race, class, and gender play in American life. The commission candidly addresses structural systems of oppression and disadvantage—and the ideological belief systems that sustain and validate these systems. Volume 2 of the report, for example, focuses on "Equal Opportunity" (President's 1947, vol. 2, ch. 3). Chapter 3 of volume 2 addresses racial and religious discrimination in higher education (President's 1947, vol. 2, ch. 3, 25–44).

This clarity is a function of an extraordinary historical moment, a rare time in our national history offering us an opportunity to reflect honestly about who we were and what we might become. The recommendations in the Truman Commission Report are linked on almost every page to the lessons learned from World War II, a conflict driven by monstrous and lethal forms of racism. We emerged from this conflict chastened, stung by criticism from other nations about our own racist history and practices—and determined to address our own cruel and antidemocratic history and conduct at home (Allen 2000; Baldwin 1992; Bateman, Katznelson, and Lapinski 2018; Bell 1992; Crenshaw et al. 1996; Douglass 1894, 2016; Kendi 2016; Lawson 2003; Lewis, Aydin, and Powell 2016; Rothstein 2018; Sharkey 2013; Whitman 2017). The Truman Commission characterized this important unresolved civic work as "democracy's unfinished business" (President's 1947, vol. 1, ch. 1, 12–14). The commission is uncompromising in its vision for fulfilling the democratic promise of higher education in the US:

> American colleges and universities must envision a much larger role for higher education in the national life. They can no longer consider themselves merely the instrument for producing an intellectual elite; they must become the means by which every citizen, youth, and adult is enabled and encouraged to carry his education, formal and informal, as far as his native capacities permit.
>
> This conception is the inevitable consequence of the democratic faith; universal education is indispensable to the full and living realization of the democratic ideal. No society can long remain free unless its members are freemen, and men are not free where ignorance prevails. No more in mind than in body can this Nation or any endure half slave, half free. Education that liberates and ennobles must be made equally available to all. Justice to the individual demands this; the safety and progress of the Nation depend upon it. America cannot afford to let any of its potential human resources go undiscovered and undeveloped. (ch. 5, 101)

For reasons linked to equity, social justice, and hope, the commission called for the establishment of a greatly expanded network of community colleges nationwide.

> To make sure of its own health and strength a democratic society must provide free and equal access to education for its youth, and at the same time it must recognize their differences in capacity and purpose. Higher education in America should include a variety of institutional forms and educational programs, so that at whatever point any student leaves school, he will be fitted, within the limits of his mental capacity and educational level, for an abundant and productive life as a person, as a worker, and as a citizen. . . . As one means of achieving the expansion of educational opportunity and the diversification of educational offerings it considers necessary, this Commission recommends that the number of community colleges be increased and that their activities be multiplied. (ch. 4, 67)

The commission theorized the modern community college not simply as a convenient, affordable, local alternative to traditional four-year institutions—but as a social justice institution with a mission and mandate to spread access to higher education more equitably across the nation. Data from the National Center for Education Statistics show that enrollment patterns changed dramatically in the early 1970s, when hundreds of community colleges were established across the nation and open-admissions policies became part of their institutional identity. Before the mid-70s, enrollment numbers for Black and Hispanic students were reported by the federal government as either "not available" or "not applicable" (United States 2016; see also Lawson 2003). Once the open-admissions revolution was underway, those numbers improved dramatically (Sullivan 2021b, 43–61; United States 2016). This development brought hope and opportunity to millions of US citizens who had been systematically excluded from higher education for centuries. It is a shining moment in the long history of higher education in our nation.

While the theoretical exigency for the modern community college system was provided by the Truman Commission, the implementation of this ideal was realized by African American and Latinx activists during the civil rights years in the 1960s and early 1970s. These movements drew inspiration from African American student activism and protests at historically Black colleges and universities decades earlier (Kendi 2012; Kynard 2014). As Carmen Kynard (2014), Ibram X. Kendi (2012), Martha Biondi (2102), and others have documented, the Black campus movement in the late 1960s and early 1970s reconstituted higher education in the US. In many ways, the system we enjoy today—and perhaps take for granted—was built by African American and Latinx student activists. This system is an enduring physical manifestation of the ideals of the civil rights movement and our efforts during this time to build a better nation and a stronger democracy.

OPEN ADMISSIONS

Open-admissions policies were a key element of this revolution, but it took considerable effort on the part of activists to convince politicians, teachers, and administrators of its revolutionary potential and value (Biondi 2012; Kendi 2012; Kynard 2014). It is still a contested public-policy innovation today (Flores 2011; Rose 2011, 2012; Sullivan 2021a). At the center of the open-admissions philosophy is the fundamental belief in every individual's worth, dignity, and potential. Open admissions is built on the core belief—now confirmed by decades of evidence and millions of community college graduates (AACC 2023)—that each of us has the luminous capacity to learn, grow, and change, a process that routinely manifests itself in remarkable ways on community college campuses. Every day on our campuses we see students rise above family history, past personal history, and unjust social and historical circumstances.

This is a revolutionary and liberatory moment in the long history of higher education in the US. Open-admissions policies boldly affirm that *it is simply not possible to predict* what great things an individual might be capable of—despite what a student's past academic history might suggest. It is a public policy that refuses to place an arbitrary ceiling on any individual's capacity or potential (Freire 1985, 1994; hooks 1994, 2003; McNair et al. 2016). This policy makes community colleges a beacon of hope and democratic promise.

BUILDING A MORE DIVERSE FACULTY AND STAFF

Unfortunately, as with most developments related to education in our history, this hopeful, promising vision for democracy and higher education has been accompanied by considerable resistance, regression, and retreat in the years since 1947 (Bell 1992; Carter et al. 2020; Hassel and Phillips 2022; Ladson-Billings 2006; Sullivan 2017; Warnke and Higgins 2018). Many areas call for attention today.

We have done a very poor job, for example, of encouraging, recruiting, training, mentoring, supporting, and hiring diverse faculty and staff at our nation's community colleges, as the editors of this volume note. We have had over seventy years to do this important work, and our teaching faculty is still rigidly segregated and stratified by race and gender. A national survey in 2019 of TYCA members conducted by the TYCA Workload Taskforce found the demographics of teaching faculty at two-year colleges to be very much out of sync with the rich diversity of community college student demographics (Suh et al. 2021). Community college students represent 38 percent of all US undergraduates and 35 percent first-time college attendees. The also represent 52 percent of all Native American, 48 percent of all Latinx, 39 percent of all African American, and 34 percent of all Asian/Pacific Islander attendees (AACC 2023). Aggregate data from this survey reveal traditional stratified patterns among our teaching faculty:

- 81 percent white
- 4 percent Latinx
- 2 percent Asian or Pacific Islander

- 2 percent Black or African American
- 2 percent other
- 1 percent multiracial
- Three respondents Native American or American Indian
- 6 percent not identified (Suh et al. 2021, 334)

Our teaching staff is also equally stratified by gender:

- 73 percent female
- 21 percent male
- 4 percent sex or gender not indicated
- 2 percent nonbinary or another identity
- 10 percent LGBTQA+ (Suh et al. 2021, 334)

This imbalance affects everything from persistence to completion.

Given how much we know about the importance of students seeing themselves reflected in faculty and staff (Figlio 2017; Kirkland 2013; Ladson-Billings 1995; Steele 2012), these data help explain the gaps we continue to see reproduced generation after generation in retention and completion trends across racial categories at all levels of higher education (Hung et al. 2020). These achievement gaps are, in fact, opportunity gaps—structural inequalities related to power, identity, and positionality that have been designed to oppress, limit, and exploit—not liberate (Bell 1992; Ladson-Billings 2006; Milner 2020; Warnke and Higgins 2018; see also Love 2020; Rothstein 2004). Many of these inequities have been written into law by state and federal governments and by Supreme Court rulings (see, e.g., Bateman, Katznelson, and Lapinski 2018; Cohen 2020; Kendi 2012; Patterson 2001; Rothstein 2004, 2018; Stevenson 2014; Whitman 2017). Students of color today are more likely to see people like themselves in technical, clerical, and service staff positions on college campuses, suggesting that professional and leadership positions are not available to them (Anyon 1980). A more diverse teaching faculty would send a very different message. A more diverse staff would provide many benefits to faculty, staff, and institutions as well, including new perspectives on assessment practices, placement protocols, and most other policies and programs (Inoue 2019; Kirkland 2013; Ladson-Billings 2013; Steele 2010).

Creating a more richly diverse teaching staff requires us to perhaps begin recruiting potential future community college English teachers as early as high school (see Jawaharlal 2022). We would also need graduate training programs in English that privilege culturally relevant pedagogy (Ladson-Billings 1995; Paris and Alim 2017), antiracist assessment practices (Inoue 2015), multilingualism (Canagarajah 2013; Horner and Lu 2010; Horner et al. 2011), equitable grading practices (Feldman 2018), and curriculum that makes two-year colleges visible to students in these programs (Calhoon-Dillahunt et al. 2017; Jensen et al. 2021; Jensen and Toth 2018; Sullivan 2020). This work is crucially important for realizing the full democratic promise of community colleges and open admissions.

Given how busy most community college faculty and staff are, however, the question is, Who will do this crucially important recruitment and outreach work?

FACULTY WORKING CONDITIONS ARE STUDENT LEARNING CONDITIONS

The 2019 TYCA survey also reported disturbing findings about community college English-faculty workload. Just as we have witnessed divestment in higher education on the state and federal level over the last forty years for college budgets overall (Century 2019; see also Bousquet 2008; Newfield 2011, 2016; Welch and Scott 2016), we have also witnessed an associated divestment in secure, full-time faculty positions at community colleges (Suh et al. 2021; see also Childress 2019; Daniel 2022; Kezar, DePaola, and Scott 2019). The community college teaching staff has been systematically deprofessionalized, adjunctified, and underfunded over the last forty years. We can view this development as an example of the resistance, regression, and retreat in relation to equity and social justice advances that have been a permanent part of our educational history in the US (see, e.g., Bell 1992; McGrew 2019; Patterson 2001; Urban, Gaither, and Wagoner 2019). As Darin Jensen and Brett Griffiths note in their introduction to this collection, the percentage of part-time instructors in some two-year college English departments is as high as 80 percent. Recent data show part-time faculty teach approximately 58 percent of all US community college classes and thus manage learning experiences for more than half of all students enrolled in community colleges (Center 2014, 2). This number is not acceptable.

The literature on persistence, completion, and student development overwhelmingly shows faculty-student interactions generate a great variety of positive benefits for students—and full-time professors have more resources, more institutional support, more time, and more professional responsibility to provide that kind of support and mentoring for individual students over the course of many years. Adrianna Kezar and Daniel Maxey (2013) summarize the current situation this way:

Changes in the composition of the American professoriate toward a mostly contingent workforce are raising important questions about the nature of non-tenure-track faculty work and connections between their working conditions and student learning outcomes. Non-tenure-track faculty, particularly part-time faculty members, face a number of challenges and obstacles in the workplace that constrain their abilities to provide a high quality educational experience and facilitate optimal student learning. Recent research suggests the rising numbers of part-time faculty, their working conditions, and the lack of support they receive from their institutions are having an adverse impact on various measures of student success. Examples include diminished graduation and retention rates, decreased likelihood of transfer from two- to four-year institutions, lower grade point averages, and greater difficulty with major selection and persistence; these outcomes were often disproportionately experienced by students who were beginning their postsecondary education, including those in developmental or remedial courses. (1)

Furthermore, as Kezar and Maxey note, "although interactions and relationships with faculty members are strong predictors of learning among nearly all groups of students, they have been found to be strongest for students of color" (3; Figlio 2017; Lundberg and Schreiner 2004). These findings make this issue one of vital importance for community colleges.

Evidence is also emerging that suggests these numbers fall into a pattern that could be characterized as "racialized austerity" (Flaherty 2021), whereby students on predominantly white campuses have more opportunities to study with full-time professors than those who attend majority minority institutions (Benton 2021; Sullivan 2022a; see also Espinosa et al. 2019; Taylor et al. 2020). Certainly, reorganization schemes like the one Joanne Baird Giordano and Holly Hassel discuss in chapter 8 of this volume, the adjunctification of community college teaching staff (Childress 2019; Kezar, DePaola, and Scott 2019), and the long-term systematic defunding of community colleges—which serve the most richly diverse cohort of students in all of higher education (AACC 2023)—suggest this is the case. Public four-year institutions have not been the target of similar interventions or austerities.

In her famous essay "Social Class and the Hidden Curriculum of Work," Jean Anyon (1980) maintains that US educational institutions "make available different types of educational experience and curriculum knowledge to students in different social classes" (67; see also Cahalan et al. 2021; Carnevale et al. 2021; Chetty 2021; Chetty and Hendren 2018; Choitz and Reimherr 2013; Goldrick-Rab 2016; hooks 1994). As Jensen and Griffiths note in their introduction, most recent US presidents have advocated that we turn community colleges into vocational training centers. This is a form of "racialized austerity" as well, offering very diverse community college students only job training and low ceilings of possibility (Rose 2012). We must resist these calls and instead advocate for education at our nation's community colleges that liberates and ennobles—education designed to promote the public good and offer students support for whatever career or life path they may choose (Goldin and Katz 2008; Griffiths 2017; Marginson 2011; McMahon 2009, 2015; Newfield 2016; Sandel 2020; Sullivan 2021b). This vision of the community college mission and mandate promotes democracy, distributes opportunity more fairly, and nurtures hope and optimism. For this work we can adopt suffrage activist Helen Todd's (1911) famous slogan: "Bread for all, and roses too" (619).

THE SHEER AMOUNT OF TIME IT TAKES TO DO ALL THE WORK

I was part of the team that conducted the national 2019 TYCA workload survey (Suh et al. 2021; Two-Year College 2022), and I was one of the coders of the data we collected. I coded hundreds of responses, and much of what I read broke my heart. I found English teachers struggling to fulfill the democratic promise of open admissions while teaching 5×5 course loads and having little or no professional-development support or funding. Many respondents to our survey had no job security beyond the end of the semester (Jensen et al. 2021; Sandel 2020; Tinberg 1997; Toth and Sullivan 2016). We asked a question about emotional labor in the survey, and these responses were particularly noteworthy (Hassel, Sullivan, and Wegner 2020). The response below from Participant #484, for example, expresses a key theme that emerged from this survey:

> The sheer amount of time it takes to do all of the work. We work on weekends and holidays providing meaningful feedback to students on their work, responding to their inquiries, representing faculty on an increasing number of committees with a decreasing number of full-time faculty, and reading and writing within our discipline in order to stay current on research both for our students and the advancement of our profession. On top of all of this, because we work with so many students who are some of the most vulnerable students in the population in terms of preparation, social support, and systemic oppression, the emotional labor of being a community college [English teacher] is enormous. Every semester, I have students who fall behind because they are working multiple jobs with shifting schedules, who are one medical or transportation bill away from being unable to make ends meet, who simply believe they don't belong in college because so much is new or unfamiliar, who lack support at home because they are the first in their families to go to college, or who don't seek treatment for anxiety, depression, or other mental illness because of

the cost, the stigma, or simply not knowing how. Providing compassion and support for these students is absolutely necessary and often rewarding, but it's also exhausting when considering all of the other work I have to do. (Two-Year College 2019)

As we know, there is a close relationship between working conditions and effective teaching and learning. The most important finding from this survey linked workload issues to student learning. I would summarize our key finding this way:

> Unsustainable workloads for teachers create less than ideal learning environments for students.

Many community colleges now resemble big-box stores run by a small number of full-time tenure-track managers overseeing an army of part-time employees. The implications of this retreat from staffing community colleges with secure, full-time faculty who have the time and institutional support to engage in professional development, research, and mentoring and advising students are significant. One of the reasons it took us so long to see the damage done by multiple tiers of developmental education beyond our own individual classrooms is because most developmental educators in community college English departments are so busy with their daily teaching responsibilities they have little time or energy to devote to this kind of ambitious, expensive, labor-intensive macrolevel research, as our survey results made very clear. Most community college English teachers also have very little institutional support and limited access to resources, including access to the kind of research libraries commonly found at four-year campuses. Many adjunct faulty have no institutional support whatsoever. Seeing the damage done by tiered developmental-course sequences required the help of an outside, philanthropically funded entity to do this work for us (Bailey, Jeong, and Cho 2009; Cho et al. 2012; Scott-Clayton and Rodriguez 2015).

The current precarious employment conditions at community colleges nationwide (Two-Year College 2022; see also Bousquet 2008; Daniel 2022; Kalleberg 2011; Kezar, DePaola, and Scott 2019; Toth and Sullivan 2016), along with austerity funding models for community colleges, actively work against many community college English teachers having the resources, time, and energy to do the important work outside the classroom our students need. This includes professional development, program evaluation, institutional research, and teacher-scholar-activism.

With 5/5 teaching loads, what can we reasonably expect community college English teachers to do, beyond keeping up with their classes? To engage the urgent equity and social justice work before us, I am calling for a 4/4 teaching load as the national standard for two-year college English teachers.

GRADING FOR EQUITY

The hegemonic role Standard Written English (SWE) has played in pedagogy and assessment practices also requires careful attention from all two-year college English teachers (Baker-Bell 2020; Canagarajah 2013; hooks 1994; Inoue 2015; Kirkland 2013; Smitherman 1977). This change in thinking about what equity means in the richly diverse context of the community college classroom is being driven by new scholarship and research about placement (Toth et al. 2019), antiracist writing assessment (Inoue 2105; Feldman 2018; Poe, Inoue, and Elliot 2019), translingualism (Canagarajah 2013), college readiness (McNair et al. 2016), and equity.

We have now come to understand, following Bettina L. Love (2020) and others, that language is "a critical component of a person's identity" (20) and must therefore be honored, respected, and valued—not erased or problematized. Scholars are calling for English teachers to commit once again to students' right to their own language in our teaching and assessment practices (Baker-Bell 2020; Kirkland 2013; Perryman-Clark, Kirkland, and Jackson 2015; Smitherman 2017). April Baker-Bell (2020) suggests, for example, that "standard English is a byproduct of white supremacy" (6) and "linguistic justice does not see White Mainstream English as the be-all and end-all for Black speakers" (7). Baker-Bell challenges our profession to "create an education system where Black students, their language, their literacies, their culture, their creativity, their joy, their imagination, their brilliance, their freedom, their existence, their resistance MATTERS" (3). The same can be said for Latinx and Native American students as well (Acevedo 2022; Diaz 2020; Lyiscott 2014, 2017; Martinez 2014). The CCCC policy brief "This Ain't Another Statement! This is a DEMAND for Black Linguistic Justice!" (College Composition 2020) is another vitally important expression of these principles.

Two-year college English teachers are being called on to develop curriculum and pedagogy that promote critical language awareness (Smitherman 2017, 10), challenges white language supremacy and monolingualism, and supports the development of culturally sustaining pedagogies (Kareem 2019; Kendi 2019; Ladson-Billings 1995; Lyiscott 2017; Minor 2017; Paris and Alim 2017; Prendergast 1998; Sealey-Ruiz 2021; Seltzer and de los Ríos 2021; Smitherman 1977; Staats 2014). These issues have become urgent in our profession, and they are particularly important in community college classrooms. We are only beginning to understand how white language supremacy becomes internalized as anti-Black linguistic racism in students of color (Baker-Bell 2020, 59–61; Kirkland 2013; Love 2020). There is obviously much important work ahead to respond to this call.

ACCESS WITHOUT SUPPORT IS NOT OPPORTUNITY

Finally, as retention specialist Vincent Tinto reminds us, "access without support is not opportunity" (Tinto 2008). Open-admissions policies addressed the issue of *access* to higher education—but they did not address the issues of *retention* and *completion* (see Goldrick-Rab and Cady 2018; Gravely 2021). To make the promise of open admissions a real opportunity for all students, we must develop programs and support services nationwide that make it possible for all community college students to stay enrolled and make progress toward meeting their educational goals. CUNY's Accelerated Study in Associate Programs (ASAP) is one such initiative. It is regarded by many as the "gold standard" of the new model of student success programs designed to offset economic inequality and structural racism (Gravely 2021). CUNY's program offers students a free unlimited MetroCard, grants to offset the cost of textbooks, scholarship support covering tuition and mandatory fees for any gap left after a student's financial-aid award, a dedicated advisor, special registration options that help students get the classes they need to fit their schedules, and opportunities to take classes with fellow ASAP/ACE students to foster community (City University 2023).

This program is working from a different and more proactive conceptual model of student support than many current programs, which often simply enroll students and then invite them to reach out to an advisor, counselor, or the local food pantry if they have questions or need support. The CUNY model and others like it acknowledge and seek to offset the complexities, inequities, and contingencies that can disrupt the lives of community college students. Such programs seek to directly address the unseen and unanticipated obstacles *outside the classroom* that disrupt students' progress toward a degree or credential (Hassel and Phillips 2022; Sullivan, Bell, and Nielsen, forthcoming). We need programs like CUNY's on every community college campus. This support—which seeks to offset economic inequality, opportunity gaps (Milner 2020), and structural racism—makes open admissions the real opportunity it should be.

CONCLUSION

It is time to chart an ambitious new course for our nation's community colleges and for the students who attend them. There are encouraging signs that the age of austerity and neoliberalism may be ending (Brink 2022; Cambero 2021; Gerstle 2022; Sullivan 2021a; Welch and Scott 2016). Let us move forward into this promising new moment as teacher-scholar-activists building a rejuvenated community college system that honors the revolutionary promise of open admissions (Lawson 2003; President's 1947; Sullivan 2021a). To do this we will need a national 4/4 teaching load, more full-time faculty (with a maximum of 25 percent adjunct faculty in any department), support programs like CUNY's ASAP program on every campus, and time built into our workdays for professional development, reflection, collaboration with colleagues, and, yes, rest, relaxation, and rejuvenation. Secretary of Education Miguel Cardona recently called for "a culture change in higher education" (Brink 2022). This change will be accomplished, Cardona suggests, by paying less attention to "elite" well-funded institutions and focusing, instead, on "institutions that serve the most students with the most to gain from a college degree"—but "have the fewest resources to invest in student success" (Brink 2022). These institutions include community colleges, HBCUs, MSIs, tribal colleges, and Hispanic-serving institutions. Two-year college English teachers have been waiting a very long time, indeed, to hear a secretary of education talk like this.

Hassel and Giordano make a similar appeal in their 2013 essay "Occupy Writing Studies," urging compositionists, educators, researchers, and legislators to put open-admissions institutions—and the millions of students who attend them—at the center of our equity and social justice work nationwide. As Hassel and Giordano note,

> Where hierarchies most stand out in higher education institutions is in the nature of the students who enroll in them. As the July 2012 *Chronicle of Higher Education* symposium, "Has Higher Education Become an Engine of Inequality?," explains, the biggest difference between our types of institutions is in the resources allocated to the students who attend them, and the social mechanisms that "sort" students into colleges and universities are the primary sources of hierarchies. For example, Richard Kahlenberg observes in "Magnifying Social Inequality" that students who have the most resources typically go to colleges with the most resources and vice versa: "Low-income and minority students are concentrated in community colleges, which spent an average of $12,957 per full-time-equivalent student in 2009, while higher-income and white students are disproportionately educated at private four-year research institutions, which spent an average of $66,744 per student." Social class also predicts a student's

likelihood of earning a degree, with 50 percent of children whose families earn more than $90,000 earning a BA by age twenty-four, while one in seventeen children whose family income is less than $35,000 will have that same educational outcome (Wolin). (123)

The Center for American Progress notes community colleges receive $8,800 less in education revenue per enrolled student than their four-year sister institutions (Yuen 2020). This "translates into a total gap of $78 billion between the two sectors" (Yuen 2020). This kind of spending has been linked to persistence, success, and completion (Fain 2019; Webber and Ehrenberg 2010).

I invite community college English personnel to begin this work right now, today, as teacher-scholar-activists. This is "democracy's unfinished business"—and there is no higher calling than engaging in this equity and social justice work.

REFERENCES

Allen, James, ed. 2000. *Without Sanctuary: Lynching Photography in America.* Santa Fe, NM: Twin Palms.

Acevedo, Elizabeth. 2022. "Afro-Latina." *Elizabeth Acevedo,* "Poetics." http://www.acevedo writes.com/poetics.

American Association of Community Colleges (AACC). 2023. "Fast Facts 2023." https://www.aacc.nche.edu/research-trends/fast-facts/.

Anyon, Jean. 1980. "Social Class and the Hidden Curriculum or Work." *Journal of Education* 162 (1): 67–92.

Bailey, Thomas, Dong Wook Jeong, and Sung-Woo Cho. 2009. "Referral, Enrollment, and Completion in Developmental Education Sequences in Community Colleges." CCRC Working Paper 15, Teachers College, Columbia University, Community College Research Center, NY. https://ccrc.tc.columbia.edu/media/k2/attachments/referral-enrollment-completion-developmental_V2.pdf.

Baker-Bell, April. 2020. *Linguistic Justice: Black Language, Literacy, Identity, and Pedagogy.* NCTE-Routledge Research Series. New York: Routledge.

Baldwin, James. 1992. *The Fire Next Time.* New York: Vintage.

Bateman, David, Ira Katznelson, and John S. Lapinski. 2018. *Southern Nation: Congress and White Supremacy after Reconstruction.* Princeton, NJ: Princeton University Press.

Bell, Derrick. 1992. *Faces at the Bottom of the Well: The Permanence of Racism.* New York: Basic Books.

Benton, Ned. 2021. "The Faculty Gap: Comparison of SUNY and CUNY Senior College Faculty/Student Ratios." https://ufsbac.commons.gc.cuny.edu/wp-content/blogs.dir/11465/files/2021/10/FacultyGap.pdf.

Biondi, Martha. 2012. *The Black Revolution on Campus.* Oakland: University of California Press.

Bousquet, Marc. 2008. *How the University Works: Higher Education and the Low-Wage Nation.* New York: New York University Press.

Brink, Meghan. 2022. "Cardona's Vision for Higher Ed." *Inside Higher Ed,* August 12.

Cahalan, Margaret W., Marisha Addison, Nicole Brunt, Pooja R. Patel, and Laura W. Perna. 2021. *Indicators of Higher Education Equity in the United States: 2021 Historical Trend Report.* Washington, DC: Pell Institute for the Study of Opportunity in Higher Education,

Council for Opportunity in Education (COE), and Alliance for Higher Education and Democracy of the University of Pennsylvania (PennAHEAD). http://pellinstitute.org/downloads/publications-Indicators_of_Higher_Education_Equity_in_the_US_2021_Historical_Trend_Report.pdf.

Calhoon-Dillahunt, Carolyn, Darin L. Jensen, Sarah Z. Johnson, Howard Tinberg, and Christie Toth. 2017. "TYCA Guidelines for Preparing Teachers of English in the Two-Year College." *College English* 79 (6): 550–60.

Cambero, Fabian. 2021. "Former Protest Leader Boric Seeks to Bury Chile's 'Neoliberal' Past." Reuters, November 17. https://www.reuters.com/world/americas/former-protest-leader-boric-seeks-bury-chiles-neoliberal-past-2021-11-17/.

Canagarajah, Suresh. 2013. *Translingual Practice: Global Englishes and Cosmopolitan Relations.* New York: Routledge.

Carnevale, Anthony P., Kathryn Peltier Campbell, Ban Cheah, Megan L. Fasules, Artem Gulish, Michael C. Quinn, Jenna R. Sablan, Nicole Smith, Jeff Strohl, and Sarah Barrese. 2021. *The Cost of Economic and Racial Injustice in Postsecondary Education.* Washington, DC: Georgetown University Center on Education and the Workforce. https://cew.georgetown.edu/wp-content/uploads/cew-the-cost-of-economic-and-racial-injustice.pdf.

Carter, Shannon, Deborah Mutnick, Stephen Parks, and Jessica Pauszek. 2020. *Writing Democracy: The Political Turn in and beyond the Trump Era.* New York: Routledge.

Center for Community College Student Engagement. 2014. "Contingent Commitments: Bringing Part-Time Faculty into Focus." Special Report from the Center for Community College Student Engagement. Austin: University of Texas at Austin, Program in Higher Education Leadership. https://www.ccsse.org/docs/PTF_Special_Report.pdf.

Century Foundation. 2019. *Recommendations for Providing Community Colleges with the Resources They Need.* https://tcf.org/content/report/recommendations-providing-community-colleges-resources-need/.

Chetty, Raj. 2021. "Improving Equality of Opportunity: New Insights from Big Data." *Contemporary Economic Policy* 39 (1): 7–41.

Chetty, Raj, and Nathaniel Hendren. 2018. "The Impacts of Neighborhoods on Intergenerational Mobility I: Childhood Exposure Effects." *Quarterly Journal of Economics* 133 (3): 1107–62. https://doi.org/10.1093/qje/qjy007.

Childress, Herb. 2019. *The Adjunct Underclass: How America's Colleges Betrayed Their Faculty, Their Students, and Their Mission.* Chicago: University of Chicago Press.

Cho, S. W., Elizabeth Kopko, Davis Jenkins, and Shanna Smith Jaggars. 2012. "New Evidence of Success for Community College Remedial English Students: Tracking the Outcomes of Students in the Accelerated Learning Program (ALP)." CCRC Working Paper 53, Teachers College, Columbia University, NY. http://ccrc.tc.columbia.edu/media/k2/attachments/ccbc-alp-student-outcomes-follow-up.pdf.

Choitz, Vickie, and Patrick Reimherr. 2013. "Mind the Gap: High Unmet Financial Need Threatens Persistence and Completion for Low-Income Community College Students." Center for Postsecondary and Economic Success. https://files.eric.ed.gov/fulltext/ED544243.pdf.

City University of New York (CUNY). 2023. *ASAP: Accelerated Study in Associate Programs.* https://www1.cuny.edu/sites/asap/about/.

Cohen, Adam. 2020. *Supreme Inequality: The Supreme Court's Fifty-Year Battle for a More Unjust America.* New York: Penguin.

College Composition and Communication. 2020. "This Ain't Another Statement! This is a DEMAND for Black Linguistic Justice!" https://cccc.ncte.org/cccc/demand-for-black-linguistic-justice.

Crenshaw, Kimberlé, Neil Gotanda, Gary Peller, and Kendall Thomas, eds. 1996. *Critical Race Theory: The Key Writings That Formed the Movement.* New York: New Press.

Daniel, James Rushing. 2022. *Toward an Anti-Capitalist Composition.* Logan: Utah State University Press.
Diaz, Natalie. 2020. *Postcolonial Love Poem.* Minneapolis: Graywolf.
Douglass, Frederick. 1894. "Blessings of Liberty and Education." Teaching American History. https://teachingamericanhistory.org/library/document/blessings-of-liberty-and-education/.
Douglass, Frederick. 2016. *Narrative of the Life of Frederick Douglass.* 2nd ed. Edited by William L. Andrews and William S. McFeely. New York: W. W. Norton.
Espinosa, Lorelle L., Jonathan M. Turk, Morgan Taylor, and Hollie M. Chessman. 2019. *Race and Ethnicity in Higher Education: A Status Report.* American Council on Education. https://1xfsu31b52d33idlp13twtos-wpengine.netdna-ssl.com/wp-content/uploads/2019/02/Race-and-Ethnicity-in-Higher-Education.pdf.
Fain, Paul. 2019. "Wealth's Influence on Enrollment and Completion." *Inside Higher Ed*, May 23. https://www.insidehighered.com/news/2019/05/23/feds-release-broader-data-socioeconomic-status-and-college-enrollment-and-completion.
Feldman, Joe. 2018. *Grading for Equity: What It Is, Why It Matters, and How It Can Transform Schools and Classrooms.* Thousand Oaks, CA: Corwin.
Figlio, David. 2017. "The Importance of a Diverse Teaching Force." Brookings, November 16. https://www.brookings.edu/research/the-importance-of-a-diverse-teaching-force/.
Flaherty, Colleen. 2021. "The Full-Time Faculty Factor." *Inside Higher Ed*, December 2. https://www.insidehighered.com/news/2021/12/02/race-and-full-time-faculty-student-ratios-suny-cuny?utm_source=Inside+Higher+Ed&utm_campaign=cdb6d8a304-DNU_2021_COPY_02&utm_medium=email&utm_term=0_1fcbc04421-cdb6d8a304-19863 5169&mc_cid=cdb6d8a304&mc_eid=559545807a.
Flores, Ray. 2011. "False Hope." *Inside Higher Ed*, February 17. https://www.insidehighered.com/views/2011/02/17/false-hope.
Freire, Paulo. 1985. *The Politics of Education: Culture, Power and Liberation.* Translated by Donaldo Macedo. New York: Bergin and Garvey.
Freire, Paulo. 1994. *Pedagogy of the Oppressed.* Rev. 20th ann. ed. Translated by Myra Bergman Ramos. New York: Continuum.
Gerstle, Gary. 2022. *The Rise and Fall of the Neoliberal Order: America and the World in the Free Market Era.* New York: Oxford University Press.
Goldin, Claudia, and Lawrence F. Katz. 2008. *The Race between Education and Technology.* Cambridge, MA: Belknap.
Goldrick-Rab, Sara. 2016. *Paying the Price: College Costs, Financial Aid, and the Betrayal of the American Dream.* Chicago: University of Chicago Press.
Goldrick-Rab, Sara, and Clare Cady. 2018. *Supporting Community College Completion with a Culture of Caring: A Case Study of Amarillo College.* Temple University, Hope Center for College Community and Justice. https://www.actx.edu/president/files/filecabinet/folder10/Wisconsin_HOPE_Lab___A_Case_Study_of_Amarillo_College__print_version_.pdf.
Gravely, Alexis. 2021. "Shifting Focus from Access to Completion." *Inside Higher Ed*, May 3. www.insidehighered.com/news/2021/05/03/biden-aims-increase-college-success-62-billion-investment.
Griffiths, Brett. 2017. "Professional Autonomy and Teacher-Scholar-Activists in Two-Year Colleges: Preparing New Faculty to Think Institutionally." *Teaching English in the Two-Year College* 45 (1): 47–68.
Griffiths, Brett M., and Christina M. Toth. "Rethinking 'Class:' Poverty, Pedagogy, and Two-Year College Writing Programs." 2017. *Class in the Composition Classroom,* edited by William Thelin and Genesea Carter, 231–57. Logan: Utah State University Press.

Hassel, Holly, and Joanne Giordano. 2013. "Occupy Writing Studies: Rethinking College Composition for the Needs of the Teaching Majority." In *Profession*, edited by Kathleen Blake Yancey, special issue, *College Composition and Communication*, 65 (1): 117–39.

Hassel, Holly, and Cassandra Phillips. 2022. *Materiality and Writing Studies: Aligning Labor, Scholarship, and Teaching*. Champaign, IL: NCTE.

Hassel, Holly, Patrick Sullivan, and McKenna Wegner. 2020. "TYCA Working Paper #7: Making the Emotional Labor of Open-Access Teaching Visible." Two-Year College English Association, TYCA Workload Task Force. https://ncte.org/wp-content/uploads/2020/11/TYCA_Working_Paper_7.pdf.

hooks, bell. 1994. *Teaching to Transgress: Education as the Practice of Freedom*. New York: Routledge.

hooks, bell. 2003. *Teaching Community: A Pedagogy of Hope*. New York: Routledge.

Horner, Bruce, and Min-Zhan Lu. 2010. "Resisting Monolingualism in 'English': Reading and Writing the Politics of Language." In *Rethinking English in Schools: Towards a New and Constructive Stage*, edited by Carol Fox, Brian Street, and Viv Ellis, 141–57. London: Continuum.

Horner, Bruce, Min-Zhan Lu, Jacqueline Jones Royster, and John Trimbur. 2011. "Language Difference in Writing: Toward a Translingual Approach." *College English* 73 (3): 303–21.

Hubrig, Ada/Adam. 2022. "Emphasizing Access in Open-Access Education: One Disabled Person's Plea to Two-Year College English Teacher-Scholar-Activists." *Teaching English in the Two-Year College* 49 (3): 193–202.

Hung, Man, William A. Smith, Maren W. Voss, Jeremy D. Franklin, Yushan Gu, and Jerry Bounsanga. 2020. "Exploring Student Achievement Gaps in School Districts Across the United States." *Education and Urban Society* 52 (2): 175–93. https://doi.org/10.1177/0013124519833442.

Inoue, Asao B. 2015. *Antiracist Writing Assessment Ecologies: Teaching and Assessing Writing for a Socially Just Future*. Anderson, NC: Parlor.

Inoue, Asao B. 2019. "2019 CCCC Chair's Address: How Do We Language So People Stop Killing Each Other, or What Do We Do about White Language Supremacy?" *College Composition and Communication* 71 (2): 352–69.

Jawaharlal, Mariappan. 2022. "Why DEI Initiatives Are Likely to Fail." *Inside Higher Ed*, July 20. https://www.insidehighered.com/views/2022/07/21/why-dei-initiatives-are-likely-fail-opinion.

Jensen, Darin L. 2020. "Dispatches from Bartertown." In *Sixteen Teachers Teaching: Two-Year College Perspectives*, edited by Patrick Sullivan, 37. Logan: Utah State University Press.

Jensen, Darin, Carolyn Calhoon-Dillahunt, Brett Griffiths, and Christie Toth. 2021. "Embracing the Democratic Promise: Transforming Two-Year Colleges and Writing Studies through Professional Engagement." *New Directions for Community Colleges* 2021 (194): 55–66.

Jensen, Darin, and Christie Toth, eds. 2018. "Symposium: Academic Freedom, Labor, and Teaching English in the Two-Year College." *Teaching English in the Two-Year College* 45 (4): 338–60.

Kalleberg, Arne L. 2011. *Good Jobs, Bad Jobs: The Rise of Polarized and Precarious Employment Systems in the United States, 1970s to 2000s*. New York: Russell Sage Foundation.

Kareem, Jamila. 2019. "A Critical Race Analysis of Transition-Level Writing Curriculum to Support the Racially Diverse Two-Year College." *Teaching English in the Two-Year College* 46 (4): 271–96.

Kendi, Ibram X. 2012. *The Black Campus Movement: Black Students and the Racial Reconstitution of Higher Education, 1965–1972*. New York: Palgrave Macmillan.

Kendi, Ibram X. 2016. *Stamped from the Beginning: The Definitive History of Racist Ideas in America*. New York: Bold Type Books.

Kendi, Ibram X. 2019. *How To Be an Antiracist*. London: One World.

Kezar, Adrianna, Tom DePaola, and Daniel T. Scott. 2019. *The Gig Academy: Mapping Labor in the Neoliberal University*. Baltimore: Johns Hopkins University Press.

Kezar, Adrianna, and Daniel Maxey. 2013. "Faculty Matter: Selected Research on Connections between Faculty-Student Interaction and Student Success." Delphi Project on the Changing Faculty and Student Success, Pullias Center for Higher Education, University of Southern California. https://pullias.usc.edu/download/faculty-matter-selected-research-connections-faculty-student-interaction-student-success/.

Kirkland, David E. 2013. *A Search Past Silence: The Literacy of Young Black Men*. New York: Teachers College Press.

Kynard, Carmen. 2014. *Vernacular Insurrections: Race, Black Protest, and the New Century in Composition*. Albany: SUNY Press.

Ladson-Billings, Gloria. 1995. "Toward a Theory of Culturally Relevant Pedagogy." *American Educational Research Journal* 32 (3): 465–91.

Ladson-Billings, Gloria. 2006. "From the Achievement Gap to the Education Debt: Understanding Achievement in U.S. Schools." *Educational Researcher* 35 (7): 3–12.

Ladson-Billings, Gloria. 2013. "Lack of Achievement or Loss of Opportunity?" In *Closing the Opportunity Gap: What America Must Do to Give Every Child an Even Chance*, edited by Prudence L. Carter and Kevin G. Welner, 11–22. New York: Oxford University Press.

Lawson, Stephen F., ed. 2003. *To Secure These Rights: The Report of President Harry S. Truman's Committee on Civil Rights*. Boston: Bedford/St. Martin's. Also available at the Harry S. Truman Library, https://www.trumanlibrary.gov/library/to-secure-these-rights.

Lewis, John, Andrew Aydin, and Nate Powell. 2016. *March: Trilogy*. San Diego: Top Shelf.

Love, Bettina L. 2020. *We Want to Do More Than Survive: Abolitionist Teaching and the Pursuit of Educational Freedom*. New York: Beacon.

Lundberg, Carol A., and Laurie Schreiner. 2004. "Quality and Frequency of Faculty-Student Interaction as Predictors of Learning: An Analysis by Student Race/Ethnicity." *Journal of College Student Development* 45 (5): 549–65.

Lyiscott, Jamila. 2014. "Three Ways to Speak English." TED video, 4:16. https://www.ted.com/talks/jamila_lyiscott_3_ways_to_speak_english?language=en.

Lyiscott, Jamila. 2017. "Racial Identity and Liberation Literacies in the Classroom." *English Journal* 106 (4): 47–53.

Martinez, Aja Y. 2014. "A Plea for Critical Race Theory Counterstory: Stock Story versus Counterstory Dialogues Concerning Alejandra's 'Fit' in the Academy." *Composition Studies* 42 (2): 33–55.

Marginson, Simon. 2011. "Higher Education and Public Good." *Higher Education Quarterly* 65 (4): 411–33.

McGrew, Will. 2019. "U.S. School Segregation in the Twenty-First Century: Causes, Consequences, and Solutions." Washington Center for Equitable Growth. https://equitablegrowth.org/research-paper/u-s-school-segregation-in-the-21st-century/.

McMahon, Walter W. 2009. *Higher Learning, Greater Good: The Private and Social Benefits of Higher Education*. Baltimore: Johns Hopkins University Press.

McMahon, Walter W. 2015. "Financing Education for the Public Good: A New Strategy." *Journal of Education Finance* 40 (4): 414–37.

McNair, Tia Brown, Susan Albertine, Michelle Asha Cooper, Nicole McDonald, and Thomas Major Jr. 2016. *Becoming a Student-Ready College*. San Francisco: Jossey-Bass.

Milner, H. Richard IV. 2020. *Start Where You Are, But Don't Stay There: Understanding Diversity, Opportunity Gaps, and Teaching in Today's Classrooms*. 2nd ed. Cambridge, MA: Harvard Education Press.

Minor, Cornelius. 2017. *We Got This: Equity, Access, and the Quest to Be Who our Students Need Us to Be*. Portsmouth, NH: Heinemann.

Mirra, Nicole. 2018. *Educating for Empathy: Literacy Learning and Civic Engagement*. New York: Teachers College Press.

Newfield, Christopher. 2011. *Unmaking the Public University: The Forty-Year Assault on the Middle Class.* Cambridge, MA: Harvard University Press.

Newfield, Christopher. 2016. *The Great Mistake: How We Wrecked Public Universities and How We Can Fix Them.* Baltimore: Johns Hopkins University Press.

Paris, Django, and H. Samy Alim. 2017. *Culturally Sustaining Pedagogies: Teaching and Learning for Justice in a Changing World.* New York: Teachers College Press.

Patterson, James T. 2001. *Brown v. Board of Education: A Civil Rights Milestone and Its Troubled Legacy.* New York: Oxford University Press.

Perryman-Clark, Staci, David E. Kirkland, and Austin Jackson, eds. 2015. *Students' Right to Their Own Language: A Critical Sourcebook.* Boston: Bedford/St. Martin's.

Poe, Mya, Asao B. Inoue, and Norbert Elliot, eds. 2019. *Writing Assessment, Social Justice, and the Advancement of Opportunity.* Fort Collins, CO: WAC Clearinghouse.

Prendergast, Catherine. 1998. "Race: The Absent Presence in Composition Studies." *College Composition and Communication* 50 (1): 36–53.

President's Commission on Higher Education. 1947. *Higher Education for Democracy: A Report of the President's Commission on Higher Education.* New York: Harper & Brothers. https://ia801506.us.archive.org/25/items/in.ernet.dli.2015.89917/2015.89917.Higher-Education-For-American-Democracy-A-Report-Of-The-Presidents-Commission-On-Higher-Education-Vol-I–Vi_text.pdf.

Rose, Mike. 2011. "Remediation at a Crossroads." *Inside Higher Ed,* April 21. https://www.insidehighered.com/views/2011/04/21/remediation-crossroads.

Rose, Mike. 2012. *Back to School: Why Everyone Deserves a Second Chance at Education.* New York: New Press.

Rothstein, Richard. 2004. *Class and Schools: Using Social, Economic, and Educational Reform to Close the Black-White Achievement Gap.* New York: Teachers College Press.

Rothstein, Richard. 2018. *The Color of Law: A Forgotten History of How Our Government Segregated America.* New York: Liveright.

Sandel, Michael J. 2020. *The Tyranny of Merit: What's Become of the Common Good?* New York: Farrar, Straus, and Giroux.

Scott-Clayton, Judith, and Olga Rodriguez. 2015. "Development, Discouragement, or Diversion? New Evidence on the Effects of College Remediation." *Education Finance and Policy* 10 (1): 4–45. https://doi.org/10.1162/EDFP_a_00150.

Sealey-Ruiz, Yolanda. 2021. *Racial Literacy: A Policy Research Brief.* Champaign, IL: NCTE. https://ncte.org/wp-content/uploads/2021/04/SquireOfficePolicyBrief_Racial Literacy_April2021.pdf.

Seltzer, Kate, and Cati de los Ríos. 2021. "Understanding Translanguaging in US Literacy Classrooms: Reframing Bi-/Multilingualism as the Norm." Champaign, IL: NCTE. https://ncte.org/wp-content/uploads/2021/04/SquireOfficePolicyBrief_Translanguaging_April2021.pdf.

Sharkey, Patrick. 2013. *Stuck in Place: Urban Neighborhoods and the End of Progress toward Racial Equality.* Chicago: University of Chicago Press.

Smitherman, Geneva. 1977. *Talkin and Testifyin: The Language of Black America.* Detroit, MI: Wayne State University Press.

Smitherman, Geneva. 2017. "Raciolinguistics, 'Mis-Education,' and Language Arts Teaching in the Twenty-First Century." *Language Arts Journal of Michigan* 32 (2): 4–12. https://doi.org/10.9707/2168-149X.2164.

Staats, Cheryl. 2014. "Implicit Racial Bias and School Discipline Disparities." The Ohio State University, Kirwan Institute. http://kirwaninstitute.osu.edu/implicit-bias-training/resources/ki-ib-argument-piece03.pdf.

Steele, Claude M. 2010. *Whistling Vivaldi: How Stereotypes Affect Us and What We Can Do.* New York: Norton.

Stevenson, Bryan. 2014. *Just Mercy: A Story of Justice and Redemption.* New York: Spiegel & Grau.

Suh, Emily, Joanne Baird Giordano, Brett Griffiths, Holly Hassel, and Jeffrey Klausman. 2021. "The Profession of Teaching English in the Two-Year College: Findings from the 2019 TYCA Workload Survey." *Teaching English in the Two-Year College* 48 (3): 332–49.

Sullivan, Patrick. 2017. *Economic Inequality, Neoliberalism, and the American Community College*. New York: Palgrave Macmillan.

Sullivan, Patrick, ed. 2020. *Sixteen Teachers Teaching: Two-Year College Perspectives*. Logan: Utah State University Press.

Sullivan, Patrick. 2021a "Composition in the Age of Neoliberalism: An Interview with Holly Hassel and Joanne Baird Giordano." *College Composition and Communication* 73 (1): 126–55.

Sullivan, Patrick. 2021b. *Democracy, Social Justice, and the American Community College*. New York: Palgrave Macmillan.

Sullivan, Patrick. 2022a. "Racialized Austerity and CSCU's 'Students First.'" *CT Mirror, March 17*. https://ctmirror.org/2022/03/17/racialized-austerity-and-cscus-students-first/.

Sullivan, Patrick, ed. 2022b. *The Community College Success Stories Project: Celebrating America's Community Colleges and the Students Who Attend Them.* https://www.communitycollegesuccessstories.org/.

Sullivan, Patrick, Abigail Bell, and David Nielsen. Forthcoming. "The Complex Nature of Student Retention at America's Community Colleges." *Community College Review*.

Taylor, Morgan, Jonathan M. Turk, Hollie M. Chessman, and Lorelle L. Espinosa. 2020. *Race and Ethnicity in Higher Education: 2020 Supplement*. American Council on Education. http://1xfsu31b52d33idlp13twtos-wpengine.netdna-ssl.com/wp-content/uploads/2020/11/REHE-2020-final.pdf.

Tinberg, Howard B. 1997. *Border Talk: Writing and Knowing in the Two-Year College*. Urbana, IL: NCTE.

Tinto, Vincent. 2008. "Access without Support Is Not Opportunity." *Inside Higher Ed*, June 9. https://www.insidehighered.com/views/2008/06/09/access-without-support-not-opportunity.

Todd, Helen M. 1911. "'Getting Out the Vote." *American Magazine* 72: 611–19. https://books.google.com/books?id=LGhEAQAAMAAJ&printsec=frontcover&source=gbs_ge_summary_r&cad=0#v=onepage&q=roses&f=false.

Toth, Christie, and Patrick Sullivan. 2016. "Toward Local Teacher-Scholar Communities of Practice: Findings from a National TYCA Survey." *Teaching English in the Two-Year College* 43 (3): 247–73.

Toth, Christie, Jessica Nastal, Holly Hassel, and Joanne Baird Giordano. 2019. "Introduction: Writing Assessment, Placement, and the Two-Year College." Special issue, *Journal of Writing Assessment* 12 (1). https://escholarship.org/uc/item/83935608.

Two-Year College English Association, TYCA Workload Task Force. 2019. Full Data Report: 2019 TYCA Workload Survey.

Two-Year College English Association, TYCA Workload Task Force. 2022. "White Paper on Two-Year College English Faculty Workload." *Teaching English in the Two-Year College* 49 (4): 292–30.

United States, National Center for Education Statistics. 2016. "Digest of Educational Statistics: Table 302.20. Percentage of Recent High School Completers Enrolled in Two- And Four-Year Colleges, by Race/Ethnicity: 1960 through 2015." https://nces.ed.gov/programs/digest/d17/tables/dt17_302.20.asp.

Urban, Wayne J., Milton Gaither, and Jennings L. Wagoner Jr. 2019. *American Education: A History*. 6th ed. New York: Routledge.

Warnke, Anthony, and Kirsten Higgins. 2018. "A Critical Time for Reform: Empowering Interventions in a Precarious Landscape." *Teaching English in the Two-Year College* 45 (4): 361–84.

Webber, Douglas A., and Ronald G. Ehrenberg. 2010. "Do Expenditures Other Than Instructional Expenditures Affect Graduation and Persistence Rates in American Higher Education?" *Economics of Education Review* 29 (6): 947–58. Also available at https://www.nber.org/papers/w15216.

Welch, Nancy, and Tony Scott, eds. 2016. *Composition in the Age of Austerity*. Logan: Utah State University Press.

Whitman, James Q. 2017. *Hitler's American Model: The United States and the Making of Nazi Race Law*. Princeton, NJ: Princeton University Press.

Yuen, Victoria. 2020. "The $78 Billion Community College Funding Shortfall." Center for American Progress, October 7. https://www.americanprogress.org/article/78-billion-community-college-funding-shortfall/.

3

IDENTITY AGENTS IN THE TWO-YEAR COLLEGE CLASSROOM

Bernice Olivas

In her closing reflection, a student writes, "I didn't think I could ever really be a college student, but this class showed me that I AM a college student and that I do belong here." This student is in her forties, raised children, acted as a contributing member of the workforce, and returned to school. From our first day together, her biggest concern was that she "didn't know how to be a college student." She didn't know how to *do* college. Our first writing assignment was a literacy narrative that included readings from Mike Rose. As she read it, she began to understand there is no one way to be a college student. In our critical analysis, she began to unravel the ways society frames college students in media and film. She concluded the social myth was there to make it easier to treat college students unfairly. By the end of the semester, she no longer referred to herself as if she existed outside the college community, but rather she was part of her community, and together with her peers, she intended to succeed in her goals. This transformation was not a happy accident that emerged randomly from her interaction with class material; this transformation was by design. I had carefully researched and chosen the class materials because of their message—one that pushed directly against the messaging that there is one right type of college student. My goal when developing this class was to act as an identity agent and help my students develop an academic identity and see themselves as belonging to the social group of academia.

FIRST-GENERATION STUDENT RESEARCH

In "Closing the Opportunity Gap: Identity-conscious Strategies for Retention and Student Success," Vijay Pendakur (2016) maps successful retention programs that merge *identity-neutral* frameworks—frameworks not centered on racial, ethnic, or generational identity, like first-year success programs—with *identity-centered* frameworks—programs developed in response to identity frameworks including race, class, or generation, like multicultural centers. Pendakur's data come from TRiO programs that actively serve first-generation students. TRiO programs are federally funded, locally situated programs intended to support the learning and education attainment of historically disadvantaged students. Using an identity-centered framework, Pendakur designs student supports to be both "identity conscious" and intersectional. He argues merging identity-conscious frameworks with larger retention programs that already exist is essential; colleges support students of color, working-class students, and first-generation students in attaining higher education benchmarks because identity-conscious frameworks are successful where identity-neutral frameworks fail. Pendakur's analysis of retention programs suggests that one of the core challenges community college students face is rooted in identity, and therefore identity must be a core component in any discussion about the success of community college students. This chapter argues that identity-conscious frameworks that work for TRiO programs can be as successful in the two-year college classroom.

In 2010, Jeff Davis (2012), author of *The First-Generation Student Experience: Implications for Campus Practice, and Strategies for Improving Persistence and Success*, observed that "the statistics describing the success of First-generation students are not good; in fact, they are succeeding at a rate roughly half that of their non-First-generation counterparts" (xiv). Further, in 2012, Vincent Tinto updated research on student retention in college with a six-year longitudinal study. In the resulting book, *Completing College: Rethinking Institutional Action*, he explains, "I have come to appreciate the centrality of the classroom to student success and the critical role the faculty play in retaining students. But I also learned that the classroom was the domain of institutional action that was given the least attention" (vii). Tinto's update highlights the overwhelming gap in attention paid to classroom design and interactions despite decades of research on higher education completion, retention, and persistence. He points out that the role the classroom and faculty play in student success gets the "least attention" despite these interactions forming the majority of interactions students have with an institution.

Thus, turning attention to how identity is constructed, reinforced, and disrupted within the space of the classroom is essential for understanding the role writing studies plays in reshaping existing structural inequities embedded in our institutions. One strong argument for identity-conscious framework and intersectional strategies in the writing classroom comes from Ann M. Penrose's (2002) "quantitative descriptive study," which examined "[first-generation college students'] perceptions of their academic literacy skills and their performance and persistence in college" (437). Penrose focused on the differences between the ways first-generation college students and continuing-generation students perceived their abilities in the areas of preparedness, retention rates, and their own academic literacy skills. Her "results indicate[d] that First-generation students' self-perceptions represent critical factors in the college experience, underscoring the importance of helping students forge identities as members of academic communities" (437).

Her resulting analysis is useful for examining how student identities both interpret and shape students' experiences in college. Penrose (2002) argues that students who fail to figure out where they belong in an academic community are much less likely to graduate because they lack a generational history—a parent's college narrative, returning to a family member's university, or connections made through their family's college networks—to help guide them through the institution of higher learning. According to Penrose, it may not be *just* lack of preparation, lack of resources, or lack of support driving Davis's terrible statistics. It may be those challenges combined with the students' struggle to situate themselves in the academic community (455–57).

Penrose (2002) argues, "Helping students see themselves as members of the academic community *may be the most important challenge* faced in the university at large and in writing classrooms in particular" (458; emphasis mine). And she concludes by saying that "writing teachers in particular should take this challenge to heart—not just because we have access and opportunity by virtue of the near-universal freshman requirement and small class size, but because the source of FG students' insecurities may be situated very specifically in composition teachers' domain of academic concern" (457). Taking such a challenge to heart, however, is daunting when our expertise is in the examination of literacy and language expression, not—we might think—identity formation. Such distinctions elude us, though, given copious position statements in our field and epistemological frameworks that link language to identity (see, e.g., *CCC*'s "Students' Right to their Own Language" [Committee on CCCC Language Statement 1974]). To bridge the gap between this tacitly accepted premise in our field and the practice of classroom teaching, I turn to identity control theory (ICT), espoused and developed by sociologist Peter Burke (2005).

IDENTITY CONTROL THEORY AND THE IDENTITY AGENT

Simply understood, identity control theory (ICT) theorizes that individuals perform distinct identities for audiences based on their group membership, perceived roles within that membership, and the expectations students perceive (Burke 2005, 5–15). The term *identity agent* helps us understand how identity develops. Burke begins by acknowledging that individuals have many identities that overlap, interact, and even conflict with each other. He suggests identities can be classified into four categories: personal, role, social, and collective. Burke suggests individuals learn to associate certain behaviors with particular identities, eventually investing more generously in those behaviors that reinforce positive roles for the individual within the group. Eventually those behaviors are seen as critical characteristics of their identity and eventually they incorporate those behaviors into how they perform that identity (Burke 2005, 5–15). Burke explains that individuals develop identity looking for the answers to "What does it mean?" questions. For example, a child's understanding of femininity is developed by the people, environments, and situations that demonstrate answers to the question "What does it mean to be a woman?" In a complicated, messy, and often unconscious process, we find the answers to those questions in the world around us. For every question the individuals ask, they eventually build an answer set that holds deep and implicit personal meaning. Once individuals invest in an answer set, they then strive to behave in ways that honor that answer set.

In the case of community college students, academic identity is a role identity. It is rooted in how they understand the role of "college student." Considering that so many community college students are first generation, hail from underrepresented backgrounds, or—as returning students—bring social capital that often goes unseen and unrecognized by their peers and instructors, they are less likely to find answers to the question "What does it mean to be a successful college student?" in their communities or in their home environments—or possibly even in school. Without such answers, students struggle to define themselves as college students, and they struggle to find a place in the academic community. This challenge makes it harder for community college students to master the institutional knowledge they need to succeed. In addition, there is rarely anyone in their home communities who can offer them narratives, images, or advice for managing their identities, navigating their positioning in their institutions, or rejecting negative stereotype threats omnipresent in myriad student-success initiatives.

Contextualizing research on first-generation students with ITC, we can extrapolate that when community college students attempt to answer the questions "What does it mean to be a successful college student?" Or "What does it mean to be a valued member of the college?," too many of them either come up empty handed or are offered images, stories, and examples they find alien and impossible to attain. By embracing the role of identity agent, writing instructors at the community college are in the position to help students develop their role identity of college student. Accordingly, identity agents exert control over behavior by intentionally influencing the ways people invest in behaviors linked to specific identities. By influencing how others see themselves in certain settings, we can influence their behavior.

In "Identity Agents: Parents as Active and Reflective Participants in Their Children's Identity Formation," Elli P. Schachter and Jonathan J. Ventura (2008), sociologists, define identity agents as members of society who use a reflective method of research and instruction to facilitate how another develops a set of meaningful answers to "What does it mean?" questions. Intentionality is the defining feature of the identity agent and what makes an identity agent more than a literacy sponsor or role model. An identity agent reflects and researches the best possible ways to encourage very specific characteristics—human interactional identity characteristics, not only academic behaviors. Identity agents are aware of their ability to affect identity formation, and they use that ability to encourage others to develop in very specific ways (449).

In "Identity Process and Transformative Pedagogy: Teachers as Agents of Identity Formation," sociologists Marinda K. Harrell-Levy and Jennifer L. Kerpelman (2010) claim teachers can be identity agents for their students. They argue, "Teachers can be purposeful co-constructors of adolescents' identities when they use a transformative pedagogical approach that involves fostering collaborative learning and empowering students to think creatively and critically." They argue that when teachers use research and reflection to devise curriculum that creates change in student identity, teachers are acting as identity agents. For example, teachers who focus on social, emotional learning are helping students develop answers to the question, "What does it mean to be compassionate?" (Harrell-Levy and Kerpelman 2010, 70–75). Yet, it is reasonable to ask how we connect the fostering of social, emotional learning—compassion—to the "skills" so many of our colleagues expect from students when they leave our classrooms. Where is the intersection of literacy education and personal enrichment? And if such a magical nexus cannot be identified, how can we verify, at least, that we are supporting the development of powerful, agentive identity roles and not only those that better serve the college and the infrastructure that churns it?

In composition studies, Deborah Brandt's (1998) literacy sponsors are partially comparable to identity agents. She says, "Sponsors, as I have come to think of them, are any agents, local or distant, concrete or abstract, who enable, support, teach, or model, as well as recruit, regulate, suppress, or withhold literacy—and gain advantage by it in some way" (166). We can expand on this definition to understand identity agents as "any agents, local or distant . . . who [use reflection and research to] . . . enable, support, teach, or model" behaviors deeply meaningful to a specific identity. In the case of writing instructors, we should consider the ways we use reflection and research to "enable, support, teach, or model" (Brandt 1988, 166) behaviors deeply meaningful to how students understand themselves as valuable members of the academic community. Adopting intersectional, identity-conscious classroom strategies is one of the most critical moves we can make to support student success at the community college.

As other authors note, queer theories suggest gender is an identity construct developed over time through a series of small choices; it is recognized, revised, and reenacted through iterative self-management. Identity is a performance; a routine we establish through a thousand little actions we perform. For folks who are queer or gender fluid, this performance requires reflection and critical thought (Butler 2002). In the same way, becoming a successful college student happens through a series of small choices made repeatedly in certain situations. Building an academic identity also requires reflection and critical thought into how one performs as a student, along with a negotiation of how to perform cultural capital. Because gender identity, like an academic identity, is a construct, queer theorists have explored the ways we construct identity and the effects of those performances. Many of these compositionists bring these concepts, ideas, and questions to the classroom to ask students to develop their understanding of how their social position interacts with the world around them.

For example, Zan Meyer Gonçalves (2005) argues in *Sexuality and the Politics of Ethos in the Writing Classroom* that identity performance, as conceptualized in queer theory, can support a pedagogical practice of building ethos and empower composition students to think through meticulously crafting rhetorical performances—in the same manner queer youth employ survival strategies in a heteronormative world. In her work with queer youth, Gonçalves witnesses writers and speakers performing carefully crafted identities to elicit certain responses from specific audiences. She realizes the value in teaching and learning rhetorical strategies that help students become aware of the ways various discourses frame identity performances. As a result, she has crafted a pedagogical praxis that provides students with the tools needed to gain rhetorical agency within those discourses. She suggests that "invit[ing] students to see themselves as agents in and subjects of multiple and competing discourses and to identify the 'truths' those discourses support" and "guid[ing] students to address the important and enduring differences in identity-based values between themselves and their audiences" (Gonçalves 2005, 91) can empower them to build ethos as social justice writers and activists.

Gonçalves's careful examination of the relationship between self-awareness and performances of identity is the foundation of her pedagogy. She writes, "If we are able to recognize, through self-reflection, how our differing identities are shaping the way we see others and perform our 'selves,' we are more likely to make conscious choices about how and for whom and for what purpose we are performing our ethos" (Gonçalves 2005, 14). She gives a very specific list of how she models the writing and thinking moves she intends her students to adopt. Modeling—a common practice in the composition classroom—is a typical strategy of identity agents. Modeling and mimicking are foundational parts of developing identity. As students begin to understand and accept that what it means to be a conscientious writer is to be socially aware, and that what it means to be socially aware includes doing certain things like examining our own social standing, actively engaging in rhetorical action that promotes social justice, and maintaining relationships with people different from themselves, they will begin mimicking these actions in order to reconcile their behaviors with their understanding of a good writer.

Gonçalves outlines four elements of an ethic that underlies her pedagogy:

- self-reflection,
- separation of judgments from observations,
- use of dialogue,
- a focus on making allies and common ground. (Gonçalves 2005, 132)

Gonçalves's methods, particularly her focus on reflection and modeling, are an example of how an identity agent might work. Just as important, Gonçalves's observations and the methods she developed from them validate the benefits of offering first-generation students' opportunities to recognize their own unique ways of contributing to the discourse of their field, opportunities to see themselves represented in academia, and opportunities to reinvest their education in their own communities.

For an instructor to act as an identity agent, they must do more than sponsor literacy. They must begin by being aware of the traits and behaviors they see as part of an academic identity. Then they must use research to craft activities and classroom interactions that show the students why these behaviors are part of an academic identity. For example, I believe part of an academic identity is understanding that we each belong to a field or discipline of scholarship and that as a member of that group we should understand the group history. As an identity agent, I would be sure to assign reading and writing that helps students understand how their field emerged, how it has changed over the years, and its complex identity. I might do that by assigning an I-search project in each student's major. The goal would be for students to emerge with a better understanding of what it means to be a historian or mathematician or compositionist.

IDENTITY AGENTS IN THE CLASSROOM

Due to the complexity of the student body the community serves, instructors who are identity agents do not have the luxury of thinking about identity as broad categories. They cannot think of their students as just white, or Black, or middle class, or disabled. They must think of the nuances of identity and must be aware of the demographics they are working with; they must be aware of all the places identities intersect, tangle up, and get messy. They must understand their class may contain white subsistence farmers, African American middle-class students, folks who have lived in a variety of different social classes due to financial loss and gain. Identity agents must be hyperaware that power does not move in simple up-and-down patterns, it just moves. They must be aware people can be both privileged and marginalized at the same time. This is not to say an identity agent must identify and understand each of their students' complex identities but that the conversation should start with demystifying the concepts of power, privilege, and marginalization for the student.

Students must explore all the many ways they exist in the complex power dynamics of the college or university, their communities, and in wider society. It is not enough to offer students Peggy McIntosh's (1995) "invisible backpack" of white privilege. If you tell a white student, who grew up in poverty, that being white makes it easier to rent a home, he will laugh at you. If you tell a white student who was a homeless teen that her white skin protected her from harassment in stores, she will laugh at you. They laugh because nothing in their lived experience corroborates those assertions. In their experience, renting a home was nearly impossible because there was no way to save the first payment, last payment, and deposit, and they never got a deposit back because a landlord could read powerlessness written into their secondhand clothes and worn shoes. At the same time, if you tell a Mexican American who has grown up in a middle-class Mexican American suburban enclave she is underrepresented and people like her rarely make it to college, she's going to scoff. Her parents did go to college, so did their friends, and she has been groomed to go to college since she was a small child.

The identity agent must design writing projects that encourage students to explore their unique academic identity. There are numerous approaches to this kind of project. For example, I might frame a writing class around the history of higher education in the US. I would begin by framing the class around exploring the development of US higher education from the colonial period to the present. That project would include exploring the founders, the student bodies, and the legislations that have shaped higher education and would offer multiple points of entry into the academic community and encourage students to build their own community. It is critical to encourage students to examine their own relationships with the academic community and their institutions from multiple perspectives so that they have a real understanding of how their institutions succeed and fail in serving students like themselves. A realistic view of their institution's strengths and weaknesses prevents the student from internalizing lack of community as a reflection on their ability. It encourages them to seek out the places where they can find community. The objective would be to help students understand the origins of higher education so they can better understand the complex community to which they belong.

The class would explore four major topics:

- changes in the purpose of higher education
- the growth and limitation of access to higher education
- the relation of higher education to the larger society
- student culture and experiences

We would examine how the university system emerged, and we would research its changing goals and how it met or failed those goals. In the first writing project, the students would write a literacy narrative that focuses on their family's traditions concerning higher education. The second might ask students to locate scholars on campus who share important identity markers with the student and to interview them about their experiences. This writing project would help students develop their identity as members of the academic community by asking them to investigate their histories to begin to understand how they fit into the larger community in the present day. The final project might ask students to research an academic community on a campus to which they belong. We would read a variety of texts both historical and contemporary about the academic community to define what we mean when we say *academic community*.

Reading about the inception and development of universities in the colonial era and in early US history and discussing legacy students, continuing-generation students, and community college students would be one way for students to examine their positions as community members in academia. From there, they could actively examine the ways their current positions in the university act to privilege or marginalize them. Finally, we could discuss how that influences their perspectives.

The writing produced in a class where the instructor is an identity agent is, by necessity, deeply focused on the writers and the ways they interact with the world. Transformative pedagogy can also offer entry points to designing an identity-conscious writing classroom. Harrell-Levy and Kerpelman (2010) specifically name transformative pedagogy as a method used by identity agents. The practices and the theoretical connections Harrell-Levy and Kerpelman make are often already reflected in community college classrooms.

Most writing teachers already agree student-centered classrooms—designed with plenty of opportunities for feedback and discussion—are the most effective environment and are already acting as identity agents. Paolo Freire and Donaldo Macedo (2005) claim reading, writing, discussion, and reflection are methods of attaining "a critical reading of reality," which is what empowers all of us to "name" our worlds (36). Research suggests reading, writing, discussion, and reflection can serve as ways to prepare students to challenge existing structures of inequality and oppression because reading, writing, discussion, and reflection are ways of demystifying the power dynamics that surround us.

Freire (2005) explains that "to surmount the situation of oppression, people must first critically recognize its causes, so that through transforming action they can create a new situation, one which makes possible the pursuit of a fuller humanity" (47). Harrel-Levey and Kerpelman (2010) define transformative pedagogy as teaching that is student-centered, that values the mutual learning of both teacher and student, and reinforces "the voice of the student body—a voice formed from the students' critical analysis of the subject, given their unique individual experiences and their unique collective experiences as a class community." Finally, they say, "that a great obstacle to this liberation is the reality that the individuals absorb" (78–79).

For many community college students, those realities are the notions that their cultures are without capital. Critical pedagogy argues that when we give students the tools to see the constructions of injustice, they use those tools to resist pressure to maintain injustice. Freire and Donaldo (2005) claim a pedagogy that includes reading, writing, discussion, and reflection is a method of attaining "a critical reading of reality," which empowers us to "name" our worlds (36). They argue such a pedagogy can serve to ready students to challenge existing structures of inequality and oppression.

Freire and Macedo (2005) tell us students need ways to "recognize various tensions" and ways to "enable them to deal effectively with them" (49), and it has always been the work of the writing teacher to help students develop literacies that make it possible for them to deal effectively with the tensions they will face as writers and citizens. Many community college writing teachers already focus explicitly in helping students develop the rhetorical tools to speak back to tensions they will face as writers and citizens; the identity agent shows students how those same tools can be applied to their own lived experiences as a way of helping them develop their role identities as writers. For example, in composition studies, most writing teachers teach a version of the rhetorical analysis because it gives students the tools to see and demystify the messages they receive from society. Ideally, the identity agent takes this move a step further and asks students to apply that same analysis to their own lived experiences in hopes the student will be more able to "recognize various tensions" that exist in their social positions. The same reasons we teach rhetorical analysis hold true for asking students to read, write, and reflect about their own experiences in context to power, privilege, marginalization, and social position and to discuss those experiences. Rhetorical analysis is a method of learning how to "see" differently. Once students begin to do the work, they will discover ways to "deal effectively" with the tensions that arise in their inquiry (Freire and Macedo 2005).

However, transformative education is not just for Freire's "oppressed." If it is to be successful, it must work for students whose experiences with privilege and marginalization are more nuanced and less obvious. Community colleges serve students from middle-class backgrounds, students of color who are coming from financially elite environments, and white students from working-class and working-poor homes. Giving students positive ways to deal with tensions that arise from their positions in society is, in some ways, even more difficult because the demystification process is not one of reaffirming revelations—unlike the underrepresented female scientist who is empowered when her experiences are validated and named as sexism, or the white male scientist who is confronted with a hard truth for which he must account. Like Freire's critical consciousness (*conscientização*), identity agents must bring students from all backgrounds to see themselves through the lenses of understanding of the self and other and the community relationship between oppressor and oppressed, and to identify and define roles that unseat deeply ingrained assumptions about roles—stereotypes and mythologies about "What does it mean to be . . . ?" However, if students are to become transformative scholars, they must be given steps they can take to deal with these tensions.

It is particularly important for community college students coming from the suburban and urban elite to be given positive ways to handle the stress placed on their identities because these students have lived experiences mostly marked by privilege outside academia. Within academia, their lived experience can make them outsiders. And due to their community college status, they still lack institutional knowledge, can still be viewed as outsiders by others, and are still part of a marginalized community. However, they will struggle to contextualize themselves in the community in very different ways. It is harder for them to understand how they are connected to the systems that create inequity, and it is harder for them to see themselves in the material they are given to read. These students' fragility often interacts with marginalization in ways that make it very difficult for them to find community or to feel comfortable in a classroom environment.

IDENTITY AGENT IN MY CLASSROOM

As a writing teacher, I claim the position of identity agent. I shape the class work around the overarching questions "What does it mean to be a writer?" and "What does it mean to be a college writer?" I have conversations about privilege and marginalization by focusing on a process of demystification. I work to demystify the variety of power dynamics and policies that may have shaped the students as writers. I tell them the strongest writers are the ones willing to question not just what they know but also how they came to know it. Then we focus on inquiring into what they know about writing, how they came to know it, and how that might affect them. In our first unit I ask students to identify a misconception about writing that has influenced their process and to investigate it. We look closely at misconceptions like the idea of creating a perfect first draft, or solitary writing. They write a literacy narrative about one or two misconceptions they have struggled with.

As an identity agent my goal is to impress upon them that writers are people who ask hard questions of themselves and their topics. This combination is important because it works to help ready students to deal with difficult and often fraught subjects. I focus on language—the right to our own ways of reading, writing, speaking, and knowing—because language connects identity and writing in very explicit and clear ways students can identify with. They understand that as writers, we choose topics and audiences connected to how we perceive our identity. From their own experience, they understand that how teachers' value student writing is connected to students' use of language. The progression from valuing the complex identities in the classroom to using them as a site of inquiry and then, in turn, using that inquiry to encourage our students is a powerful process. It also offers plenty of opportunities to discuss privilege, marginalization, and power, and opportunities to push students to be critical thinkers about the social issues confronting them.

By asking the students to locate a personal connection to the topic before I allow them to research, I reinforce the idea that writers can and should research the ways they formed their beliefs. I also reinforce the idea that writers see their lived experiences as valid and important because they have shaped us in ways that give us a unique voice, which allows me to reinforce their unique voice as valuable to the community of readers and writers. More importantly, as an identity agent, I am creating access for marginalized writers to claim their identities as writers.

REFERENCES

Brandt, Deborah. 1998. "Sponsors of Literacy." *College Composition and Communication* 49 (2): 165–85.
Burke, Peter. 2005. "Identity Control Theory." In *Blackwell Encyclopedia of Sociology*, edited by George Ritzer. Oxford: Blackwell.
Butler, Judith. 2002. *Gender Trouble: Tenth Anniversary Edition*, 2nd ed. London: Routledge.
Committee on CCCC Language Statement. 1974. "Students' Right to Their Own Language." National Council of Teachers of English.
Davis, Jeff. 2012. *The First-Generation Student Experience: Implications for Campus Practice, and Strategies for Improving Persistence and Success*. Sterling, VA: Stylus Publishing.
Freire, Paolo. 2005. *Pedagogy of the Oppressed*. 30th ann. ed. New York: Continuum.
Freire, Paulo, and Donaldo Macedo. 2005. *Literacy: Reading the Word and the World*. London: Routledge.
Gonçalves, Zan Meyer. 2005. *Sexuality and the Politics of Ethos in the Writing Classroom*. Carbondale: Southern Illinois University Press.

Harrell-Levy, Marinda K., and Jennifer L. Kerpelman. 2010. "Identity Process and Transformative Pedagogy: Teachers as Agents of Identity Formation." *Identity: An International Journal of Theory and Research* 10 (2): 76–91.

McIntosh, Peggy. 1995. "White Privilege: Unpacking the Invisible Backpack." In *Women: Images and Realities: A Multicultural Anthology*, edited by Amy V. Kesselman, Lily D. McNair, and Nancy Schniedewind, 264–67. Mountain View, CA: Mayfield.

Pendakur, Vijay, ed. 2016. *Closing the Opportunity Gap: Identity-Conscious Strategies for Retention and Student Success*. Sterling, VA: Stylus Publishing.

Penrose, Ann M. 2002. "Academic Literacy Perceptions and Performance: Comparing First-Generation and Continuing-Generation College Students." *Research in the Teaching of English* 36: 437–61.

Schachter, Elli P., and Jonathan J. Ventura. 2008. "Identity Agents: Parents as Active and Reflective Participants in Their Children's Identity Formation." *Journal of Research on Adolescence* 18 (3): 449–76.

Tinto, Vincent. 2012. *Completing College: Rethinking Institutional Action*. Chicago: University of Chicago Press.

4
TRANSLATING HABITS OF PERSISTENCE
Supporting Generation 1 Learners in Community College

Emily K. Suh

Her name is Labiba. She was a sixth grader when she was forced to flee her homeland of Afghanistan during the 1979 Soviet invasion and the murder of her cousin at the hands of the Mujahideen. Outside Afghanistan, her family's previous political and social connections meant nothing, and as she matured and raised her own six children, Labiba struggled to provide for and protect her young family as they moved between countries seeking safety and peace. After spending several years as refugees abroad, Labiba's family immigrated to the United States. Nearly two decades after their arrival, she continues to draw upon the perseverance with which she protected her family from the Taliban and other "bad men," believing this same determination will ensure her ability to complete a college education.

His name is Olan. He was in his mid-twenties when he and his bride immigrated to the United States from Iraq seeking physical safety and economic opportunity. However, his heart remained in the Sinjar mountains, where his family had been forced to seek refuge in tents to escape Islamic State militants. Olan dreams of returning to his homeland. He speaks Kurdish to his two young sons who were born in the United States, and his family gathers in their modest midwestern apartment with friends to celebrate *Sere Sal,* the Yazidi new year. There are several friends with whom to celebrate, as many Yazidis, like Olan, resettled in the same town through the Special Immigrant Visa program for interpreters supporting US armed forces in Iraq. Like Olan, these friends served alongside US troops only to wait helplessly for US intervention to save their families in Iraq. Olan's friends understand the hardships of Olan's past and his hopes for a brighter future. He calls upon them frequently for advice about his plans to enroll in the local community college.

ORIENTING POSITIONS AND QUESTIONS

I first met Labiba and Olan in 2014 while working as a developmental reading and writing instructor at their community college. I had previously taught adult ESL at the college, and I was a faculty member in developmental English when I met Olan and Labiba and asked them to participate in an ethnographic case study I was conducting about how adult immigrant learners (whom I refer to as Generation 1 learners) transitioned from adult ESL into credit classes at the college (Suh 2017).

Reflecting my own guiding assumptions during my time as a community college English instructor, this chapter explores the culturally relevant (Ladson Billings 2014; see also Sullivan 2015; Sullivan, this volume) pedagogical position that all learners possess and should be encouraged to draw upon their nonmaterial resources and experiences for achieving their college goals. For example, familiarity with US academic participation expectations, such as raising one's hand before speaking or taking notes during lectures, is believed to be highly relevant to being a college student. Experience using word-processing applications or writing a five-paragraph essay is similarly highly valued since it is assumed these experiences can be translated to the tasks of being a college student. These resources and experiences are referred to as *symbolic capital*, a phrase suggesting their socially assigned but nonmonetary value (Bourdieu 1991). The recognition and positive valuation of learners' previous experiences and knowledge are especially relevant in community college contexts, where students from historically marginalized backgrounds can struggle to define themselves—and be recognized by others—as college students (Olivas, this volume). In this chapter, I apply the lens of symbolic capital to examine the experiences of Labiba and Olan as they drew from and were encouraged to share forms of *symbolic capital* applicable to their academic success in college. Although I have written about these learners and grappled with specific but related questions in previous work (see Suh 2018, 2021; Suh, McGee, and Owens 2021; Suh and Shapiro 2020), my exploration in this chapter is intended to be broader and guided by the research questions, What symbolic capital do learners like Olan and Labiba bring to the two-year college? How do they attempt to apply their symbolic capital? And how do instructors and students (re)frame students' identities and apply their experiences as symbolic capital?

Labiba's and Olan's experiences in the community college adult ESL course offer insight into the ways Generation 1 learners can apply—or struggle to apply—necessary knowledge and experience to their institutional environments. In this chapter, I explore how instructors, in the service of honoring students' past experiences and identities, may fail to validate students' desired future identities or the symbolic capital deployed in enacting those identities. Through Labiba's and Olan's stories, I offer examples of the ways instructors and other members of students' learning environments (i.e., tutors, fellow students) can misapply students' experiences as symbolic capital college professionals believe will translate into academic success. In such instances, the faculty and staff can fail to provide appropriate supports for students' transfer of knowledge and overall success. I conclude with suggestions for supporting learners' translation of their *symbolic capital* into forms relevant to and powerful in the two-year college. Like Patrick Sullivan and Bernice Olivas (both in this volume), I call upon two-year college faculty to reenvision their support of students' identity development as members of the academic community.

Ultimately, this chapter examines ways community college educators can better serve their immigrant students. Immigrant-background students are more likely to enter higher education through community college than four-year institutions (Teranishi, Suárez-Orozco, and Suárez-Orozco 2011). In their journeys to the United States, Labiba, Olan, and multitudes of other refugees demonstrate courage, resilience, and determination. The ongoing triple pandemic of COVID-19, structural racism, and economic inequality continue to challenge community college students, the majority of whom live what Mike Rose (1990) refers to as "lives on the boundary" (1). Instructors wishing to engage students may feel drawn to students' narratives of persistence through often-harrowing experiences. However, assuming learners' previous personal persistence will ensure their academic success, and the empathy from which that assumption can stem, may be insufficient to support the students' educational goals, including their ability to establish an academic identity.

THEORY

In this chapter, I bring together three theories of language acquisition as a lens for understanding and responding to the specific strengths and needs of Generation 1 learners. The first theory, Pierre Bourdieu's theorization of "symbolic capital," or socially valued resources, is frequently applied in second language-acquisition research to understand how learners enact desired identities as language users and members of various imagined communities (e.g., Becker 2011; Curry 2008; Norton 2013). Bourdieu explains how *symbolic capital* is socially constructed; in other words, experiences or knowledge are recognized as being relevant or irrelevant to college success because they are labeled as such. This ability to label or assign value is referred to as "symbolic power." Most frequently, *symbolic power* rests with college faculty and staff, while students like Labiba and Olan possess varying levels of *symbolic power* to assign value to the experiences they bring to college.

Drawing from Bourdieu, Bonny Norton (2013) explores how learners' identities are locally situated, enmeshed within a system of representational resources and contexts. Norton argues that learners assign value to language-learning experiences and their identities as language learners, making intentional and deliberate choices about how to apply their various resources to gain membership into the communities in which they desire membership. Rather than simply accepting the power of college faculty and staff to determine which experiences and knowledge are valuable forms of *symbolic capital*, Norton's theory of investment highlights how individual language learners intentionally deploy their *symbolic capital* to enact their desired identity. Learners like Olan and Labiba actively attempt to apply their *symbolic capital* to be recognized as belonging as college students within the subjective and dynamic site of identity development that is the two-year college.

Like investment theory, Malcolm Knowles's (1968) theory of andragogy presents several assumptions about how adults learn. Knowles explains that adults' previous experiences are a rich source of resources for their learning and that they are motivated to learn based on their desired social roles. This self-direction is manifested as internal motivation to gain necessary skills or knowledge, or what investment theorists would refer to as the symbolic capital for legitimizing the learners' participation in the imagined community. Researchers (Almon 2015; Becker 2011; Csepelyi 2012; Rumbaut 2004) recognize life experiences as important resources for adult ESL students to assert their legitimate participation within US educational contexts (Almon 2015; Norton 2013; Suh 2016, 2017). Such work may inadvertently imply that learners control the symbolic value of their previous experiences. However, as Labiba's and Olan's stories illustrate, current interpretations of the theory that view experience as *symbolic capital* may be insufficient for guiding instructors through the complex power dynamics involved in labeling learners' experiences as *symbolic capital*. While investment theory and andragogy foreground the learners' roles, these students' identities develop within complex systems that do not privilege learners and college professionals equally. The faculty role in supporting—but not determining—which experiences are most valuable and which identities are most desirable cannot be overstated.

Indeed, while applying theorizations of *symbolic capital* to the work of teaching and researching in the two-year college facilitates our recognition of the untapped academic value of the personal experiences Generation 1 learners can apply as *symbolic capital* to achieve academic goals, our recognition of the range of students' past experiences is by itself insufficient. Bourdieu (1991) notes that *symbolic capital* does not automatically ensure the *symbolic power* necessary to manifest a particular desired identity. As I explain elsewhere with Shawna Shapiro, not all *symbolic capital* is valued or valuable: not all experiences are relevant to learners' desired college student identity (Suh and Shapiro 2020).

As two-year college faculty, we must acknowledge the power we wield when we declare certain experiences and knowledge to be relevant to enacting a college-student identity. Instead of labeling students' experiences, we must first acknowledge, and then decenter, the implicit power that allows us to identify which experiences hold valuable *symbolic capital*. Within students' complex identity negotiations, a critical disjuncture exists between how adult-arrival immigrant students and their instructors conceptualize and recognize the students' identities and symbolic resources. Labiba's and Olan's cases illustrate how college personnel's privileging of certain identities (e.g., Army interpreter or refugee) can unduly impact the legitimacy of some students' participation within the college community.

Finally, separate from the theoretical framework I outline above, I point to the prevalence of *bildungsroman*, the literary genre focused on a character's moral growth. This genre is common in the developmental English classroom, where stories of persistence are emotionally appealing and can become a form of symbolic capital translatable to academic success (Harklau 2000). At times, learners' efforts to apply their available symbolic capital can become misaligned with others' perceptions of the learners, and in such instances, learners can struggle to establish their legitimacy within the college, an imagined community in which not all individuals know each other directly but all share a sense of identity connected to the college. This misalignment can occur because narratives of overcoming by themselves do not provide the narrator with the necessary symbolic power to guarantee others' recognition of their chosen identity. Symbolic capital is only valuable insomuch as other members of the imagined community of the college agree to its value. Indeed, the *bildungsroman* can become dangerous if misapplied in the classroom, and Joseph Slaughter (2007) cautions against what he refers to as a "sentimental" or "humanitarian reading" of such based on their "tendency to become a patronizing humanitarianism that is enabled by and subsists on socioeconomic and political disparities" (325). When readers valorize students' written accounts of personal development, they risk falsely equating students' character growth with their academic knowledge. Learners' symbolic resources can thus perpetuate the misrecognition of their chosen identities if others negatively assess the learners' *academic capital*, or their education and academic experiences relevant to future academic and social success.

LOCATING GENERATION 1 LEARNERS WITHIN THE TWO-YEAR COLLEGE

Two-year colleges serve as "critical gateways" for educating immigrant and refugee populations in the US (Casner-Lotto 2011, 1), and two-year colleges have an essential role in advocating for adult ESL students and providing them with educational resources (Chisman 2008). However, the two-year college response to English-language learners remains an understudied area within higher education research (Bunch and Endris 2012). The National Center for Education Statistics estimates that nearly one-quarter of degree-seeking students in two-year colleges come from an immigrant background (Horn, Nevill, and Griffith 2006), and in 2014, there were 667, 515 students enrolled in state-administered adult ESL classes, many of which are offered in the two-year college (Institute n.d.). Unfortunately, this number aggregates former adult English as a second language (ESL) students, English-dominant second-generation students, and the so-called Generation 1.5 students who completed their K–12 education in the United States. The immigration scholar Rubén Rumbaut (2004) advocates for distinguishing between immigrant groups by age and life stage at arrival, arguing scholars and researchers must acknowledge a subgroup within the larger population of immigrants to effectively serve them. This study responds to calls for additional research into two-year college support for adult English-language learners (Bunch and Endris 2012).

Given the diverse practical and epistemological traditions of the instructors teaching students in adult ESL and credit-level courses, the Generation 1 label serves as a heuristic for beginning conversations across disciplines regarding our support for the same population. The Generation 1-learner label encompasses the intersection of the learners' subjectivities—past, present, and future—and the ways others (scholars and practitioners alike) recognize the symbolic resources these learners, like Olan and Labiba, acquired through their varied lived experiences as immigrants/refugees, family caretakers, community elders, employees or employers, and students in previous learning environments, among other identities.

METHODS

The cases of Olan and Labiba come from a multiple-case study of six Generation 1 learners transitioning into developmental English courses at a community college (Suh 2017). I collected data during the learners' first term as credit-seeking students and included observations, interviews, and document collection as I observed the learners attending classes, studying, and meeting with advisors and tutors. Triangulation occurred through multiple data sources, including member checking with learners and college personnel. I examined Olan's and Labiba's experiences transitioning to developmental education, defined by the National Organization for Student Success (n. d.) as extending beyond the remedial classroom to include advising, tutoring, and placement testing. Through thematic analysis (Clarke and Braun 2014), I examined the first term through a lens of learners' desired identities and previous experiences to illuminate how Generation 1 learners and others draw upon the learners' experiences as symbolic capital.

Because I was both an instructor at the college and a researcher, my positionality was complex and layered. My interpretation of Olan's and Labiba's experiences was shaped by my own first-generation-immigrant status and the facets of my identity as a woman of color, researcher, and former adult ESL teacher. At the time of data collection, I also taught as a developmental English instructor at the learners' community college. My own position as a faculty member at the college is of relevance, as I attempt to present here my own complicity in the ways faculty and staff interactions with Labiba and Olan shaped their experiences at the college.

OLAN AND LABIBA: UNPACKING LEARNERS' SYMBOLIC CAPITAL AS IDENTITY INVESTMENT

Olan

Olan's upbeat manner belied the stress of providing for his young family in a foreign country with only a part-time job setting up for events and cleaning at a downtown hotel. When he began taking college classes, he dreamed of becoming an ultrasound technician. Although he tested out of developmental reading, Olan was placed into developmental writing. He registered for an integrated reading and writing course on the advice of friends, who shared Olan's experiences as a Yazidi interpreter. Like Olan, they were brought to the United States through the Special Immigrant Program, a visa program established to expedite the immigration of individuals who served as military interpreters in Iraq and Afghanistan. A native speaker of Kurdish, Olan first learned to read and write in Arabic. However, Olan saw no academic connections between his experiences studying Arabic and studying English. Olan described the Iraqi educational system as rife with corruption and linguistic, ethnic, and political discrimination. Despite these challenges, he described himself as thriving academically: "Back in my country, whenever teacher explain to me, sometime I do homework but not really a lot, not really well. When they teach me, when explain, I know everything." In effect, Olan presented the identity of a naturally gifted student and language expert who accessed significant *social capital* (i.e., the social network and the relationships Olan could apply to enacting his desired identity and achieving his academic goals) through the local Yazidi diaspora. He could also access significant *academic capital* through his natural intelligence and work ethic; however, he refused my efforts to get him to acknowledge how these experiences as a student who had learned to read and write in one colonial second language and was undergoing similar learning in an additional colonial language were symbolic resources relevant to his college transition.

Olan reflected on his experiences in Iraq during one of my observations of his study sessions in his apartment.

It was an afternoon typical of Olan's days off from the hotel: Olan read while his children played nearby and his wife cooked food for a dinner party. Olan frequently paused to interact with his family and to share with me his plans to return to Iraq as a health-safety inspector for a foreign company (a job his friend assured him would pay highly). As I watched, Olan paused in reading a new word. He carefully reread the surrounding sentences until he felt he understood enough of the context to keep reading. This process was one of the many strategies Olan taught himself but that went unobserved by faculty. At the same time, the significance of Olan's identity as a Yazidi went unrecognized. Olan's instructor noted Olan's disengagement with a problem-solution essay requiring him to critique his workplace. She appeared unaware of discrimination in Iraq that prevented Yazidis from attending college or entering their desired profession. Although Olan had little to say for the assignment, he openly discussed his experiences as an oppressed Yazidi with me. These exchanges illustrated how our efforts to connect Olan's previous experiences and college expectations frequently perpetuated a misrecognition of those experiences most meaningful to Olan. Bourdieu (1991) explains that certain forms of symbolic capital, such as Olan's military service, are arbitrarily assigned symbolic value through a process of "misrecognition" in which certain "cultural arbitraries," that is, constructs or beliefs seen as representative of a cultural group, are perceived to be valuable based not upon intrinsic worth but rather people's recognition of worth.

My final interaction with Olan further illustrated the discrepancies between the symbolic resources Olan claimed and those college personnel believed to be available to him. Olan and I met on campus three weeks into his third term. After completing two developmental English courses, Olan enrolled in English composition. Unfortunately, he missed the first two classes because of transportation issues. Still, Olan intended to submit his missed assignments, as he wanted to show his instructor his commitment to the course and his education. He borrowed a friend's notes because he didn't have the syllabus. He also arranged to borrow another friend's textbook because he could not afford to purchase the text. He explained all of this during our meeting, adding he was unsure whether he would get credit when he submitted the assignments he missed. I recommended he speak with the instructor, whose office was located just down the hall from us. Olan dismissed my recommendation, stating he only had a short amount of time away from work and rationalizing the instructor (who was an adjunct) was unlikely to be in her office.

When it came to academic guidance, language learning, and educational resources, Olan avoided asking for assistance from college personnel, preferring instead to talk with other former Yazidi interpreters. Olan felt a strong personal connection to these men who shared his language, culture, homeland, previous work, and dreams for the future. It seemed natural that Olan preferred the *social capital* available to him through these relationships rather than that offered by college personnel who tended to overacknowledge his experiences as a refugee/immigrant or interpreter. Olan's privileging of advice from other Yazidis indicates that for some Generation 1 learners, the source of advice may be as important as the advice itself, as learners enact their student identities by aligning with certain groups.

There were significant discrepancies between Olan's and his instructor's (and my own) perceptions of Olan's chosen identities—and the *symbolic capital* (Bourdieu 1991) they afforded. While Olan's instructor and I emphasized Olan's identity as a former interpreter, Olan was uninvested in this capital. Instead, he invested heavily in his identity as a gifted student and language expert through social capital amassed through his relationships within the Yazidi community and academic capital derived from his natural intelligence and work ethic. For Olan, these resources held the greatest significance, and his choice to apply his *symbolic capital* as a gifted student rather than an army interpreter illustrated the complexities of his identity negotiations.

Oftentimes, Olan's chosen identities and the experiences and resources he attempted to draw upon went unacknowledged by others within the college. College personnel did not recognize those resources as being relevant to being a college student. In other words, his resources, experiences, and identities had limited symbolic power and were therefore not recognized as symbolic capital. In Olan's case, we as faculty failed to acknowledge the identities he claimed. Nor did we explain our rationale for applying alternative experiences for him to claim as *symbolic capital*. For example, had Olan been encouraged to choose a problem of personal relevance in his problem-solution essay, he might have been more engaged in his writing and better able to enact his desired identity as an empowered Yazidi.

Labiba

Like Olan, Labiba experienced a disconnect between efforts to access her experiences as symbolic capital and college personnel's recognition of the symbolic value of those experiences. Labiba was born into a politically and socially connected family, but the 1979 Soviet invasion of Afghanistan and her cousin's murder by the Mujahideen forced Labiba and her mother to flee the country. Labiba was a young girl at the time; she would spend the next several decades as a refugee, learning six different languages as she and her mother continued their transnational migrations.

More than fifty years after her initial flight from Afghanistan, Labiba entered college through the Bridging Lab (B-Lab), a support center housed within a midwestern community college for students preparing for college. In college, Labiba frequently and proudly shared her stories of her life abroad. Labiba tenaciously pursued assistance from college personnel, and the lab staff praised her work ethic and frequent questions. Labiba was particularly encouraged by the math tutor's positive response to her habit of walking up to the board to ask questions during lectures, and as a result, she increased her already frequent interruptions. Labiba and lab personnel alike believed her willingness to seek assistance and her previous personal persistence would ensure her success in college. When she enrolled in her first college term, Labiba had already adapted an intensive study routine of taking copious notes in multiple languages from the reading before soliciting tutoring assistance to complete assignments. She quickly applied this routine to her developmental English class and the writing center, which she visited daily to seek assistance with her assignments.

As she did in the B-Lab, in class, Labiba frequently shared stories of overcoming personal trauma in other academic spaces in the college. For example, during Labiba's first book-report presentation, instead of summarizing her book about World War II, Labiba told stories of running across rooftops with her children to escape the Taliban. Everyone remained engaged in Labiba's slide show of family pictures and images of her war-torn hometown. Neither the instructor nor the students appeared concerned that her presentation ran nearly ten minutes over the allotted time or even asked her questions about the book, which she had barely described. Instead, classmates expressed praise and admiration.

Through these emotional revelations, Labiba's previous experiences became symbolic capital everyone in the college (especially Labiba) assumed would directly translate to overcoming academic challenges. Labiba frequently drew from the symbolic resources of her identity as a persevering refugee and multilingual learner to bolster her legitimacy as a college student. Surely the same tenacity by which Labiba immigrated to the US and single-handedly raised her children would allow her to master such innocuous tasks as reading comprehension and academic writing.

However, Labiba struggled with the vocabulary and volume of the assigned readings and the length and foreign modes of college writing. The writing tutors felt underprepared to support a student they perceived as lacking study skills and self-initiative, and Labiba's instructor, who was respected throughout the college as a patient and approachable educator, grew increasingly concerned by Labiba's frequent interruptions and unwillingness to work independently. College personnel felt these behaviors indicated Labiba's ignorance of US educational norms and inadequate English reading and writing skills.

As Labiba's academic struggles mounted, she clung more fiercely to her identity as a refugee and survivor, and she fought to transform her symbolic capital as a refugee into recognition of her perseverance as a college student. She shared her past widely in hopes of gaining access to the community of college students. However, instead of exemplifying her persistence, Labiba's stories became evidence to others of her traumatization as a refugee. Whereas the B-Lab and writing center had once been a refuge from the stresses and uncertainties of college, Labiba found herself increasingly at odds with staff whose expectations of independent work seemed to oppose the very skill she had cultivated in the B-Lab: persistence in seeking assistance.

Faculty and staff, including myself, believed Labiba's survival of trauma would directly translate into academic persistence. However, her persistence as a refugee and immigrant was not directly applicable to the classroom, and it was insufficient to support her instructional needs. We failed to address the discontinuity between Labiba's demonstrated persistence as enacted symbolic capital and our expectations that Labiba persist independently. We did not discuss with Labiba how to translate her symbolic capital into a form appropriate to college, and as a result she experienced further distance from the college community. Committed to honoring Labiba's lived experience, faculty and staff allowed Labiba to direct instructional moments away from academic-skills development to focus on her past persistence, even as they failed to acknowledge how, untranslated, this symbolic resource proved insufficient for establishing her identity as a college student. Had we explored with Labiba the connection between our academic expectations and her desired identity of a college student, we might have been able to help Labiba identify how her existing skills at persistence could be applied to her academic endeavors.

Recognizing her trauma narrative as symbolic capital led Labiba to identify as a victim rather than as a member of the academic community. While her trauma narrative did bring her sympathy, and even admiration, it did not translate into academic capital, nor did it help her gain access to the academic community. Instead, it limited her perceived identity (both to herself and others) as one dimensional. Even more concerning, her continued reliance on her trauma narrative emotionally and cognitively linked her academic identity to her previous victimization. Her experience illustrates the care with which instructors must respond to trauma narratives to avoid learners' potential retraumatization. Although Labiba was unable to translate her trauma narrative into academic capital, her daily visits to the writing center and extensive support from her instructor did pay off. Labiba passed her English course and planned to enroll in the subsequent developmental education course the following term.

This study extended investment theory to illustrate how students' identities are dependent in part upon their ability to convince others (i.e., faculty and staff) of their legitimate membership within the imagined community. Olan's and Labiba's experiences demonstrate both the potential symbolic power of Generation 1 learners' past experiences and the dangers of instructors mapping their own values onto those experiences.

Theoretical explanations of language choice include examinations of how language learners possess the agency to (re)negotiate their identities and available symbolic resources. Sandra Lee McKay and Sau-Ling Cynthia Wong (1996) explain,

> As subjects with agency and a need to exercise it, the learners, while positioned in power relations and subject to the influence of discourses, also resist positioning, attempt repositioning, and deploy discourses and counterdiscourses. In general, they constantly conduct delicate social negotiations to fashion viable identities. (603)

In sharing their academic and professional goals as well as the symbolic resources they felt were most relevant to their success as college students, Olan and Labiba engaged in complex identity negotiations about the meaning and ways of being a college student. Like Olan's stories of personal persistence, Generation 1 learners' symbolic capital has increased power when deployed within discourses valued by the academy. With an understanding of the academic community, Generation 1 learners can, therefore, strategically position themselves within discourses of immigration, race, and belonging.

ACKNOWLEDGING AGENCY: IMPLICATIONS FOR THEORY AND PRACTICE

Before discussing the conclusions from this study, it is necessary to highlight some limitations of this work. Due to space limitations, only two of the study's original six cases are presented here; the study's full triangulation through instructor and staff interviews, document analysis and observation, and the cross-case analysis among six learners are absent from this chapter (Suh 2017). Additionally, although not an inherent limit to the study, the complexity of my position as both an instructor and researcher at the community college certainly impacted my interpretation of the institutional support available to Olan and Labiba.

Despite these limitations, this chapter illustrates how faculty and staff efforts to honor student experience can become misdirected by an inappropriate focus on student persistence. In our interactions with Olan and Labiba, college faculty and staff—myself included—failed to acknowledge the complexity of their identity negotiations. We ignored their self-positioning within discourses of persistence and academic success, engaging in what Bourdieu (1991) would refer to as "misrecognition," or arbitrarily and falsely identifying certain resources as being forms of *symbolic capital*—despite their lack of relevance to the learners. Important, both Olan and Labiba were refugees, which profoundly impacted how they and others perceived the relevance of their experiences to becoming college students. Future research must examine the applicability of the theorization of Generation 1 learners' identity enactment to nonrefugee immigrants, such as love migrants, economic migrants, or educational migrants who arrive in the receiving community with access to different forms of symbolic capital by virtue of their reasons for immigrating (Catalano 2016). However, Olan and Labiba share several points of commonality with other two-year college students, particularly in the era of COVID-19, who have persisted through personal hardship and who seek to develop academic skills relevant to enacting their desired identities as college students, future professionals, and educated citizens.

Working with Olan and Labiba led me to reflect upon my own assumptions as a teacher and a researcher of multilingual and English-only students, encouraging me to rethink my own teaching practices to commit to the following practices as English faculty:

- Recognize the symbolic capital learners wish to highlight in the classroom.
- Assist learners in distinguishing between their previous experiences and their aspirational identities.
- Collaboratively coconstruct with learners the meaning they seek to assign to their personal experiences within the institution.

By engaging in these practices through a framework of teaching for agency (Shapiro et al. 2016), I, and other two-year college English faculty, can assist students' intentional development of the necessary skills for enacting their chosen identities within the college.

First, we must recognize the symbolic resources students wish to draw upon within the institution. In contrast to deficit framing of some students as "underprepared" or "at-risk," I encourage two-year college English faculty to recognize learners' wealth of previous experiences—and the value learners themselves assign to those experiences (Suh 2018, 2016; Suh and Shapiro 2020). The classroom should be an inclusive space where learners are encouraged to make personal connections to the course content.

Second, although previous experiences are a rich learning resource, students benefit from a clear and explicit distinction between their past experiences and their desired identities. While being mindful of the risk of assigning value to students' experiences for them, instructors must still help learners differentiate between their collected abilities (e.g., personal persistence) and the objectives associated with their aspirational identity (such as meeting course outcomes or assignment parameters). In reflecting upon instructor and staff interactions with Olan and Labiba, I recognize how we college personnel erroneously assumed that if we named and praised learners' past experiences, they would automatically know how to translate that knowledge into strategies for enacting their desired social identities. Just as the field recognizes the necessity of "deliberate, mindful abstraction of skill or knowledge from one context for application to another" in genre-knowledge transfer (Perkins and Salomon 1988, 25), so, too, must we understand that the transfer of *symbolic capital* requires reflective thought and intentionality. As instructors, we should discuss with students how their *habits of persisting*—rather than the past persistence itself—are relevant to overcoming academic obstacles and then strategize with them about how to apply those habits towards the achievement of their academic goals (Suh and Shapiro 2020).

Finally, because English class (either developmental or composition level) is frequently one of students' first college experiences, two-year English faculty play an essential role in introducing the participation norms of the academic discourse community. This is not to say instructors are—or should be—responsible for teaching students to conform to these expectations. Rather, all students can benefit from explicitly examining both college expectations and their agency within the college to make informed choices about how they wish to engage. Such *cultural capital* is especially relevant for Generation 1 learners who have no previous experience with the academic expectations of the US K–12 system. As my colleagues and I discovered, college personnel must be cautious not to overexercise our authority in defining certain experiences as *symbolic capital* without the input of our students. Instead, by listening carefully and affirming the value learners assign to their own experiences, we can invite students into collaborative negotiations of their intersectional and evolving identities, thereby widening the community of those who possess the authority to legitimate *cultural arbitraries* as valued *symbolic capital* (Bourdieu 1991).

Acknowledging unequal symbolic power within the institution is essential to engaging in the "revolutionary and inescapably political" work of campus and community change (Sullivan 2015, 327). At the institutional level, full-time and adjunct two-year college faculty can collaboratively establish values-driven change (Higgins and Warnke 2019). At the classroom level, Shawna Shapiro, Michelle Cox, Gail Shuck, and Emily Simnitt (2016) outline a change process, referred to as "teaching for agency," in which faculty acknowledge students' resources and goals while simultaneously honoring supporting students' development of their awareness and control over available opportunities for action. Shapiro and her colleagues describe how this pedagogical strategy can be used to invite students to critically examine their college-student identity (31). When instructors teach for agency, students like Olan and Labiba are better supported in applying their experiences as symbolic resources for interrogating institutional values, such as personal persistence, and determining whether and how they want to participate as members of the college community by upholding or resisting such values (Shapiro et al. 2016). Such a practice reframes our understanding of the work from making students college ready to making colleges student ready (McNair et al. 2020). This reframing is essential to applying the culturally relevant and culturally sustaining pedagogy (Ladson-Billings 2014; Paris and Alim 2014) we seek to apply in community colleges (see also Kareem in this volume). This chapter focuses on two Generation 1 learners, but there are countless more. Ultimately, honoring Generation 1 learners' experiences requires that all members of the two-year college community view learners as participants within conversations about the institution's cultural spaces (see Olivas this volume) and that faculty and staff in particular make sure the institution is ready to hear our students' voices and perspectives.

REFERENCES

Almon, Cate. 2015. "College Persistence and Engagement in Light of a Mature English Language Learner (ELL) Student's Voice." *Community College Journal of Research and Practice* 39 (5): 461–72.

Becker, Leza. 2011. "Noncredit to Credit Transitioning Matters for Adult ESL Learners in a California Community College." *New Directions for Community Colleges* 2011 (155): 15–26.

Bourdieu, Pierre. 1991. *Language and Symbolic Power.* Edited by John B. Thompson. Translated by Gino Raymond and Matthew Adamson. Boston: Harvard University Press.

Bunch, George C., and Ann K. Endris. 2012. "Navigating 'Open Access' Community Colleges." In *Linguistic Minority Students Go to College: Preparation, Access, and Persistence*, edited by Yasuko Kanno and Linda Harklau, 163–83. New York City: Routledge.

Casner-Lotto, Jill. 2011. *Increasing Opportunities for Immigrant Students: Community College Strategies for Success.* Community College Consortium for Immigrant Education. http://hdl.handle.net/10919/87023.

Catalano, Theresa. 2016. *Talking About Global Migration: Implications for Language Teaching.* Bristol, UK: Multilingual Matters.

Chisman, Forrest. 2008. *Findings in ESL: A Quick Reference to Findings of CAAL Research on ESL Programs at Community Colleges.* New York: Council for Advancement of Adult Literacy.

Clarke, Victoria, and Virginia Braun. 2014. "Thematic Analysis." In *Encyclopedia of Quality of Life and Well-Being Research*, edited by Alexandros C. Michalos, 6626–28. Netherlands: Springer.

Csepelyi, Tünde. 2012. "Transition to Community College: The Journey of Adult Basic Education English Language Learners from Non-credit to Credit Programs." PhD diss., University of Nevada. ScholarWork.

Curry, Maryanne J. 2008. "A 'Head Start and a Credit': Analyzing Cultural Capital in the Basic Writing/ESOL Classroom." In *Pierre Bourdieu and Literacy Education*, edited by James Albright and Allan Luke, 279–98. New York: Routledge.

Harklau, Linda. 2000. "From the 'Good Kids' to the 'Worst': Representations of English Language Learners across Educational Settings." *TESOL Quarterly* 34 (1): 35–67.

Higgins, Kristen, and Anthony Warnke. 2019. "Reform as Access, Reform as Exclusion: Making Space for Critical Approaches to the Neoliberal Movement." *Basic Writing e-Journal* 16 (1): 1–27.

Horn, Laura, Stephanie Nevill, and James Griffith. 2006. *Profile of Undergraduates in U.S. Postsecondary Education Institutions, 2003–04: With a Special Analysis of Community College Students.* Statistical Analysis Report NCES 2006-184. Washington, DC: National Center for Education Statistics.

Institute of Education Sciences, National Center for Education Statistics. n.d. "Table 502.20: Participants in State-administered Adult Basic Education, Secondary Education, and English as a Second Language Programs, by Type of Program and State or Jurisdiction: Selected Fiscal Years, 2000 through 2014." Accessed January 22, 2018. nces.ed.gov/programs/digest/d15/tables/dt15_507.20.asp?current=yes.

Knowles, Malcolm. 1968. "Andragogy, Not Pedagogy." *Adult Leadership* 16 (10): 350–52.

Ladson-Billings, Gloria. 2014. "Culturally Relevant Pedagogy 2.0: a. k. a. the Remix." *Harvard Educational Review* 84 (1): 74–84.

McKay, Sandra Lee, and Sau-Ling Cynthia Wong. 1996. "Multiple Discourses, Multiple Identities: Investment and Agency in Second-Language Learning among Chinese Adolescent Immigrant Students." *Harvard Educational Review* 66 (3): 577–608.

McNair, Tia Brown, Susan Albertine, Nicole McDonald, Thomas Major Jr., and Michelle Asha Cooper. 2020. *Becoming a Student-Ready College: A New Culture of Leadership for Student Success.* Hoboken, NJ: John Wiley.

National Organization for Student Success. N.d. "About Developmental Education." Accessed June 13, 2016. http://www.noss.net/aboutdeved.html.

Norton, Bonny. 2013. *Identity and Language Learning: Extending the Conversation.* 2nd ed. Bristol, UK: Multilingual Matters.

Paris, Django, and H. Samy Alim. 2014. "What Are We Seeking to Sustain through Culturally Sustaining Pedagogy? A Loving Critique Forward." *Harvard Educational Review* 84 (1): 85–100.

Perkins, D. N., and Gavriel Salomon. 1988. "Teaching for Transfer." *Educational Leadership* 41 (1): 22–32.

Rose, Mike. 1990. *Lives on the Boundary: A Moving Account of the Struggles and Achievements of America's Educationally Underprepared.* New York: Penguin Books.

Rumbaut, Rubén G. 2004. "Ages, Life Stages, and Generational Cohorts: Decomposing the Immigrant First and Second Generations in the United States." *International Migration Review* 38 (3): 1160–1205.

Shapiro, Shawna, Michelle Cox, Gail Shuck, and Emily Simnitt. 2016. "Teaching for Agency: From Appreciating Linguistic Diversity to Empowering Student Writers." *Composition Studies* 44 (1): 31–52.

Slaughter, Joseph. 2007. *Human Rights, Inc.: The World Novel, Narrative Form, and International Law.* New York: Fordham University Press.

Suh, Emily. 2016. "Language Minority Student Transitions." *Journal of Developmental Education* 40 (1): 26–28.

Suh, Emily. 2017. "'Off from Lost': Generation 1 Learners' Transition from Adult ESL to Developmental Education." PhD diss., University of Nebraska.

Suh, Emily. 2018. "Counting Backwards toward the Future of Community College Immigrant Students: Conceptualizing Generation 1 Learners." *Basic Writing e-Journal* 15 (1): 1–41.

Suh, Emily. 2021. "Literacy Strategy Use and Identity Enactment: Generation 1 Learners' Emergent Competence in College." *Journal of College Literacy and Learning* 47 (1): 21–43.

Suh, Emily K., Barrie McGee, and Sam Owens. 2021. "When Bootstraps Break: Re-examining Assumptions about the Symbolic Capital of Immigrant Students' Persistence Narratives." *Journal of Basic Writing* 40 (1): 68–98.

Suh, Emily. K., and Shawna Shapiro. 2020. "Making Sense of Resistance: How Adult Immigrant Students Apply Symbolic Capital in the College Classroom." *TESL Canada* 37 (3): 27–46.

Sullivan, Patrick. 2015. "The Two-Year College Teacher-Scholar-Activist." *Teaching English in the Two-Year College* 42 (4): 327–46.

Teranishi, Robert, Carola Suárez-Orozco, and Marcelo Suárez-Orozco. 2011. "Immigrants in Community Colleges." *Future of Children* 21 (1): 153–69.

5
"I'VE NEVER BEEN A GOOD WRITER"
Disrupting Raciolinguistically Marginalized Students' Negative Writerly Self-Image

Jamila M. Kareem

Over the last decade I've been teaching, there have probably been at least two instances per semester in which a student has said to me, after receiving an unexpectedly high rating and positive feedback on an assignment, something along the lines of, "Wow, I've never been a good writer. This is the first time anyone's ever said anything nice about my assignments." A few times, the student has belonged to the dominant raciolinguistic community, but mostly, they have been multilingual or multidialectical students of color, sometimes from the US but sometimes not. Rather than providing ways to help our supposedly linguistically deficient students assimilate to raciolinguistic appropriateness (Flores and Rosa 2015), I argue for applying critical race culturally sustaining pedagogies to convert multilingual and multidialectical students' self-perceptions that their writing is bad to perceptions that their own already-adaptable repository of social-rhetorical linguistic practices as a viable college-ready asset. The language ideologies of these students reflect the systemically racist rhetoric perpetuated by broader societal attitudes about the place of linguistic diversity in our raciolinguistic social systems.

By examining rhetorics of race through critical race theory's (CRT) race-shaping and race-narrativizing tenets, I expose the embedded racial ideologies in some of composition studies' most beloved critically conscious practices to show the limitations of higher education practices, policies, and strategies in valuing and supporting raciolinguistic diversity. I follow this examination with a review of the CCCC resolution Students' Right to Their Own Language (SRTOL), a common solution to addressing our limited engagement with students' linguistic lives, and present the shortcomings of this resolution, arguing for disruptively better approaches to engaging raciolinguistically subjugated student identities in writing-centric college curricula. I close by offering an example of raciolinguistically diverse writing about writing as a culturally sustaining orientation to teaching college-level writing.

CRT RACE MAKING AND RACE NARRATIVIZING

For those unfamiliar, the goal of CRT is to critically examine, name, and respond to racist ideas and actions in the legal system, as well as in other policymaking contexts in society, including education. I am interested in the ways we can borrow from CRT to make influential changes to our teaching perspectives and practices in writing-intensive college courses because, as A. Suresh Canagarajah (2006) proclaims, "The classroom is already a policy site; every time teachers insist on a uniform variety of language or discourse, we are helping reproduce monolingualist ideologies and linguistic hierarchy" (587). Some writing studies scholarship has taken CRT approaches to the ways we research the intersections of race and language with writing, writers, and the teaching of writing (Baker-Bell 2020; Baker-Bell, Butler, and Johnson 2017; Johnson 2018; Kareem 2018, 2019; Martinez 2014; Prendergast 1998; Young 2007). These studies have generally focused on the standardization of racist ideologies and action in English language arts (Baker-Bell, Butler, and Johnson 2017; Johnson 2018;), literacy (Baker-Bell 2020; Prendergast 1998; Young 2007), first-year writing (Kareem 2018, 2019), and graduate composition studies, education, and writing-pedagogy research methodologies (Martinez 2009). That makes sense, as two additional CRT tenets submit that (1) racism is the normal business of US society, and, therefore, appears as the natural way of things to participants in that society and (2) racism is challenging to eliminate, as it advances the interests of the whole US culture—"materially" and "psychically" (Delgado and Stefancic 2006); further, these interests converge through racist norms (Bell 1980; Kareem 2019). To more clearly grasp how language-diversity ideologies in the teaching of first-year writing (FYW) and beyond are influenced by the racist rhetoric and ideologies of larger raciolinguistic social systems, I turn to two other CRT major tenets.

The first theorizes that the social powers that be—for example, judges, legislators, curriculum developers, and media company executives—condition us to associate specific material and social factors with specific racial formations (Omi and Winant 1986) to maintain their position in society. These include the social factors correlated to language, discourse, and rhetoric in education practices that benefit the textbook publishers, standardized-test developers, college and university leaders, board members, and stockholders for higher education institutions, as well as teachers and legislators. These beneficiaries create racial distinctions about language that allow them to designate the appropriate time and place of language practices. For example, discursive practices that value controlled, culturally decontextualized writing (Barnett 2000; Inoue 2016; Kincheloe 2008) are projected as correct, good, or proper without any recognition of their Eurocentric cultural and colonizing roots. Shaping and mobilizing these practices, and others I discuss later, as standard rather than culturally derived allows the raciolinguistic culture from which they are derived to be positioned as natural. Therefore, when composition studies teachers, researchers, and administrators promote these practices as objectively accurate, we are perpetuating the stance that practices of Euro-American whiteness are universal or natural and any other raciolinguistics are only situation-specific or *unnatural.*

The other CRT tenet I suggest can structure our understanding of racialized ideologies of linguistic diversity states that images and narratives about different racial groups change over time based on the needs of the dominant social group, in this case Eurocentric-American English-speaking, middle-class, Judeo-Christian male social groups. As I indicate in "A Critical Race Analysis of Transition Level Writing Curriculum to Support the Racially Diverse Two-Year College" (Kareem 2019), the stakeholders of higher education overwhelmingly represent the values and customs of the dominant racial social group. Therefore, images of language difference in the academy and in civic life are depicted based not on what truly reflects the sociorhetorical communication needs of groups and communities practicing nondominant discourses but rather on the discursive requisites of the dominant raciolinguistic group. Prevalent narratives about race and language have shifted over time as more ethno- and raciolinguistically diverse teacher-scholars with language ideologies divergent from established norms have spoken and written publicly about these matters. For example, during the early beginnings of the discipline, linguistic diversity could be seen as a threat to the dissemination of white patriarchal mainstream discourses supported by the academy. Because the foremothers and -fathers sustained discourse practices reflective of English-language-literate middle-class Eurocentric masculinity as the ultimate sign of US social mobility (Brereton 1996, 9, 21), primacy images and narratives of raciolinguistic appropriateness fit this identity (Royster and Williams 1999). Educators and scholars within Black American, Latinx, and Indigenous communities were often teaching and learning mainstream discourses alongside the marginalized discourses that reflected students' multiple community identities, but these ideologies and epistemological perspectives had not made their way into the collective intelligence of early composition studies.

The absent presence of race (Prendergast 1998) has been critical to the ideological and epistemological shaping of composition studies. Until recently, and even still for the majority of teaching approaches today, nondominant forms of American English have been situated as having little to no value in formal writing contexts (Perryman-Clark 2012a). As I outline in "A Critical Race Analysis" (Kareem 2019), Catherine Prendergast (1998) offers the absent presence of race as the evasion of racialized implications in the work of our field (274). The white racial habitus—a "set of discursive and performative dispositions" (Inoue 2016, 146) that has shaped the discursive practices of the academy—primarily functions by maintaining a perpetual invisibility. Racial invisibility disguised as objectivity and universality sustains the social relation of whiteness and Eurocentrism as dominant. It helps portray the image of *browner* patterns of expression, that is, those honored and wielded by cultures of primarily African, Indigenous, Mesoamerican, and API descent, as lower scale linguistically. As I demonstrate in the forthcoming section, composition studies has contributed to such portrayals through its rhetorical positioning of language and race matters in the teaching of writing in the two-year college.

PREJUDICE IN COMPOSITION STUDIES' TWO-YEAR COLLEGE LINGUISTIC RACE RHETORICS

Lamar L. Johnson (2018) argues for applying a critical race English education (CREE) framework to guide our teaching and research of English language arts curriculum. Johnson suggests CREE can be put to use in exploring and responding to the contemporary and historical contexts of current race relations and their connection to racial justice matters in ELA classrooms. While the CRT principles I espouse here are but one dimension of CREE, which also draws from Black critical theory and critical literacy theory frameworks, I see CREE as an important contribution to investigating and responding to racial justice efforts in the transitional English and composition classroom, as well as to becoming proactive with these efforts.

Rhetorics of race—messages or implications, both implicit and explicit, about racial identities and cultures—have been key to two-year college scholarship about the language use of its students. The hidden racialized curriculum of mainstream education (Ladson-Billings 1998; Leonardo 2004) permits policy makers all the way down to teaching assistants the opportunity to infiltrate racist rhetorics about language in the teaching of reading and writing. The majority of the racially subjugated population of college students in the US attend two-year institutions (Kirklighter, Cárdenas, and Wolff 2007, 7; Toth and Jensen 2017, 30), so research regarding the impact of raciolinguistics on students' writing practices is essential. It is also essential to examine and challenge where necessary the ways we narrativize and enact the links among language, discourse, and race.

Consider the rubrics traditionally used when grading compositions in community college FYW courses. While these assessment documents might vary to some extent across courses and institutions, they tend to have the same rhetoric about language use and proper academic writing. They is some variation on the following (for a high-scoring essay):

- demonstrates evidence of careful proofreading and editing
- organizes effectively
- exhibits minimal usage errors
- demonstrates effective diction in Standard American English
- uses appropriate spelling, punctuation, and sentence structure

Oftentimes in two-year institutions, rubrics are systemic, unable to be altered by the individual instructor. But there are always opportunities to discuss these expectations with our students and how they affect their perceptions of themselves as writers. What do they struggle with and why? In my own FYW courses, I often have students draft a profile of themselves as writers that, with an antiracist approach, includes a discussion of which writing rules create roadblocks for them and which racial rhetorical traditions they associate those rules with. As Carmen Fought (2006b) illustrates, our society has created linguistic and social correlates to being white, such as middle classness and intelligence (115), and our rubrics reflect these social correlates through linguistic expectations.

At colleges and universities, language ideologies that privilege Euro-American academic reading and writing practices reflect the race shaping that benefits the dominant social group's social relations. Siskanna Naynaha (2016) explains, "What Latinx students find in community colleges is a culture that is finely tuned to the needs and interests of a historically white student body, faculty, and staff" (198). Staci Perryman-Clark (2012a) offers one example of such relations in "Africanized Patterns of Expression: A Case Study of African American Students' Expository Writing Patterns across Written Contexts." There, Perryman-Clark exemplifies that the linguistic diversity of Black American students' home language patterns is more accepted in some, namely informal, academic literacy situations than in other more formal situations. The prevalence of this perspective is so pervasive many see it as a given: if I, as a professional trained in teaching and evaluating writing, do not recognize the stylistic and rhetorical purposes of your home language patterns, then they do not fit the social language standards. This ideological framework aligns with the racial narrativizing thesis of CRT, because it creates a narrative that tells these students that, currently, some of their useful, culturally relevant language practices are unacceptable in white-dominated spaces.

The discipline of composition studies has sometimes consciously and sometimes unconsciously poached the dominant race rhetoric about linguistic traditions. In 1992, Maxine Hairston observed a disturbing trend in freshman composition that "puts dogma before diversity, politics before craft, ideology before critical thinking, and the social goals of the teacher before the educational needs of students" (180). The author claims this approach does not "take freshman English seriously in its own right" but instead "envisions required writing courses as vehicles for social reform rather than as student-centered workshops designed to build students' confidence and competence as writers" (180). Specifically, the article identifies difference-centered ideological approaches to the teaching of first-year composition as "politically-focused" (181) and separate from the conventional composition course that is writing focused. Yet Lynn Z. Bloom (1996) implies that all first-year composition is ideological and political in "Freshman Composition as a Middle-Class Enterprise." Bloom brazenly asserts, "Yes, freshman composition is an unabashedly middle-class enterprise," a social identity linked to whiteness, per Fought (2006b), and that aspect influences "its aims of enabling students to think and write in ways that will make them good citizens of the academic (and larger) community, and viable candidates for good jobs upon graduation" (655). This classist orientation of composition courses "reinforces the values and virtues embodied not only in the very existence of America's vast middle class, but in its general well-being-read promotion of the ability to think critically and responsibly, and the maintenance of safety, order, cleanliness, efficiency" (655) and, therefore, cannot be apolitical. Hairston's (1992) implicit whiteness rhetoric is coded under the pretense of a nonpresent, invisible, unraced, neutral, objective engagement with writing. This rhetorical stance is rooted within a white racial habitus. Part of the emphasis "on the individual in a contractual relationship with other individuals[,] . . .

individual rights are more important and non-political, whereas socially-oriented values and questions are less important and often political (bad) by their nature" (Inoue 2016, 147). Just as "middle-class standards may operate for the worse, particularly when middle-class teachers punish lower-class students for not being, well, more middle class" (Bloom 1996, 655), faux apolitical attitudes and resultant practices in composition curriculum development lead to raciolinguistic discrimination that impacts in-school writing experiences to the detriment of many marginalized student populations, especially multilingual ones.

Even the ways researching and teaching in the discipline converse about literacy and language holds raciolinguistic implications. The insider/outsider metaphor of acquiring linguistic literacies often targets teachers of racially and linguistically subjugated students (Bartholomae 1986; Mutnick 1996; Noe 2009). Carmen Kynard (2013) calls for those in the fields of composition and literacy studies to question "the very terms we use to talk about literacy when we imagine ourselves to be talking about multiple locations, academic literacy/discourse communities, schooling, and marginalized communities" (63). These concepts include liberation, freedom, access, sponsorship, stewardship, and tools. Literacy is situated as a means to access liberation and freedom. Particularly from the two-year college perspective, prevailing narratives about literacy indicate that versatility in whiteness-validated literacies is a necessary tool for rhetorical and material survival, whether transferring to universities or joining the workforce. We position ourselves—teachers, department chairs, and upper-level administrators—as stewards of these literacies, even as we fail to contend with the "deep political and ideological shifts that have left structured inequalities and violence firmly in place, especially in reference to, but not solely based on, race" (64) and literacy practices.

STUDENTS' RIGHT TO THEIR OWN LANGUAGE AND MORE CURRENT RESOLUTIONS

As a subfield of composition studies, two-year college English teachers must understand the impact of negative raciolinguistic self-images on students' writing practices and goals. To do so, these teacher-scholars should examine the most prevalent approaches to language difference in teaching two-year college composition. As Staci Perryman-Clark (2012a), Carmen Kynard (2007), A. Suresh Canagarajah (2006), and Valerie Kinloch (2005) suggest, the Students' Right to Their Own Language (Conference 1975) resolution is limited in its exclusion of students' own language practices from formal academic writing exercises. Traditional critical pedagogies are similarly limited in that they promote speaking truth to power through teaching and learning practices, but they fail to invite and sustain multilingual practices in mainstream academic spaces. These solutions, intentionally or unintentionally, often align with dominant raciolinguistic cultures in practice.

I have found that students' racialized writerly self-images often reflect the narratives and images about race, language diversity, and writing we have imposed through our own pedagogies and college-prep advice extending all the way from secondary education to early elementary education and into the communities that support our students. The most enduring of these narratives might be the Conference on College Composition and Communication's 1974 resolution on Students' Right to Their Own Language (SRTOL) (Committee 1975). SRTOL achieves a lot of cultural-inclusion objectives, but it has never been implemented in the ways the creators likely intended. In fact, a search of the most prominent journals on two-year college teaching and research—*Community College Review, Community College Journal of Research and Practice,* and *Teaching English in the Two-Year College*—reveal only sixteen articles even mentioning SRTOL, despite its relevance to the student bodies at these institutions. The Conference on College Composition and Communication (CCCC) collaborators on the SRTOL resolution, the Committee on CCCC Language Statement, wanted to practically theorize "the claim that any one dialect is unacceptable [and] amounts to an attempt of one social group to exert its dominance over [others]" (2–3). The affirmation of the resolution further argues, "A nation proud of its diverse heritage and its cultural and racial variety will preserve its heritage of dialect" (3). The democratic linguistic and literacy goals here are laudable. Many educators in composition and literacy studies have moved beyond holding this resolution as an ideology and have tested the belief system through practice in first-year composition and basic writing classrooms (Barbier 2003; Gilyard and Richardson 2001; Kinloch 2005; Looker 2016; Perryman-Clark 2012b). After clarifying the limitations of SRTOL and its resultant pedagogies through a critical race analytical lens, I discuss more recent raciolinguistic-focused teaching resolutions forwarded by NCTE, resolutions that seem to be more relevant to two-year college faculty and administrators.

Besides its lack of implementation, the other limitation I see with SRTOL in realistically supporting students' raciolinguistic diversity in composition and English coursework at the transitional level is that it prolongs the ideology that non-CDE (Culturally Dominant English) language users or raciolinguistically minoritized discourses are problematic in academic environments. The statement reads, "Empathy with the difficulties often faced by such speakers can be appreciated in indirect analogies with other situations which make one an outsider. *But the most vivid sense of the students' problem is likely to come from direct experience*" (Committee 1975, 18; emphasis mine). Advocating a sort of voyeuristic approach for teachers to "experience" unfamiliar dialects, the resolution suggests teachers of writing "be wholly immersed in a dialect group other than their own" or "liste[n] to tapes and records as well as interviewing sympathetically speakers who use minority dialects" (18). This suggestion is chalked up to the race relations of the US at the time SRTOL was written, no matter how progressive the statement proved at that time. In the FYC community college classroom, this approach might include a teacher calling on the few brown English-language learners to share their experiences with speaking and writing in the dominant English-language dialect, or asking students to freewrite about these experiences but not actually engaging those freewrite responses or open discussions through the course content.

The support for what would eventually become known as code switching, or expecting students to set aside their home or other preferred social languages when writing for academic purposes, further diminishes the progressive capacity of the statement. And although SRTOL argues that "dialect is not separate from culture, but an intrinsic part of it," it also asserts that "the question [is] . . . whether [students] can step over the hazily defined boundaries that separate dialects" because "dialect switching is complicated by many factors, not the least of which is the individual's own cultural heritage" (Committee 1975, 8). That is, a person's presumably nondominant culture *hinders* their ability to learn the dominant English dialect. But a significant amount of scholarship published well after CCCC forwarded the resolution (Canagarajah 2006; Kynard 2008; Perryman-Clark 2012a; Young 2007, 2009) highlights the racist implications of code switching, additionally demonstrating how, at a broad societal level, images and narratives about race and language have changed over time, always shaped by the acceptance of these narratives and images in dominant racial contexts.

Scholarship on composition in the two-year college has advised comparably limited engagement with students' language rights due to limited perspectives about the effectiveness of non-DAE dialects. In a 1977 issue of *Community College Review,* Nancy J. Iredell and Jerry Parsons wrote that even though raciolinguistically marginalized students' "unique dialects must not be judged as good or bad, appropriate or inappropriate, acceptable or unacceptable" (44), in the end, "students who are unable to use standard English have a cultural deficiency" (46). These suggestions follow the authors' acknowledgment that language traditions are tied to racial, ethnic, and socioeconomic backgrounds. Pedagogies based in the theoretical perspectives of SRTOL cannot help but portray similar kinds of prejudices, despite the best efforts of any practitioner.

Although more linguistically and racially aware of the prejudice embedded within mainstream college literacy-based course curriculum, the CCCC Statement on Second Language Writing and Multilingual Writers (SOSL) (Conference 2001) fails to go far enough to disrupt dominant raciolinguistic narratives and images. It does, however, establish ways faculty and administrators might productively navigate and interrogate these stories we tell and pictures we paint of language practices and identity alignment in our instruction.

STATEMENT ON SECOND LANGUAGE WRITING AND MULTILINGUAL WRITERS

SOSL was introduced to the CCCC community twenty-seven years after the first publishing of SRTOL because the field needed clearer rhetorical support of its evolving diversity and more actionable steps to reflect this support. Like SRTOL, this statement has yet to be implemented on a systemic policy-making level within colleges and universities across the country, let alone within state legislatures. In fact, I'd be willing to wager that many of the two-year college faculty and administrators reading this are unfamiliar with the statement. However, SOSL surpasses affirmation and doublespeak to provide specific research-based practices aimed to support multilingual writers—"international visa holders, refugees, permanent residents, and undocumented immigrants, as well as naturalized and native-born citizens of the United States and Canada" (Conference 2001, para. 3)—in the classroom, through program administration, and across the curriculum.

The goal of the document is "to provide broad research-based guidelines for teachers and administrators to advocate for multilingual writers in all spaces of universities and colleges, including first-year writing, undergraduate and graduate courses across the curriculum, writing centers, and intensive English programs" and "to promote social justice for all multilingual members of the academic community, students, faculty, and staff in order to make visible otherwise underutilized linguistic and literacy resources" (Conference 2001, para. 1). Unlike the linguistic accommodationist ideologies of SRTOL, SOSL promotes language ideologies based in raciolinguistic multiculturalism. Valerie Balester (2012) describes accommodationist pedagogies and assessment practices as those that "give students a stake in mainstream culture, often by using home language as a bridge to teaching Edited American English" (67). In other words, this ideology advocates code switching. For Balester, multiculturist approaches "advocate providing instruction in the dominant forms of academic discourse, [but also] education in the politics of language and making room for alternative discourses" (71). SOSL attempts to evolve CCCC's own collective thinking as an organization by throwing out the former attitude about the obstacles of home and social languages in favor of seeing "languages as integrated, so that multilingual writers have the ability to draw on their full linguistic repertoire for communication and meaning-making" (Conference 2001, para. 6). Having come to mainstream education consciousness later than SRTOL, perhaps pedagogies such as critical language awareness closed some of the ideological gaps left by the CCCC resolution. Still, critical pedagogical processes have their limitations.

Particularly for the two-year college population, the goal is to inculcate these students with the social standards of our society, which, as has been described in detail, is invested in maintaining the racial hierarchy of superior whiteness and inferior Black/Brownness. These pedagogies carry on with mobilizing narratives of racial cultural dominance because their objective is to only dissect the dominance with the hopes of improving writers' own critical literacy skills. Note that "improve" in this case usually means to align more closely to discourses of whiteness (Inoue 2016), language practices we as a field convey as objectively, universally good. This attribute has allowed these resolutions to gather support from a large segment of the mainstream-education sector, as it continues to sustain the benefits of dominant racial social relations. Instruction focuses on questions about culture as opposed to sustaining or remaining relevant to marginalized cultures.

These kinds of curricula depict race and language in a way that both adds to and subtracts from dominant racial ideologies. While students might be exposed to the critiques of racial linguistic attitudes, they aren't necessarily encouraged to put them into practice in a way that is sustained by AAL, AAVE, Spanglish, Navajo, Tagalog, or any other non-DAE linguistic practice. Putting raciolinguistic sovereignty into practice, as well as critiquing white-supremacist ideologies about language in academic spaces, seems to be one of many goals of CCCC's latest position statement on language, This Ain't Another Statement! This Is a DEMAND for Black Linguistic Justice! (Conference 2020).

THIS AIN'T ANOTHER STATEMENT! THIS IS A DEMAND FOR BLACK LINGUISTIC JUSTICE!

A list of demands was drafted by the 2020 CCCC Special Committee on Composing a CCCC Statement on Anti-Black Racism and Black Linguistic Justice, Or, Why We Cain't Breathe! in response to "current historical and sociopolitical context," which includes being "in the midst of a pandemic that is disproportionately infecting and killing Black people" and "witnessing ongoing #BlackLivesMatter protests across the United States in response to the anti-Black racist violence and murders . . . [of] a growing list of Black people at the hands of the state and vigilantes" (Conference 2020). The committee laid it down that "as language and literacy researchers and educators, we acknowledge that the same anti-Black violence toward Black people in the streets across the United States mirrors the anti-Black violence that is going down in these academic streets" (Conference 2020). Formerly in 2018's "Where Do We Go from Here? Toward a Critical Race English Education," Lamar Johnson—one of the writers of the document—questions, "As a Black male English educator and language and literacy scholar, how am I implicated in the struggle for racial justice and what does it mean for me to teach literacy in our present-day justice movement?; (2) How are Black lives mattering in ELA classrooms?; and, (3) How are we using Black youth life histories and experiences to inform our mindset, curriculum, and pedagogical practices in the classroom?" (102). "This Ain't Another Statement!" asks, "How has Black Lives Mattered in the context of language education? How has Black Lives Mattered in our research, scholarship, teaching, disciplinary discourses, graduate programs, professional organizations, and publications? How have our commitments and activism as a discipline contributed to the political freedom of Black peoples?" (Conference 2020)

Directed at CCCC as an organization with policy-negotiating, policy-changing power, the committee first recognizes the foundational work but mostly the deficiencies of SRTOL, similar to what I do in this chapter. The majority of "This Ain't Another Statement!" confronts the ways CCCC's challenges to anti-Black linguistic racism have failed systemically. In response, the document proclaims, "We cannot say Black Lives Matter if decades of research on Black Language has not led to widespread systemic change in curricula, pedagogical practices, disciplinary discourses, research, language policies, professional organizations, programs, and institutions within and beyond academia!" (Conference 2020) These assertions and their resulting actionable demands exceed the work of not only SRTOL but SSOL as well. Although "This Ain't

Another Statement!" emphasizes anti-Black linguistic racism in the academy and the discipline, its calls to action could lead to comprehensive changes towards equity for all students, teachers, and administrators from marginalized raciolinguistic communities:

- teachers stop using academic language and standard English as the accepted communicative norm, which reflects White Mainstream English!
- teachers stop teaching Black students to code-switch! Instead, we must teach Black students about anti-Black linguistic racism and white linguistic supremacy!
- political discussions and praxis center Black Language as teacher-researcher activism for classrooms and communities!
- teachers develop and teach Black Linguistic Consciousness that works to decolonize the mind (and/or) language, unlearn white supremacy, and unravel anti-Black linguistic racism!
- Black dispositions are centered in the research and teaching of Black Language!

Within the discussion of each of these stipulations, DEMAND! "This Ain't Another Statement!" (Conference 2020) uses Black American discursive patterns, putting into action the Black dispositions discussed in the document. "This Ain't Another Statement!" May have the most potential to impact change in the two-year college in its direct address "to all the upper-level college administrators, mid-level college managers, WPAs, deans, department chairs, superintendents, school district leaders, principals, school leaders, curriculum coordinators, state and national policymakers, and editors"—essentially those inheritors of Euro-Western raciolinguistic dominance.

In the next section, I detail specific pedagogically disruptive practices that can be added to a critical race approach to vindicate, not assimilate, subjugated raciolinguistic customs as part of two-year college curriculum.

INSTRUCTIONAL PRACTICES THAT DISRUPT STUDENTS' NEGATIVE RACIOLINGUISTIC WRITERLY SELF-IMAGES

Recently, teacher-scholars have turned to culturally relevant and culturally sustaining pedagogies to consider practical applications of critical race theory in composition or writing-intensive courses. They have furthered the goals of critical pedagogies—more socially just methods for engaging multilingual cultural practices in the writing classroom. This is an area in which two-year institutions overall have missed the mark. Even as a significant majority of students of color and students of multiethnic, multilingual backgrounds in higher education attend community and technical colleges, the nature of these missions and identities of these institutions often result in faculty of a literacy-based curriculum preparing students from Eurocentric ideologies of literate practice. When the goal is to prepare students for transitioning into four-year institutions or into the workforce, where so many of the ideologies about language and race are invested in maintaining raciolinguistic structures of power, it is no surprise these institutions have not systematically worked to sustain marginalized language practices. When the message given through the curriculum is "we need to make you sound more white, more American, more middle-class, more male," or at least as close as possible to these identities, students who do not meet these sociocultural criteria reject their own images as writers.

SRTOL and critical pedagogies offer some limited teaching and curricular methods for faculty to design socially equitable materials, but other than theoretically granting students the right to use the languages of their nurture (Conference 2001) and critiquing the social controls of race and language, these practices do little to truly build positive writerly images across situations for language difference in racially and ethnically underrepresented students. Nelson Flores and Jonathan Rosa (2015) suggest these additive approaches that "affirm nonstandard varieties of English and nonstandard varieties of languages other than English as practices that are appropriate for out-of-school contexts" and "valorize students' diverse linguistic repertoires by positioning their skills in languages other than Standard English as valuable classroom assets to be built on" (153) also treat "racialized speaking subjects . . . as linguistically deviant" (150), as missing a part of culture.

One of the simplest ways to implement raciolinguistically positive teaching practices is to be explicit with students about what cultural perspectives so-called standard English is promoting. They should understand its connection to raciolinguistic and cultural dominance that is the result of a history of cultural conquest, colonizing, pilfering, and eradication. This acculturation to whiteness as a discourse (Barnett 2000; Inoue 2016) must be addressed directly to begin to confront negative raciolinguistic images about the writing of multilingual students. While institutional changes may not be reachable, Canagarajah (2006) reminds all composition teachers that classrooms are a policy-making sites, and we have the capability to affect change from our positions of authority there. Some practices I use in my own classes that translate well across institutions and may be modified for any curricular approaches are (1) a syllabus statement on academic cultural language standards, (2) mini units on multiple raciolinguistic rhetorical traditions, and (3) assigned readings on language myths and ideologies.

ACADEMIC CULTURAL LANGUAGE SYLLABUS STATEMENT

Aiming for an even more antiracist FYW curriculum than I had previously administered, in the fall 2020 semester, I added an Academic Cultural Language Statement to my syllabus for both the introductory FYW course and the research-intensive FYW course. The statement reads:

> This course and others you take in college may call on you to write compositions in Culturally Dominant English. You might know this as Standard English, Standard American English, Formal English, or school English. This dialect is not objectively superior to other English dialects or other languages; however, it is based in the historical cultural dominance assigned to middle-class European-descended English-speaking American communities and most valued by academic environments. There is nothing wrong with Culturally Dominant English, but in this course, I do not value this language ideology above others. You may freely choose to compose your writing in another dialect with the same attention to rhetorical means and practices one would put to writing in Culturally Dominant English. You will be evaluated with the same intent as those who choose to write in Culturally Dominant English. Like any polished piece of writing, you should demonstrate that you understand the way syntax, semantics, rhetoric, and discourse operate in that dialect and overall, it should be free of error in the dialect. Any questions may be directed to your instructor or to the Department of Writing and Rhetoric at [e-mail address excluded].

This practice moves beyond the race-evasive, "discourse stacking" (Delpit 1995, 65) ideologies of SRTOL and aligns with many of the ideologies of the SOSL and "This Ain't Another Statement! This Is a DEMAND for Black Linguistic Justice!" It's a practical way "to advocate for multilingual writers in all spaces of universities and colleges, including first-year writing," as well as a way "to promote social justice for all multilingual members of the academic community" (Conference 2001). The learner-centered statement honors and recognizes the linguistic validity of non-Euro-American discourse practices by outwardly affirming they do have syntactic and rhetorical value in all sociolinguistic spaces. It recognizes the limitations of discourses of whiteness in rhetorically preparing all students for the lives they lead and want to lead. While it does not grant "widespread systemic change in curricula, pedagogical practices, disciplinary discourses, research, language policies, professional organizations, programs, and institutions within and beyond academia," it can move teachers on a linguistic justice path in which we "stop using academic language and standard English as the accepted communicative norm, which reflects White Mainstream English" (Conference 2020). The statement also lends itself to antiracist assessment practices by establishing language about evaluation regardless of a student's chosen raciolinguistic tradition.

MINI UNITS ON MULTIPLE RACIOLINGUISTIC RHETORICAL TRADITIONS

My research-intensive FYW courses include one-week units on the discourse features developed out of the rhetorical traditions of Latin American, Black American, Indigenous American, and Eurocentric American cultures. Because I want students to be able to interrogate the raciolinguistic cultural practices present in their own writing, it's necessary that they understand the basis for those practices. I also like to put my pedagogy where my mouth is, so with the Academic Cultural Language Statement, to not teach multiple cultural rhetorical traditions or practices would be irresponsible. I begin with "African American Rhetoric and Rhetorical Traditions," as the legacy of Black culture in the American imagination (Morrison 1992) and possibly the global imagination means many students, if not all, are familiar with the discourse features. Many of these are those discussed by Keith Gilyard and Elaine Richardson (2001) (see also Smitherman 1993), including the following:

- narrativizing: dramatic retelling of facts or events, sequenced to make a specific point;
- testifying: telling the truth using story;
- signifyin': using indirection to make an argument (usually a put-down or "diss");
- call-and-response (structure): returning to the question being asked, prompt given, or previous point made repetitiously to check for constant connection;
- tonal semantics or repetition: repeating sounds or structures to stress meaning (similar to parallel structure but more purposeful);
- rhythmic language and ethnolinguistic idioms: using language that has strong meaning in Black/African American communities;
- image making or evocative imagery: applying metaphors and stimulating imagery;
- mimicry: overexaggerating an imitation of a person or situation to make a point;
- jubilee/tragic undertone: contrasting a feeling of utter joy with a feeling of tragedy or despair to evoke emotion.

I teach Euro-American/Euro-Western rhetorical tradition last of all the units because it is the one students are most accustomed to from prior educational experiences and the tradition venerated by public discourse in general. As I've confronted in " 'When the Looting Starts, the Shooting Starts': Anti-Black Higher Ed Pedagogical Ideologies and Practices" (Kareem 2021), this familiarity isn't because these features are better or universal, it's because everything dealing with whiteness is most honored in the mainstream social sphere (e.g., Why does my Black beautician have to learn how to style EVERY type of hair, including white hair, but I can walk into a white salon and these award-winning fools don't even know what shampoo or moisturizer to use on my hair?). So, yes, I use Eurocentricism as a kind of unteaching lesson. But more on that in a moment.

After Black American rhetorical traditions, I discuss Latinx/Latin American rhetorical traditions. These features include the following:

- visual rhetorics: use of graphic images to convey important ideas; emphasis on significance of visual elements alongside textual elements;
- border rhetorics: expression of multiple identities simultaneously through linguistic expression; representation of multiple locations ("How to Tame a Wild Tongue")
- code meshing: combination of two or more linguistic varieties or patterns of expression in writing or speech;
- codex rhetorics: pictographic communication with use of symbols, icons, and figurative representations to convey visual messages;
- deviations from a main topic due to elaboration: conscious departure from central thesis or current point of discussion to provide further context, often without signaling change;
- elaborative structures/flowery language: persistent use of run-ons, complex analogies, or ornate language choices;
- subtlety of language/indirection: writing with messages between the lines and without explanations for clarity; directness can be seen as rude.

Because I work at an HSI, a kind of institution found most commonly as a two-year college, this lesson may be especially critical. Many of the Latinx-, Hispanic-, Chicanx-identifying students reflect on their usage of some of these discourse features, including stories of being rewarded or ridiculed. I pair with the TED Talk "Identifying Yourself through Language" by Robyn Giffen (2015) with excerpts from Damián Baca's (2009) article "The Chicano Codex: Writing against Historical and Pedagogical Colonization" to discuss the link between what we value and devalue in writing usage as a social culture. This discussion can prove useful in the two-year college composition classroom, where many students are using its concepts within their lives as a way to access the literacies of the academy. It might help them understand the narratives their birth, native, or home cultures convey about their own written expressions and the ways these expressions have been shaped by dominant discourses of whiteness. It also gives them some of the tools to critique dominant raciolinguistic ideologies about the discourse features and their use.

The following week, we explore the rhetorical traditions common to Indigenous American communities. The discourse features we discuss are

- rhetorical sovereignty: determining own communicative purposes rather than appropriating mainstream, Euro-Western-developed purposes for communication;
- survivance (not survival!): Indigenous culture survival through endurance and continuance of Native stories and cultural practices, and resistance to polite and violent assimilation;
- visual rhetorics;
- relationality: interconnection with individuals, cultures, and environmental ecological systems;
- storying: emphasizing there is inherent value in stories for the sake of the story, not other purposes such as argument.

Like HSIs, most tribal colleges in the US are two-year institutions, so this lesson might hold particular relevance for many community and technical college faculty. I will note that, for me, this lesson is probably the most difficult to prepare since it's the one culture with which I have the least linguistic familiarity, which makes it markedly essential to include. For many teachers reading this who are entrenched in the dominant raciolinguistic expression, constructing these lessons may feel daunting or even impossible. I approached the development of the Indigenous American lesson by first researching works on Native American and Indigenous rhetorics from composition and literacy scholars (Alexie 1997; Cole 2011; Lyons 2000; McDougall and Nordstrom 2011; Powell 2002), as well as scholarship in cultural rhetorics about meaning making in Indigenous communities. The goal is to present the information about rhetorical and discourse features with the same degree of dedication with which we have approached Euro-American raciolinguistic culture in the classroom.

Finally, I end this examination of raciolinguistic rhetorical traditions with a discussion of Eurocentric/Euro-American rhetorical practices. These will likely be the ones you are most familiar with. In my lesson, I include the following:

- appeals: modes of persuasion, focused on moving the audience to rhetor's stance or action:
    * ethos: ethical appeal to establish credibility of rhetor's character;
    * logos: logical appeal to establish rationality of argument or message;
    * pathos: emotional appeal to establish connection to audience's needs and experiences;
- low-context/decontextual: writer's assumption of readers' limited knowledge of topic; information disconnected from social, cultural, and political contexts; privileging of originality above tradition;
- hyperindividualist: reliance on self for knowledge development and distribution; lack of connection to other individuals, larger cultural context, or environment;
- alphabetic modalities: textual presentation valued above all other forms of expression (graphic, sound, movement);
- emotional distance: dissemination of information disconnected from feelings of rhetor; audience feelings only focused on pathos appeal.
- linear argument structure: organization revolving around main idea and evidence presented in simple-to-follow order.

These identifying features of Eurocentric, typically academic-oriented writing features come from several resources (Baca 2009; Fought 2006b; Inoue 2016; Thaiss and Zawacki 2018; Villanueva 1999, 2015). I also draw on these resources to establish a social context for this raciolinguistic tradition. This aspect is critical to dismantle the notions of norms and standardization students bring with them about "proper writing," read whiteness-validated writing practices. Key to establishing the social context is to emphasize these practices are not raceless, void of cultural context, or universally correct. Rather, as I explain to students, they are sociolinguistically dominant in US, Canadian, and Western European societies and colonies.

CONTENT ON LANGUAGE IDEOLOGIES AND MYTHS

Example articles and chapters I assign include but that are not limited to these:

- Rosina Lippi-Green's "The Standard Language Myth" (1997)*
- Chris Thaiss and Terry Myers Zawacki's "What Is Academic Writing? What Are Its Standards?" (2006)*
- Paul Kei Matsuda's "The Image of College Students and the Myth of Linguistic Homogeneity" (2006)*
- Rusty Barrett's "Rewarding Language: Language Ideology and Descriptive Language" (2014)*

- Threshold concept chapters from Linda Adler-Kassner and Elizabeth Wardle's *Naming What We Know: Threshold Concepts of Writing Studies* (2015): Victor Villanueva's "Writing Provides a Representation of Ideologies and Identities"; Kevin Roozen's "Writing is Linked to Identity"; Paul Kei Matsuda's "Writing Involves the Negotiation of Language Differences"; and Tony Scott's "Writing Enacts and Creates Identities and Ideologies."
- Vershawn Ashanti Young's "The Problem of Linguistic Double Consciousness" (2018)*
- Carmen Fought's "Are White People Ethnic? Whiteness, Dominance, and Ethnicity" (2006a)*
- H. Samy Alim's "Hip Hop Nation Language" (2018)*

The asterisked items can be found in Samantha Looker-Koenigs's (2018) edited collection *Language Diversity and Academic Writing*, which I frequently assign in my courses.

Two-year colleges are the most raciolinguistically diverse institutions of higher education in the nation, yet so many of the literacy-education goals in FYW or English composition center on assimilationist or acculturationist approaches. Such approaches seek to eradicate students' raciolinguistic difference and, in the process, cause them to develop negative writerly self-images about their aptitude for discoursing within the dominant Euro-American way of doing language. In our efforts to prepare diversely languaged and racially subordinated student populations for further education or professional life, we fail to contend with the deep, rich cultural heritage of their raciolinguistic practices and force them to conform to a single, colonizing raciolinguistic perspective at the cost of writerly agency and self-perceptions. A critical race approach to teaching FYW in the two-year college can help us as teacher-scholar-activists disrupt the detrimental work of the mainstream education sites that precede us. We can disrupt this attitude that has told our students the white way is the right way to write so they may generate more positive, confident self-images about the impact of their raciolinguistic varieties in and out of school.

REFERENCES

Adler-Kassner, Linda, and Elizabeth Wardle, eds. 2015. *Naming What We Know: Threshold Concepts of Writing Studies*. Logan: Utah State University Press.

Alexie, Sherman. 1997. "The Joy of Reading: Superman and Me." In *The Most Wonderful Books: Writers on Discovering the Pleasures of Reading*, edited by Michael Dorris and Emilie Buchwald, 3–6. Minneapolis: Milkweed Editions.

Alim, H. Samy. 2018. "Hip Hop Nation Language." In *Language Diversity and Academic Writing*, edited by Samantha Looker-Koenigs, 74–87. Boston: Bedford/St. Martin's.

Baca, Damián. 2009. "The Chicano Codex: Writing against Historical and Pedagogical Colonization." In "Writing, Rhetoric, and Latinidad," special issue, *College English* 71 (6): 564–83.

Baker-Bell, April. 2013. "'I Never Really Knew the History behind African American Language': Critical Language Pedagogy in an Advanced Placement English Language Arts Class." *Equity and Excellence in Education* 46 (3): 355–70.

Baker-Bell, April, Tamara Butler, and Lamar Johnson. 2017. "The Pain and the Wounds: A Call for Critical Race English Education in the Wake of Racial Violence." *English Education* 49 (2): 116–29.

Baker-Bell, April. 2020. *Linguistic Justice: Black Language, Literacy, Identity, and Pedagogy.* New York: Routledge.

Balester, Valerie. 2012. "How Writing Rubrics Fail: Toward a Multicultural Model." In *Race and Writing Assessment*, edited by Asao B. Inoue and Mya Poe, 63–77. New York: Peter Lang.

Barbier, Stuart. 2003. "'The Reflection of 'Students' Right to Their Own Language' in First-Year Composition Course Objectives and Descriptions." *Teaching English in the Two-Year College* 30 (3): 256–67.

Barnett, Timothy. 2000. "Reading 'Whiteness' in English Studies." *College English* 63 (1): 9–37.

Barrett, Rusty. 2018. "Rewarding Language: Language Ideology and Descriptive Language." In *Language Diversity and Academic Writing*, edited by Samantha Looker-Koenigs, 130–38. Boston: Bedford/St. Martins.

Bartholomae, David. 1986. "Inventing the University." *Journal of Basic Writing* 5 (1): 4–23.

Bell, Derrick. 1980. "Brown v. Board of Education and the Interest-Convergence Dilemma." *Harvard Law Review* 93 (3): 518–34.

Bloom, Lynn Z. 1996. "Freshman Composition as a Middle-Class Enterprise." *College English* 58 (6): 654–75.

Brereton, John C. 1996. *The Origins of Composition Studies in the American College, 1875–1925.* Pittsburgh: University of Pittsburgh.

Canagarajah, Suresh A. 2006. "The Place of World Englishes in Composition: Pluralization Continued." *College Composition and Communication* 57 (4): 586–619.

Cole, Daniel. 2011. "Writing Removal and Resistance: Native American Rhetoric in the Composition Classroom." *College Composition and Communication* 63 (1): 122–44.

Committee on CCCC Language Statement. 1975. "Students' Right to Their Own Language." *College English* 36 (6): 709–26.

Conference on College Composition and Communication. 2001. "CCCC Statement on Second Language Writing and Multilingual Writers." https://cccc.ncte.org/cccc/re sources/positions/secondlangwriting.

Conference on College Composition and Communication. 2020. "This Ain't Another Statement! This Is a DEMAND for Black Linguistic Justice!" https://cccc.ncte.org /cccc/demand-for-black-linguistic-justice.

Delgado, Richard, and Jean Stefancic. 2006. *Critical Race Theory: An Introduction.* New York: New York University Press.

Delpit, Lisa. 1995. *Other People's Children: Cultural Conflict in the Classroom.* New York: New Press.

Flores, Nelson, and Jonathan Rosa. 2015. "Undoing Appropriateness: Raciolinguistic Ideologies and Language Diversity in Education." *Harvard Educational Review* 85 (2): 149–71.

Fought, Carmen. 2006a. "Are White People Ethnic? Whiteness, Dominance, and Ethnicity." In *Language and Ethnicity*, by Carmen Fought, 112–132. Cambridge: Cambridge University Press.

Fought, Carmen. 2006. *Language and Ethnicity.* Cambridge: Cambridge University Press.

Giffen, Robyn. 2015. "Identifying Yourself through Language." YouTube video. Posted by TEDx Talks. August 7, 2015.

Gilyard, Keith, and Elaine Richardson. 2001. "Students' Right to Possibility: Basic Writing and African American Rhetoric." In *Insurrections: Approaches to Resistance in Composition Studies*, edited by Andrea Greenbaum, 37–51. Albany: SUNY Press.

Hairston, Maxine. 1992. "Diversity, Ideology, and Teaching Writing." *College Composition and Communication* 43 (2): 179–93.

Inoue, Asao B. 2016. "Friday Plenary Address: Racism in Writing Programs and the CWPA." *WPA: Writing Program Administration* 40 (1): 134–54.

Iredell, Nancy J., and Jerry Parsons. 1977. "Should English Teachers Allow Student Dialects?" *Community College Review* 5 (1): 44–48.

Johnson, Lamar L. 2018. "Where Do We Go from Here? Toward a Critical Race English Education." *Research in the Teaching of English* 53 (2): 102–24.

Kareem, Jamila. 2018. "Transitioning Counter-Stories: Black Student Accounts of Transitioning to College-Level Writing." *Journal of College Literacy and Learning* 44: 15–35.

Kareem, Jamila. 2019. "A Critical Race Analysis of Transition Level Writing Curriculum to Support the Racially Diverse Two-Year College." *Teaching English in the Two-Year College* 46 (4): 271–96.

Kareem, Jamila. 2021. "'When the Looting Starts, the Shooting Starts': Anti-Black Higher Ed Pedagogical Ideologies and Practices." *Teacher-Scholar-Activist* (blog). January 28, 2021. https://teacher-scholar-activist.org/2020/07/20/when-the-looting-starts-the-shooting-starts-anti-black-higher-ed-pedagogical-ideologies-and-practices.

Kincheloe, Joe L. 2008. *Knowledge and Critical Pedagogy: An Introduction*. Germany: Springer Netherlands.

Kinloch, Valerie Felita. 2005. "Revisiting the Promise of Students' Right to Their Own Language: Pedagogical Strategies." *College Composition and Communication* 57 (1): 83–113.

Kirklighter, Cristina, Diana Cardenas, and Susan Wolff, eds. 2007. *Teaching Writing with Latino/a Students: Lessons Learned at Hispanic-Serving Institutions*. Albany: SUNY Press.

Kynard, Carmen. 2007. "'I Want to Be African': In Search of a Black Radical Tradition / African-American-Vernacularized Paradigm for 'Students' Right to Their Own Language,' Critical Literacy, and 'Class Politics.'" *College English* 69 (4): 360–90.

Kynard, Carmen. 2008. "Writing while Black: The Colour Line, Black Discourses and Assessment in the Institutionalization of Writing Instruction." *English Teaching: Practice and Critique* 7 (2): 4–34.

Kynard, Carmen. 2013. "Literacy/Literacies Studies and the Still-Dominant White Center." *Literacy in Composition Studies* 1 (1): 63–65. http://licsjournal.org/OJS/index.php/LiCS/article/view/17/19.

Ladson-Billings, Gloria. 1998. "Just What Is Critical Race Theory and What's It Doing in a Nice Field Like Education?" *Qualitative Studies in Education* 11 (1): 7–30.

Leonardo, Zeus. 2004. "The Color of Supremacy: Beyond the Discourse of 'White Privilege.'" *Educational Philosophy and Theory* 36 (2): 137–52.

Lippi-Green, Rosina. 2018. "The Standard Language Myth." In *Language Diversity and Academic Writing*, edited by Samantha Looker-Koenigs, 212–19. New York: Bedford/St. Martin's.

Looker, Samantha. 2016. "Writing about Language: Studying Language Diversity with First-Year Writers." *Teaching English in the Two-Year College* 44 (2): 176–98.

Looker-Koenigs, Samantha, ed. 2018. *Language Diversity and Academic Writing*. New York: Bedford St./ Martin's.

Lyons, Scott Richard. 2000 "Rhetorical Sovereignty: What Do American Indians Want from Writing?" *College Composition and Communication* 51 (3): 447–68.

Martinez, Aja Y. 2009. "'The American Way': Resisting the Empire of Force and Color-Blind Racism." *College English* 71 (6): 584–95.

Martinez, Aja Y. 2014. "A Plea for Critical Race Theory Counterstory: Stock Story versus Counterstory Dialogues Concerning Alejandra's 'Fit' in the Academy." *Composition Studies* 42 (2): 33–55.

Matsuda, Paul Kei. 2006. "The Image of College Students and the Myth of Linguistic Homogeneity." In *Language Diversity and Academic Writing*, edited by Samantha Looker-Koenigs, 312–16. New York: Bedford/St. Martin's.

Matsuda, Paul Kei. 2015. "Writing Involves the Negotiation of Language Differences." In *Naming What We Know: Threshold Concepts of Writing Studies*, edited by Linda Adler-Kassner and Elizabeth Wardle, 68–70. Logan: Utah State University Press.

McDougall, Brandy Nālani, and Georganne Nordstrom. 2011. "Ma Ka Hana Ka 'Ike (In the Work Is the Knowledge): Kaona as Rhetorical Action." *College Composition and Communication* 63 (1): 98–121.
Morrison, Toni. 1992. *Playing in the Dark: Whiteness and The Literary Imagination.* New York: Vintage Books.
Mutnick, Deborah. 1996. *Writing in an Alien World: Basic Writing and the Struggle for Equality in Higher Education.* Portsmouth, NH: Boynton/Cook.
Naynaha, Siskanna. 2016. "Assessment, Social Justice, and Latinxs in the US Community College." *College English* 79 (2): 196–201.
Noe, Mark. 2009. "The Corrido: A Border Rhetoric." In "Writing, Rhetoric, and Latinidad," special issue, *College English* 71 (6): 596–605.
Omi, Michael, and Howard Winant. 1986. *Racial Formation in the United States from the 1960s to the 1990s.* New York: Routledge.
Perryman-Clark, Staci. 2012a. "Africanized Patterns of Expression: A Case Study of African American Students' Expository Writing Patterns across Written Contexts." *Pedagogy: Critical Approaches to Teaching Literature, Language, Composition, and Culture* 12 (2): 253–80.
Perryman-Clark, Staci. 2012b. "Toward a Pedagogy of Linguistic Diversity: Understanding African American Linguistic Practices and Programmatic Learning Goals." *Teaching English in the Two-Year College* 39 (3): 230–46.
Powell, Malea. 2002. "Rhetorics of Survivance: How American Indians Use Writing." *College Composition and Communication* 53 (3): 396–434.
Prendergast, Catherine. 1998. "Race: The Absent Presence in Composition Studies." *College Composition and Communication* 50 (1): 36–53.
Roozen, Kevin. 2015. "Writing Is Linked to Identity." In *Naming What We Know: Threshold Concepts of Writing Studies,* edited by Linda Adler-Kassner and Elizabeth Wardle, 50–51. Logan: Utah State University Press.
Royster, Jacqueline Jones, and Jean C. Williams. 1999. "History in the Spaces Left: African American Presence and Narratives of Composition Studies." *College Composition and Communication* 50 (4): 563–84.
Scott, Tony. 2015. "Writing Enacts and Creates Identities and Ideologies." In *Naming What We Know: Threshold Concepts of Writing Studies,* edited by Linda Adler-Kassner and Elizabeth Wardle, 48–49. Logan: Utah State University Press.
Smitherman, Geneva. 1993. " 'The Blacker the Berry, the Sweeter the Juice': African American Student Writers and the National Assessment of Educational Progress." Paper presented at National Council of Teachers of English Annual Convention, Pittsburgh, PA, November 1993. https://files.eric.ed.gov/fulltext/ED366944.pdf.
Thaiss, Chris, and Terry Myers Zawacki. 2018. "What Is Academic Writing? What Are Its Standards?" In *Language Diversity and Academic Writing,* edited by Samantha Looker-Koenigs, pp. 288–292. Bedford St./ Martin's.
Toth, Christie, and Darin Jensen, eds. 2017. "Responses to the TYCA Guidelines for Preparing Teachers of English in the Two-Year College." *Teaching English in the Two-Year College* 45 (1): 29–32.
Villanueva, Victor. 1999. "On the Rhetoric and Precedents of Racism." In "A Usable Past: CCC at 50: Part 2," special issue, *College Composition and Communication* 50 (4): 645–61.
Villanueva, Victor. 2015. "Writing Provides a Representation of Ideologies and Identities." In *Naming What We Know: Threshold Concepts of Writing Studies,* edited by Linda Adler-Kassner and Elizabeth Wardle, 57–58. Logan: Utah State University Press.
Young, Vershawn Ashanti. 2007. *Your Average Nigga: Performing Race, Literacy, and Masculinity.* Detroit, MI: Wayne State University Press.
Young, Vershawn Ashanti. 2009. " 'Nah, We Straight': An Argument Against Code Switching." *JAC: A Journal of Rhetoric, Culture, and Politics* 29 (1/2): 49–76.
Young, Vershawn Ashanti. 2018. "The Problem of Linguistic Double Consciousness." In *Language Diversity and Academic Writing: A Bedford Spotlight Reader,* edited by Samantha Looker-Koenigs, 325–334. Boston: Bedford/St. Martin's.

6

INSTITUTIONAL THINKING FROM THIRDSPACE
A Case Study of Interactional Inquiry into 2YC Student Learning Outcomes

Rhonda Grego

SPACE IS OUR FRONTIER

The word *space* is used nearly fifty times throughout this collection (not including this chapter) to name an institutional place in US higher education for diverse student bodies to exist and thrive. Teacher-scholar-activists herein invoke making space, holding space, giving space, fostering space, creating space, providing space within which the diversities of which Jim Corder (1985, 31–32) speaks can be welcomed—and many point to two-year colleges as an institutional place where such space is most likely to be found.

But these authors also call our attention to the difficulties of institutionalized space, particularly where labels integral to our disciplinary identity become "naturalized," separated from specific location and attendant history, and "business as usual." Even when individuals' intentions are good, labels and attendant binaries used to identify long-standing divisions—such as *basic writer, first-year composition* (FYC), and *two-year college* (2YC)—maintain existing power structures via the silences those labels allow about the diversity of institutional conditions, faculty labor, and student backgrounds these labels elide—and via the attention deflected from often unnamed counterparts. Indeed, much scholarship centers on parsing such labels to do better justice to the complexities. Patrick Sullivan and Christie Toth's 2017 *Teaching Composition at the Two-Year College* is a pertinent example—the categories for the "Background Readings" therein highlight specific dimensions of 2YC life, including history and mission, access, preparing to teach, translating theory into practice, diverse student populations, and "the profession" (faculty identities). The section titled "Rethinking 'Business as Usual'" interestingly includes chapters on a diverse range of topics, from busting stereotypes associated with current-traditional pedagogy (five-paragraph essays and grammar), all the way to "developmental education" and an excerpt from Mike Rose's book *Back to School* titled "A Learning Society" (2017) that locates 2YC/community college most broadly in the lives of citizens as "second chance institutions." The collection provides a convincing portrait of 2YC composition faculty's value to society and to our larger profession as front-line FYC teachers, but recognizing and affirming that value is different from distinguishing our expertise so it is not subsumed—or silenced—by the predominance of "FYC-anywhere."

And as Darin Jensen and Brett Griffiths make clear in their rationale for this collection, 2YC faculty do regularly face a variety of situations in which our professional expertise is silenced and/or erased. As scholars have begun to investigate this 2YC silence, they have identified obstacles to greater voice and shifts in positioning and types of spaces that can foster productive change.

- Christie Toth and Patrick Sullivan (2016) document substantive and systemic barriers that create and reinforce the professional isolation of even experienced 2YC faculty, including lack of time, incentive and support, funding, and access to scholarly publication and difficulties locating research relevant to the circumstances of their work (258–59). They envision local "communities of practice" as supportive spaces within which 2YC faculty can help each other recognize and give voice to their experiential knowledge.
- Joanne Giordano, Holly Hassel, Jennifer Heinert, and Cassandra Phillips (2017) describe the "complexities of writing program development at access institutions," including shifts in student populations and college readiness across a multicampus system without dedicated writing program administrators or cohesive faculty development. The multifaceted plan they enacted required changes in position descriptions, use of data to support connections between faculty development and student retention, and finding ways to value "ongoing course redesign and continual reflection" (90).
- Anthony Warnke and Kirsten Higgins (2018) look at silence within an institutional setting as the result of a "bind" that occurs when neoliberal "enthusiastic reformers" (often promoted by administrators and nonprofit organizations championing 2YC student research) and faculty "reform resisters" create "conflict—us versus them—that leaves some instructors feeling unmoored and conflicted . . . [longing] for a 'third space' of resistance to both corporatization and the instructional status quo . . . a position of critical engagement with issues of reform" (363). Warnke and Higgins outline scenarios and questions "critical reformers" can ask, particularly in reference to issues of basic writing, student equity, and access, with the hope of opening up that space.

The picture these scholars bring into focus is that the relative silence of 2YC professionals (relative, that is, to our numbers and reach of our work with students) is constructed by messy layers of past and present scenarios, contexts, and institutional systems that differ—in and of themselves and/or in the particular mixture of influences and history at a given site—from those within which 4YC faculty live and work. In my state, 2YC faculty work is governed by budgets, expectations, and requirements set by our accrediting agency (SACS), our state legislative bodies, the Commission on Higher Education (CHE), the State Board for Technical and Comprehensive Education, our college's Board of Commissioners (business owners, politicians, and community members), upper-level administrators, and enrollment and finance departments—all of which exert a mix of influence over placement, scheduling, loading, hiring, and, thereby, teaching and curriculum. In my previous 4YC life (even at a private open-admission HBCU [historically Black college or university]), being in an English Department located within 4YC institutional and disciplinary history lent a "buffering" effect and certainly more connection to faculty governance than I have seen in our state's 2YC system, where (in this "right-to-work" state) governance and labor often feel like taboo topics.

As Brett Griffiths (2017) reports in her study, "Professional Autonomy and Teacher-Scholar-Activists in Two-Year Colleges," many 2YC faculty are not prepared by prior training to "think institutionally"—to engage with colleagues and administrators across their institutional context for the improvement of teaching and working conditions—so they/we "limit the influence of their [our] own pedagogical knowledge to [our] courses" (63). When the institutional dynamics are patently different from faculty's previous higher ed existence (from undergraduate to graduate degrees earned in 4Y institutions), and when there is no experience or preparation, the apparent choice for 2YC compositionists is to speak to those aspects of our work we hold in common with 4YC FYC colleagues (in the classroom) and to avoid or ignore the (institutionalized) differences. There are many reasons our classrooms may feel like a safe space. When we find ourselves located in institutional history and bureaucracies (like the nexus of agencies and authorities outlined above) honed to maintain the *status quo*, focusing intellectual energies on the classroom—and on pedagogy shared with 4YC FYC—can be a self-protective move, even an unconscious one with roots in unvoiced institutional grievance. As Warnke and Higgins (2018) describe, faculty can be resistant to change or reform because they suspect the motives of institutional reformers or feel misunderstood due to labor issues at their institutional sites.

In a 2YC-setting, the work of thinking institutionally requires a good bit of inside understanding of the history and forces exerting influence over very localized stakeholders and their ever-shifting interactions and balances of power. 2YC faculty who are new and/or contingent often don't have access to contextualizing information needed to parse the forces at work—perhaps academic affairs or faculty-council minutes are circulated by email, but processing these reports requires a good bit of reading between the lines and background knowledge of institutional history. In such settings, institutional thinking voiced aloud can feel transgressive, like a risky kind of talking back—even when one might just be wondering how a decision to change placement, for example, was made, when, and by whom.

Simply sharing information within and across 2YC institutions can feel risky even for full-time faculty with some measure of permanence in their positions. At a 2014 statewide annual meeting of English Department colleagues across our sixteen-college two-year system—affectionately known as "No Frills"—our English Department acted as host campus. We set up "table-talk" sessions designed for colleagues to share information about circumstances at their 2YC institutions on professional topics such as class size, loading, placement, adjunct working conditions, online-teaching practices, dual-enrollment courses, and so forth—each table resourced with copies of relevant professional statements from NCTE (1982, 1997, 1999, 2004, 2008, 2009), WPA (Council 2011), and both TYCA's *Guidelines for Academic Preparation* (2004a), and *Research and Scholarship* (2004b). As groups reported out on their discussions and comparisons across institutions, questions and concerns arose, and an older colleague anecdotally recounted early history of the "No Frills" effort when 2YC administrators at a sister institutions saw such information-sharing discussions as challenging to their authority (perhaps as a precursor to unionizing?) and withdrew support from the statewide meeting; this colleague noted that a similar organizing effort by math faculty across our system's colleges years prior had been "shut down" by administrators, who discouraged faculty from taking a day from teaching to attend, would not reimburse mileage for travel, and so forth.

As these situations and scenarios indicate, it is likely the silencing of 2YC professional expertise and focus on the classroom is inherited and embedded in institutional/ized policies and practices and systemic barriers internalized by successive generations of 2YC faculty and supported by isolation across 2YC environments. Certainly this *habitus* (Bourdieu 1977) contributes to the absence of the "departmental cultures" Toth

(2014) argues are needed to support greater 2YC faculty connection to professional organizations and publications. And as Griffiths (2017) argues, any retreat to the classroom as a space of independence will not gain authority for our 2YC voices and expertise. Her study of 2YC professional autonomy leads Griffiths to conclude that this tendency "will likely continue to limit the status and autonomy of writing instructors who teach at two-year colleges." Her survey findings argue for creating ways to help faculty "identify and value their own knowledge, to assert authority based on that knowledge, and to engage with the institutional systems that make up their colleges" (63).

What frameworks might support such engagement, might help 2YC faculty open up space, time, and access for our knowledges and experience? What commodious language will make visible the connections between student learning and faculty labor and place those connections at the heart of our FYC work at a 2YC? As I look at the scholars who have opened up conversations about 2YC silence, authority, and agency, what I note in their proposals is a need to create new connections and alternative spaces in which to foster metadiscourse. In that spirit, this chapter describes how a thirdspace methodology and language drawn from writing studio work provides one way to think institutionally about connections that swirl among student learning, pedagogy, and faculty labor in a 2YC. After examining interactional inquiry and thirdspace as frameworks, I provide a case study of FYC program work undertaken with colleagues in a 2YC English Department, exploring the knowledges produced as an example of institutional memory work that demonstrates the potential for thinking institutionally and professing the realities of both student and faculty lives in a 2YC setting.

THIRDSPACE AS OUR PLACE

In her award-winning 2018 article, "Epistemic Authority in Composition Studies: Tenuous Relationship between Two-Year English Faculty and Knowledge Production," Holly Larson applies feminist standpoint theory to the issue of two-year college faculty's professional representation and identifies "third space" as a place where the professional knowledge of two-year college faculty lives. In the early 1990s, Nancy Thompson and I (Grego and Thompson 2008) were drawn to feminist frameworks that call attention to this space as a place of "being" with students. In our case we applied the SPUJJ Collective's "theorizing the cross-section" (Crawford et al. 1992), as well as "participatory inquiry" from Peter Reason and John Rowan (1981)—and later the concept of thirdspace from cultural geographers Edward Soja (2009) and Doreen Massey (2004)—to realize the radical way the space of writing studio programs can be a support for student writers and their teachers. Our conception of thirdspace was and is closely akin to the opening of spaces referred to by other authors in this collection.[1]

Our adoption of this approach and formulation of a collaborative research method was connected to other access work foundational in both our lives. When we first met, Nancy was a long-time faculty member at the southeastern R1 where I had just been hired as a new faculty member for their composition and rhetoric graduate program. Nancy is a white working-class woman originally from a midwestern farm community; she went to school in a one-room schoolhouse, where her mother served as teacher. She entered the R1's English Department via a doctoral degree in educational research after originally being hired during desegregation to teach in a new school created by the university to use curricula based on alternative media as an entry point for African American students. I was a white working-class first-generation college student from the southeastern US who'd attended historically Black middle and high schools during desegregation; benefitted from talented African American teachers in a tight-knit community that valued education; earned a scholarship to attend a small, predominantly white 4YC in Charleston, South Carolina; and then entered Penn State's English Department as a graduate student in 1981, where my difference from the white middle- to upper-middle-class predominantly male students there made me hyperaware of context and sensitive to language.

As outsiders will do, Nancy and I shared certain skepticisms; we first met in 1989 when I was hired by Nancy's R1 to join graduate faculty in their relatively new composition and rhetoric doctoral program, specifically to teach a research-methods seminar. While in PSU's composition and rhetoric doctoral program, I had taken a typical research-methods seminar that surveyed approaches from experimental to anthropological. I remember learning about the "controlled" experimental approach in educational research and wondered at the idea that an education institution could be like a laboratory, that social systems could be so easily likened to physical properties, that the differences of space and place could be controlled. Nancy had actually completed her doctoral work and dissertation using those methods of controlled versus "experimental" applications, but the experience left her certain of the inefficacy of those approaches as she began her work in higher education. A year after

---

1. As Nancy Thompson and I drew primarily on Soja's work, we adopted his spelling—"thirdspace" instead of "third space"—and have stayed with that spelling.

I was hired as graduate faculty, the SC Commission on Higher Education abolished developmental coursework for credit at the state's public 4YCs, and I joined Nancy and a group of dedicated graduate students who had previously taught both basic writing and first-year composition to explore this mandate and its consequences for our students. That group was the seed ground for what was to become our first writing studio program, and this whole set of circumstances pushed my own investigation of research methods for the graduate seminar into the realm of participatory inquiry and feminist research approaches, and ultimately into postmodern cultural geography. Because context matters.

In the writing studio program that emerged, student small groups and facilitators operating outside but alongside enrollment in a writing course (or a course requiring intensive writing) help students develop agency through exploring students' interactions with the conceptions of academic discourse and culture they encounter in FYC classrooms and with instructors at that institution. We named this hybrid of participatory research (Reason 1988; Reason and Rowan 1981) and memory work (Crawford et al. 1992) "interactional inquiry" (Grego and Thompson 2008), and over several years and institutional sites, we explored this approach for opening up thirdspaces where perceptions of everyday reality that have been subsumed, silenced, or suppressed by institutional and disciplinary secondspace conceptions (akin to what feminist and postcolonial theorists term "master narratives" and what Sullivan and Toth's 2017 collection identifies as "business as usual") can surface, and be heard.

Nancy and I engaged in writing studio work over several decades as I moved across institutions (Nancy remained at the R1 where we first met until her retirement), and in every case we encountered conflicting desires and histories swirling around institutional labels and positionings of "basic writer."

- As mentioned, in the early 1990s at our R1 institution, Nancy and I wrote a proposal and cleared out a forgotten storeroom (one with a mural painted by a student years before along one wall) to make literal space for our first writing studio program after the SC Commission on Higher Education declared in the early 1990s that there would be no remedial courses at four-year state-supported institutions. The course and label *basic writing* were banished from those institutions, but we knew there would still be ENG 101 students—and their graduate TA teachers—who would need support.
- In 1996 I moved to a local HBCU and obtained a FIPSE (Fund for the Improvement of Post-Secondary Education) grant, with Nancy Thompson and Marie Wilson-Nelson as consultants, to begin another writing studio program—the Bridges Writing Program. There

- I cleared out cabinets and boxes (again), cleaning and moving in tables and chairs over a couple of weekends to make ready a room for another studio program, though this time at an institution with (as I came to learn) a decades-long history of many different supplemental support programs forged to fill the gaps ignored by mainstream, white-centric institutional labels and hierarchies.
- After lobbying and writing proposals for several years at my next institution—a 2YC where I have been since 2006—I became department chair, then moved back to faculty status where I eventually worked with colleague Mark Sutton (a former doctoral student of Nancy's recently hired as faculty) to renovate and repurpose a one-credit-hour course to again make space for a writing studio program we officially began at this institutional site in fall 2017. With the advent of multiple measures in fall 2019, basic writing course offerings at our 2YC (ENG 100 Introduction to Composition) has shrunk from twenty-five sections in spring 2019 to five sections in fall 2022, while Guided Pathways implementation in fall 2020 and its support for corequisite courses (Bailey, Jaggars, and Jenkins 2015, ch. 4) have increased need and institutional support for our writing studio weekly small-group program.

Over the years since 1992, writing studio programs have come and gone at many institutions, some persisting and some not, including programs by John-Paul Tassoni and Cynthia Liewecki-Wilson (2005) at Miami University–Middletown (the oldest continuously running program), by Joanne Baird Giordano and Holly Hassel at the University of Wisconsin (discussed in this volume), and by many others, including those discussed in authors in Mark Sutton and Sally Chandler's (2018) collection *The Writing Studio Sampler*, which grew out of years of discussion at our annual Studio+ Special Interest Group meetings at CCCC. Writing studio's alternative approach has sparked related programs as well; most well known would be the accelerated learning programs, or ALPs, begun by Peter Adams after a visit with our Studio SIG (See Adams et al. 2017.) ALPs also provides support for students working "outside but alongside" participation in a regular first-year composition course, though there are two key writing studio elements not typically featured in ALPs: (1) studio programs enroll students from several different courses and teachers in a single small-group session (facilitated by someone familiar with the course overall but not their specific teacher) so that students in that group are able to compare and discuss differences in the way the same course or similar curriculum is implemented by different teachers and experienced by different students, and (2) studio programs create an important "studio studio" via regular staff meetings for studio group facilitators themselves to compare notes and deliberate on what we can learn from our studio students and their experiences across a variety of FYC sections.

Both these elements—mixing across classrooms and making space for faculty metadiscourse—are vital to institutional memory work, to recovering what is elided by secondspace labels, to opening a thirdspace wherein the institutional contexts and attendant rhetorical exigencies are made more visible for examination and reflection. In the next section I focus on how—when I was a 2YC English Department chair—interactional inquiry became a managerial approach to thinking institutionally, to calling attention to context in ways that help open space and time in which to recognize and recollect our professional expertise and foster productive change and growth specific to our 2YC circumstances.

INSTITUTIONAL MEMORY WORK: RECOLLECTING STUDENTS

It was previous studio work with thirdspace and the potential of interactional inquiry that gave me heart in June 2008 as I moved from instructor into the role of department chair (until 2015) of a 2YC department that, particularly in 2008–2009, seemed overrun by outside interests, trajectories, and demands, which were enacted via unexamined secondspace conceptions and labels that aided and abetted the continued overlooking of (and silences about) 2YC faculty labor.

- In 2008–2009, in the midst of a serious national financial recession and rapidly shrinking state funding for SC two-year colleges (moving from approximately 40 percent to less than 10 percent of funding from the state that created our sixteen-college system in 1974), our college's administration and commissioners decided it was economically necessary to raise the teaching loads of full-time faculty from 5/5 (fall/spring) to 6/6.
- In 2008–2009 our college was readying for SACS reaccreditation, and all areas were required by the new SACS standards to implement quantitative student learning outcomes (SLO) assessment. In the first two years we were charged with collecting SLO data on every student in every course every semester (fall and spring).
- As a part of the new SLO implementation, the English Department was charged with semester-by-semester assessment of not only the expected written communication and humanities competencies but also information literacy.
- At the same time, our lead academic advisors and transfer coordinators outlined widespread changes 4YCs and universities in our state were making to their FYC curriculum. In several cases (e.g., at the College of Charleston and Clemson University), 4YC English Departments were moving from a two-course FYC sequence in which

the second course was an introduction to literature to a one-course FYC requirement focusing on rhetoric/argument and research.

In 2008, the conceptions of our work by those in higher positions—both state- and college-level administrations—had voice that our own realities did not. And these voices had far-reaching effects on our department. Increased loading meant full-time faculty were teaching more FYC courses and sections (though FYC sections were capped at twenty-two to twenty-three students, in part by making use of the National Council of Teachers of English 1999 position statement). This department had already (admirably) affirmed its commitment to teaching FYC via a long-standing departmental policy that all full-time faculty should teach at least one section of our first-year courses every year, including ENG 100 Introduction to Composition (our pre-college-level writing course), ENG 101 English Composition I (then a literary nonfiction-based writing course), and ENG 102 English Composition II (then an introduction to poetry, short fiction, and drama). Two hundred-level literature survey courses (capped at twenty-five per section) were taught on a three-year rotation to ensure all faculty had the chance to teach a literature course. Each full-time English faculty member, as well as adjunct faculty who taught a full load of courses, now faced fall and spring semesters with up to 138 FYC students—or, if one FYC was replaced by a 200-level course, then 135–140 students in writing- and reading-intensive courses.

Being assigned responsibility for teaching and assessing the additional competency of information literacy (a learning competency tied to separate library-sciences instruction at the nearby R1 university and at other 4YC and universities in our state) also meant increased attention to developments in the online world and new media genres—in a department in which over half the nineteen full-time faculty (in fall 2008) were within five to seven years of retirement, and many of those were decidedly not comfortable with online tech. At that time, the majority of fifty-plus adjunct faculty had earned graduate degrees several decades earlier; most of these faculty also were not comfortable with online worlds and multimedia communication. Department full-time and adjunct faculty makeup was typical of that described by Christie Toth and Patrick Sullivan (2016)—there were a handful of doctorates, but most faculty had master's degrees, the majority in American and British literature, with one to three from each of the areas of linguistics, comparative literature, creative writing, and English education. I was the first department member with a degree in rhetoric and composition, though faculty with more recent degrees hired in the early

2010s brought graduate TA training in that field (particularly hires from Clemson's master's program). This faculty makeup meant the requirement to quantify student achievement and "value added"—in other words, to collect data/numbers and calculate percentages of students "meeting benchmark"—as part of our SLO assessment system, though not intended in this way, read to most faculty like a further tech school devaluing of their literature-as-humanities-focused professional identities.

Faculty backgrounds also made the addition of "argument" and "rhetoric" as these were found at that time in FYC at 4YCs in our state (to which many of our associate in arts/associate in science program students sought transfer) a challenge. Our college's ENG 101 and 102 courses had long been based on an unquestioned (and arhetorical, current-traditional) business-as-usual nonfiction/fiction divide, with the SC Technical College System's *CAC* (*Catalog of Approved Courses* n.d.) course descriptions that had appeared in our college's catalogue as far back as 1974 when our 2YC college was founded:

- **ENG 101 Catalog Description:** This college transfer course emphasizes the study of composition in conjunction with appropriate literary selections, with frequent theme assignments to reinforce effective writing skills. A review of standard usage and the basic techniques of research are also presented.
- **ENG 102 Catalog Description:** This is a college transfer course in which the following topics are presented: development of writing skills through logical organization, effective style, literary analysis, and research. An introduction to literary genre is also included.

When I came into the department in 2006, ENG 101 was taught using literary nonfiction ("Once More to the Lake" was a staple), and ENG 102 was taught as an introduction to poetry, drama, and fiction—as they had been for many years. In fact, those same course descriptions still appear in the state *CAC*, in our MTC catalog, and in our course syllabi. The state *CAC* is meant to provide guidance for SC public colleges and universities with a goal of keeping courses transferable across public state higher ed institutions, but in reality only 2YC colleagues in our sixteen-college system seem to be held to the course listings in this catalog; English departments at our state's 4YCs were busy at that time revising first-year writing course sequences and curriculum based on the privilege afforded by their institutional contexts and accompanying authority.

As I mention earlier, my previous managerial training was as a studio builder with faculty colleagues at two previous 4Ycs, so in my new role

I adapted what I knew about how to respect and engage faculty. Our 2YC department did not have a formal WPA position, but there was a history of coordinator positions in the department, with both full-time and adjunct faculty members having served as bookstore liaisons and ENG 100 and ENG 101 coordinators in previous years, sometimes with course releases but typically as "service." The call for SLO data collection needed for SACS reaccreditation provided impetus (and budget arguments with administration) for expanding this system to include coordinators for ENG 100, 101, 102, and 200-level courses; and I argued that these coordinators receive course releases in proportion to student and faculty populations served, using the release time to not only provide sample course curricula but also to chair their respective course committees comprised of faculty who met to

1. design SLO performance measures for the communication and information literacy (ENG 100, 101, 102) or humanities (200-level literature and genre survey courses) competencies each course was now responsible for assessing;
2. discuss and interpret SLO data after they were collected;
3. draft SLO reports for the college that included plans for actions to be taken to improve areas of weakness (not meeting benchmark) identified in the SLO data;
4. enact professional- and curriculum-development plans outlined in those reports in connection with our SLO assessment findings.

Increased course release helped create time and room for faculty voices, while student SLO data helped firstspace realities disrupt secondspace conceptions and labels. In addition to making faculty labor visible to our college administration via course releases for this work, I knew from directing previous studio programs that my role was to provide all manner of needed supports—from technological to professional to psychological—for implementing this system so faculty could focus their limited time and energies on discussions (i.e., interactional inquiry) with each other. In interactional-inquiry systems, administrative labor is directed towards reducing the labor needed by participants (in this case, faculty) to bring firstspace realities to the table. To that end, I constructed Excel workbooks in which each instructor at the end of every semester holistically rated their students' achievement on a range of performance measures decided upon by each course committee, and I also set up a system of training sessions for both full-time and adjunct faculty (assisted by course coordinators) to discuss, share, and calibrate scoring and demonstrate how to open, fill in, and save these workbooks.

I collected workbooks at the end of every semester and compiled the resulting data (stripping away any teacher- or student-identifying information) in summary tables I then provided to each coordinator and committee for discussion. In a department where the majority of instructors are adjuncts, this was an important "reflecting back" of patterns from data, and it helped disrupt secondspace assumptions about student learners and business-as-usual attitudes about what students' writing said about their work ethic, preparedness, or abilities.

In the beginning semesters of this process, I also attended course committee meetings, took notes on faculty discussions, assisted course coordinators in drafting initial SLO reports, revised our departmental fall in-service meeting (which previously focused on issues such as parking and copy codes) to focus on pedagogical initiatives for the year, organized an annual spring best-practices in-house conference featuring short presentations and workshops by departmental full-time and adjunct faculty, and initiated creation of D2L (our learning-management system) course shells as a 24/7 space to provide and house resulting "ENG Faculty Resources." These were important vehicles to enable the communications required for actions to be taken decided upon by course coordinators and their faculty committees. But even more important, all these actions were a way to make visible our expertise to each other and develop our 2YC professional knowledges in ways that moved beyond those less productive assumptions about student learners and writers.

Course committee meetings each semester in 2008–2009 and 2009–2010 (and at least annually thereafter) brought faculty together (with refreshments, in whatever classrooms were available) to examine SLO data tables that compiled all course sections and instructors' perceptions of their students' level of achievement on a range of communication- and information-literacy performance measures from the previous semester. These intensive discussions focused on the possible *whys* behind patterns our assessment statistics revealed about areas of strength and weakness in student writing and research. Over and over I stressed to faculty that despite the accountant-like quantification of student learning found in the data tables and required for reporting, the heart of this system was *their* perceptions and interpretation of the trends in our data, based on the considerable knowledge and experience *they* brought to the table from their courses and classrooms—the SLO reports and actions we decided to take were *our* story to tell. Though I did not at the time phrase it in this way, we set out to theorize the cross-section of student learning represented by the SLO data in combination with faculty's classroom-based experiences.

The SLO reports we wrote were filed within a college-wide online system that was a part of the SACS reporting process, not only for our initial reaccreditation in 2010 but also annually each year thereafter for the five-year report (and ten years later, our reaccreditation in 2019). Those reports followed a standard structure across all college courses, including charts and sections for summarizing results, analyzing strengths and weaknesses in student performance, discussing the impact of changes implemented as a result of the previous cycle (i.e., actions previously taken), as well as impact of other factors on student performance during this cycle, before ending with an outline of actions to be taken before the next cycle of data collection. The summaries of our faculty course committees' interactional-inquiry discussions provided by coordinators in these report sections stressed over and over establishing the *connections* between professional- and curriculum-development actions and what we knew (and documented) about our student writers.

The actions we took—including faculty-designed workshops and inservice meetings, D2L teacher resource sites and readings sponsored by curriculum-development grants, and textbook-committee work—all prompted ongoing cycles of interactional inquiry with department colleagues, cycles that continue today. Below I highlight just two (of several) key areas where our initial interactional inquiry facilitated explicit focus on previously submerged or unarticulated aspects of our work and faculty labor—and contributed to institutional thinking for change.

INSTITUTIONAL MEMORY WORK: RECOLLECTING RHETORIC

In order to arrive at reasonable actions to be taken, we had to begin asking questions and hypothesizing about *why* student writing exhibited the patterns of strength and weaknesses documented by our SLO data collection (not just laziness or ignorance—those business as usual labels applied to student behavior when there is not a framework for understanding student actions as *writerly* action) and thinking about the professional and curriculum development that was (or was not) in place to support *all* instructors (not just the very experienced or full-time faculty). As I look back on the SLO reports from 2009 to 2013 in particular, I can see how our interactional inquiry began to question previously accepted (and naturalized) dichotomies such as the nonfiction/fiction divide (which tended to position students as passive consumers rather than active producers) and the current-traditional focus on skills and skill building many faculty brought with them from graduate student teaching in the 1970s/80s at the then R1 where I had begun my career so many years ago. This questioning opened up a thirdspace for other possible explanations and approaches, for looking at other possible connections.

Because SLO performance measures for our composition courses ranged from higher-order (organization, focus, revision, evaluation, and integration of sources) to lower-order concerns (editing, use of a documentation system), we looked at connections between those concerns and saw that our students needed more explicit experience with how audience and purpose influence text production and consumption in not only academic but also everyday contexts. So, for example, in the post-fall 2009 SLO report for ENG 010 Introduction to Composition (at that time a "fast-track" three or four-week version of ENG 100, our basic writing course), Coordinator Julie Nelson and her ENG 010/ENG 100 Committee members had this to say about the fall-to-fall student weaknesses in performance measures for writing, including "use of thesis" (PM 2), "topic sentences" (PM 3), and "use of evidence" (PM 4):

> Because ENG 010 is a compressed course, taught in 3 or 4 weeks' time, skills related to structure and development may be difficult for students to develop in such a short time. PM 2 (thesis), PM 3 (topic sentences), and PM 4 (evidence) may seem like basic composition skills, but in longer, more traditional writing courses, students have more time to practice and improve these skills. *It may be that instructors of ENG 010 assume their students know how to structure an essay, when in fact skills like writing a thesis (PM 2) and writing topic sentences (PM 3) are as much related to development of ideas as they are to structure. Further discussion with instructors about the skills of incoming students and how to create a framework for the course that takes those skills into consideration may be helpful.*[2] (emphasis added)

In this excerpt from an ENG 010 report, the connection between "poor structure" and "time" needed to develop ideas was one that called into question the efficacy of the three–four-week essay-writing "bootcamp" approach that undergirded this course at that time. But the need for a framework that went beyond isolated skills and the problem of how to reframe skills in a more coherent way for students (and for less experienced teachers) arose across several FYC course SLO reports. The framework our course committees turned to across ENG 010, ENG 100,

---

2. Student Learning Outcomes (SLO) reports quoted in this section and the next are internal documents and not publicly available. SLO reports for each course in the English Department at Midlands Technical College are archived digitally in the Department's English SLO Documents D2L resource site and submitted annually to an internal college O:Drive.

and eventually ENG 101 and ENG 102 was provided by rhetorical study: committee members talked about why students had trouble evaluating and using sources, why they struggled to identify different genres of online sources, and why they struggled to take ownership of their essay content and structure—and the answers all pointed to the need for further explicit attention to audience, purpose, and context as the motivation for choices of form and genre. Both reading and writing as active pursuits needed to be more fully contextualized for students—they needed rhetoric's connection to *why*.

But having taught ENG 101 and 102 based on the nonfiction/fiction divide for twenty-five-plus years, instructors were not familiar with rhetoric. Professional development and our annual Spring Best Practices in-house conference was born, as described by a part of the ENG 101 (English Composition I) "Actions to be Taken" section of the post-fall 2009 report:

> The English Department organized its Spring 2009 Best Practices Conference for full-time and adjunct instructors with breakout sessions on ways to include more rhetorical emphasis in ENG 101 assignments. The inaugural conference was held on January 8, 2009 and included sessions that focused on emphasizing audience and purpose to motivate and direct revision and ways to motivate more focused reading and analysis across courses. One session specifically illustrated how to design smaller research assignments across ENG 101 so that research is framed not as a separate activity, but as part of the overall rhetorical situation of reading and writing in academic culture. This session targeted both communication and information literacy competencies.

Subsequent annual best-practice conferences presented sessions offered by both full-time and adjunct faculty demonstrating a variety of rhetorical terms, assignments, strategies, and course units as our interactional inquiry fostered collaboration among faculty. This "rhetorical turn" opened up space by 2012 for faculty to investigate and embrace work emerging on genre systems and by fall 2014 to put in place a new framework for ENG 100, ENG 101, and ENG 102 as true companion courses—with a focus on audience and purpose (ENG 100: Introduction to Composition), rhetorical awareness (ENG 101: Freshman Composition I), and genre awareness (ENG 102: Freshman Composition II) in ways compatible with a variety of teacher backgrounds. This new framework interwove faculty backgrounds and student learning needs, making both visible and placing faculty's professional expertise in conversation with developments championed by professional organizations (including TYCA).

INSTITUTIONAL MEMORY WORK: RECOLLECTING FACULTY LABOR

SLO reporting and widening cycles of inquiry and collaboration across the department prompted connections to societal movements and institutional issues outside our department that intersected with work by professional organizations. For example, in examining areas where SLO data showed student writers to be weaker across courses—particularly integration of source materials and revision—our discussions and reports outlined connections to larger societal shifts in print/digital literacies, the complicated nature of synthesis, and the work of understanding students' dispositions towards writing formed in previous educational experiences. Closer to home, we started questioning the full-time/adjunct divide: our SLO reports required all departments to report the percentage of students successful on performance measures in sections taught by full-time versus those taught by adjunct faculty, but fairly early in our SLO interactional inquiry process, we started mixing considerations of experience and notes about working conditions in ways that disrupted the rigid binary offered by the institutional labels of *full-time* versus *adjunct* faculty, as this section from the post-fall 2009 ENG 010 SLO report exemplifies:

> For further analysis, student performance data was compiled according to instructor and level of experience. Due to the difficulty of scheduling and the length of sessions (3-4 weeks total), ENG 010 is a course taught almost exclusively by adjuncts. In Fall 2009, 16 of 17 sections were taught by adjunct faculty, and only 1 section was taught by a full-time faculty member. But, when the experience level of all faculty is taken into account, all 17 sections of ENG 010 were taught by instructors with at least one semester of experience teaching the course. This is in stark contrast to Fall 2008, when 12 of 26 sections—nearly 50 percent—were taught by instructors who had not previously taught the course.
>
> 94 percent of students in the one ENG 010 section taught by a full-time faculty member met the benchmark, while 79 percent of students taught by adjunct faculty met the benchmark. This may be due to limited access for adjuncts to instructional resources and professional development opportunities, as well as less experience and calibration for some of those instructors.
>
> Within the adjunct faculty instructor population, all adjunct faculty teaching ENG 010 in Fall 2009 had taught the course at least once before, while in 2008, 12 of 26 sections were taught by first-time ENG 010 instructors. So it is likely that the improved performances [in Fall 2009] were in part due to having a more experienced group of instructors, all with a better understanding of the course and its requirements.

There is privileging here of full-time faculty experience: in the second paragraph, the full-time instructor's experience level is not questioned.

But I also note this passage mixes thinking about status versus experience in a way that demonstrates rhetorical struggle with institutional labels and rigid binaries that was and is an important part of interactional inquiry's thirdspace in our 2YC setting. In instances like these across our SLO reports, course committees—including adjunct-faculty volunteer members—looked at student data not just to look at student deficiencies in the ways SLO analysis was originally presented to faculty across our college: in discussing *why*, our gaze turned not only inward to our own professional experience but also outward to our institutional environment and issues of labor in new ways, articulating new connections and questioning status quo assumptions.

There were specific times in the SLO reports when faculty did focus attention on full-time faculty versus adjuncts and issues of institutional working conditions. As our interactional inquiry progressed over several semesters of discussion, coordinators increasingly used the "Other Factors Impacting Student Performance" section of the college's SLO report template to argue the impact of labor conditions, as this extended passage from our 2012 ENG 101 and ENG 102 SLO reports demonstrates:

> We must also note that (a) full-time faculty loading [which since the recession of 2008 had been moved from 5/5 to 6/6 course sections per fall/spring semester], and (b) less than ideal adjunct faculty working conditions are both environmental factors that greatly determine the extent to which faculty are able to communicate with each other on a regular basis.
>
> Having down-time in between classes for consulting with other faculty, schedules that allow informal meetings and discussions, office spaces in close proximity, time apart from class prep, grading, and advising—all these are a part of working conditions which allow college faculty time and energy to come together in unscripted ways to discuss, question, and develop shared assumptions, expectations, and ideas about student work—and their own.
>
> Currently MTC English full-time faculty teach 6 courses each fall and each spring, and 4 during the 10-week summer session, in addition to significant advising duties and service commitments. Time is definitely a factor for full-time faculty. NCTE 1999 (National Council of Teachers of English) recommends no more than 20 students per writing course (fewer if students are developmental, as in our ENG 100) and that no single writing teacher have more than 60 students in first-year writing courses in any given semester.
>
> MTC full-time and some adjunct faculty regularly have 5–6 sections of first-year writing, with 22 students per section, for a minimum of 110–132 students, twice the number of students recommended, twice the number of assignments on which to give feedback, twice the number of classroom communities to care for while working at a two-year college where many students are "at risk" due to a range of socioeconomic and cultural obstacles.

Adjunct faculty have situations that vary, depending on whether an adjunct is retired and teaching 1–2 sections per semester, works during the day as a high school English teacher, or is cobbling together something resembling a full-time living by teaching full loads of 4–6 sections (or more) at MTC and at other institutions (often with considerable driving times between institutions). MTC provides workrooms, but no real office spaces for meeting privately with students or having extended discussions with other faculty about teaching issues, even should adjunct faculty have the time for such discussions.

These working conditions make it all the more difficult to foster a departmental professional life within which those shared values can develop and flourish. Two meetings each year during which full-time and adjunct faculty can meet to share and talk (fall in-service and spring best practices conference), plus the online resources and communications which attempt to "fill the gap" on a weekly basis throughout the academic year are certainly worthwhile, but they are not enough.

Originally, we were told that this "Other" section for reporting SLO results was where we should note events that impacted student learning, such as college closures due to hurricanes or floods, campus computer outages, and so forth. But our interactional inquiry had affirmed a connection between professional development (i.e., time and space to realize professional knowledges) and improvement in student learning outcomes as a key part of our actions to be taken year after year. That connection allowed faculty in their discussions and in our reporting to assert the impact of institutional work environment as a kind of climate over which we had little control but that must also be acknowledged. In 2015 when our Faculty Council chair was preparing a presentation on the impact of the 6/6 loading for our MTC Board of Commissioners, our department was able to provide data collected from our SLO work to show that the increase in loading that began in 2008 resulted in lower retention across our FYC courses when compared to pre-SLO data years. While it is likely many other factors impacted our MTC Board of Commissioners' eventual decision to return loading to 5/5, being able document impact and contribute to those arguments was an affirming step for our department faculty's growth in institutional thinking.

INSTITUTIONAL MEMORY WORK: RECOLLECTING PROFESSIONAL IDENTITIES AND ORGANIZATIONS

In fact, issues related to labor conditions sparked some of the first connections in our department reports, workshops, in-service sessions, and presentations to organizations and publications in the larger field. For example, a spring 2010 departmental-coordinator PowerPoint presentation to our vice president for academic affairs included an annotated bibliography of sources referenced in our presentation to lobby

- against use of standardized testing instead of our then in-house writing placement test based on actual student writing (NCTE 2008, 2009; Sullivan 2008);
- against increasing class size and workload (Lee 2009; NCTE 1999);
- against increasing use of adjunct faculty (Klausman 2010; NCTE 1982, 1997) and for increased attention to professional development and preparation (TYCA 2004a, 2004b), particularly in the areas of technology and twenty-first-century literacies (Millward 2008; Yancey et al. 2004; Swenson et al. 2005; Warnock 2009).

And a 2011–2012 internal report on the activities of an in-house FYC study group (formed in fall 2011 to follow up on faculty reports of changes in FYC curriculum across colleges in the region) made further connections to recently published professional statements, including the WPA's original "FYC Outcomes Statement" (Council 2014) and WPA, NCTE, and NWP's *Framework for Success in Postsecondary Writing* (Council 2011), which coincided with our college-wide QEP (Quality Enhancement Plan) consultant Dr. Saundra McGuire's focus on metacognition (an approach developed in her subsequent book *Teach Students How to Learn*).

One of the first orders of business of our 2011–2012 FYC Study Group (formed by volunteer faculty representing a range of departmental years and areas of expertise) was to decide upon professional readings and to apply for curriculum-development funding to purchase books for the group and all other faculty (full-time and adjunct) who wished to join these discussions. Our first read was Howard Tinberg and Patrick Sullivan's 2011 *What Is "College-Level" Writing?*, and notes from the meeting record that faculty connected immediately to Sullivan's (2011) opening discussion of the emotional labor of FYC instructors (9) and to Michael Dubson's (2011) discussion of the "emotional distance [2YC students place] between themselves and the work they do, doing work they may emotionally disown in order to preserve a tenuous sense of self, and to survive" (97). Acknowledging the role our emotions—and those of our students—play in our 2YC lives further challenged the institutional us/them, teacher/student binary and echoed parallels our interactional inquiry was already drawing between what was happening in student writing and what was happening (or not) in faculty's professional and institutional lives. Articulating connections not typically found in institutional or disciplinary scripts—such as those among labor conditions, emotional distances, and daily life—is an important part of memory work's thirdspace.

Such thirdspaces helped us move past other hypostatizing divides, including the nonfiction/fiction divide and an accompanying adversarial stance towards rhetoric as what some faculty had previously labeled "just a trend." The FYC Study Group tackled readings that helped us further unbind the study of genre from rigid instantiation in the categories of poetry, drama, and fiction (and course outlines comprised solely of long lists of titles for reading). In 2012–2013 we read and discussed Anis Bawarshi and Mary Jo Reiff's 2010 *Genre: An Introduction to History, Theory, Research, and Pedagogy*. In spring 2012, I presented at TYCA–SE in Virginia Beach on "FYC at a Two-Year College in the Twenty-First Century" (Grego 2012) on the groundwork our department had forged for curriculum revision, and in March 2013, I was joined at TYCA–SE in Greenville, South Carolina, by colleagues Ashley Buzzard, Jessica Graves, Amy Hausser, Keith Higginbotham, Jon McCarter, Julie Nelson, and Andrea West in "FYC in Two-Year Colleges: Where Have We Been? Where Are We Going?" in which faculty each provided examples from their own revised ENG 100, 101, and 102 course units (Buzzard et al. 2013). Our fully revised FYC sequence, implemented in fall 2014, focused on introducing ENG 100 students to ideas about audience and purpose as aids to both production and critical reading of texts, moving to a focus on rhetorical awareness in ENG 101 and what we termed "critical genre awareness" in ENG 102, and spreading work on evaluating and integrating sources into different kinds of projects, including multimodal work, across the FYC sequence.

IN CONCLUSION: ON SILENCE AND SILENCING

In many ways this story of interactional inquiry, recollection of our professional knowledges, and institutional thinking echoes Toth and Sullivan's (2016) ideas about forging a "community of practice" as well as Joanne Giordano et al.'s (2017) arguments for cohesive support of faculty development across both assessment- and course-redesign activities. Readers will also see ways our department implemented a kind of "interest convergence" (Lamos 2011) and worked to remain flexible when faced with mandates from both inside and outside our institutional context, using "our hybridity [as] a source of power for navigating complicated conversations and initiatives" (Warnke and Higgins 2018, 379). Deliberate repositioning of departmental-management structures to support recursive interactional-inquiry cycles and thirdspace work helped us dive deeply and collaboratively.

Certainly, our journey has not been as smooth or easy as this necessarily truncated history makes it sound, and of course what we have *not* changed is the reality that there are many outside factors and agents that influence how our 2YC work is conceived, by whom, and when. But the stronger the connections we made in our interactional inquiry, the more our institutional thinking and professional identities evolved, and the more we looked to see what professional organizations and publications said and how we might use them to support our own authority and conclusions. Opening up a thirdspace for resisting hegemonic scripts of erasure and articulating connections between student learning and 2YC faculty labor generated the rhetorical exigence for our department's progressively stronger connection to professional organizations and publications. Interactional inquiry made visible our insights, and published work contributed to our own conversations and our search for framing. Life within business-as-usual secondspace conceptions does not make visible faculty expertise, does not empower faculty, and provides no intrinsic motivation to seek out new potential frameworks. But repeated cycles of interactional inquiry have helped us occupy our 2YC space in ways that honor—and connect—our knowledges.

This journey strikes me as quite different from the approaches, timelines, and publications based on the life cycle of those who move from graduate programs into 4YC tenure-track positions located within institutional settings and departmental histories quite different from those in many 2YCs. Like other genres, professional academic genres are shaped by the spaces in which conversations grow—and as an institutional "border crosser," I've felt how lack of concerted disciplinary attention to institutional context enforces silence about the privilege thus enjoyed by those who live and publish in 4YC contexts often assumed to be the norm. If the *we* of our larger discipline want to work against the silence and silencing of 2YC faculty expertise, we must think critically about (1) how the rhetorical exigencies and kairotic moments that motivate, inform, and shape our conversations and knowledge differ across *the entire range* of institutional environments for FYC in the US, and (2) how the publication opportunities and genres available must *acknowledge* the role of those differences in shaping professional discourse. We all have institutional memory work to do.

COVID-19 CODA

In May 2019 our college's administration announced adoption of the Guided Pathways Model (Bailey, Jaggers, and Jenkins 2015) and directed faculty to carve out several programs of study to implement in fall 2020. In March–April 2020, I had just become dean of the (newly created) School of English and Humanities when COVID-19 and lockdown descended. As at most colleges and universities, our 2YC faculty had to quickly navigate the move to virtual teaching and then ride a roller coaster of change in teaching and pandemic management—from all virtual to partial on-ground/online/virtual lives with social distancing and masking, then just masking, then just masking indoors, until no masking by May 2022—all during a time fraught with political upheaval and growing social unrest and protest over racial disparities in our country, and in a state whose government was determined to minimize the pandemic's impact on business (as usual).

Despite COVID-19, our 2YC moved forward with implementing Guided Pathways in fall 2020. We navigated new programs, new structures, the divide between two previously separate departments and faculty, the inadequacy of f2f pedagogies in virtual classrooms, our students' previously documented lack of success in online/asynchronous courses, the college's decision to remove attendance requirements, administration's concern over loss of enrollment and lack of student (and faculty) presence on campus, and faculty and staff's pervasive sense of loss and uncertainty. As did many others, we saw how COVID-19 threw into even greater relief the struggles our 2YC students already faced with financial issues, housing and food insecurities, family care, healthcare, employment, and a host of other basic needs—not to mention mental-health strains. All this amplified by the emotional distances and fatigue of meetings via zoom.

On so many levels, business as usual has left the building. Certainly, our secondspace conceptions of teaching and learning, of enrollments and engagement, of faculty labor and student lives, have been seriously challenged by firstspace realities that are still evolving. My memories of early weeks as a COVID-19 dean are of radical self-doubt. What policies and practices were best for the health and safety of teachers and students? (And why hadn't I stayed in my teaching comfort zone for my remaining years before retirement?) In such a maelstrom, I wondered how we might begin to recollect ourselves and our students, to think institutionally. When I'd been hired as dean, administration had made clear they wanted deans to build "identity" for their new schools of study. A key starting point was to realize that building identity for two liberal arts departments in a 2Y technical college environment meant we needed to make visible the empowering importance of our disciplines. So, we started with that.

In 2020–2021, when our marketing area mandated a series of Facebook Live! sessions focused on each new school of study, we titled ours the "Pandemic Prism" and focused on students, their pandemic experiences, and how the areas of art, music, writing, literature, and history brought meaning to those experiences. That year we recorded student performances and presentations at events such as a *Bread, Boxes, and the Virus* spoken-word night, and we moved an annual English-Department student conference online and turned it into a school-wide event. In 2021–2022, we held even more student events in on-ground/outdoor and online/zoom modes, including National Day on Writing graffiti walls outside our libraries on two campuses, a *Coffee House Open Mic Nite* on a student-center patio, and an inaugural *MTC Speaks!* evening of student speeches in a large auditorium with zoom streaming.

I knew from previous experiences with studio work that my job was to scaffold and organize all manner of supports for what began growing in this thirdspace moment. I threw myself into behind-the-scenes work needed to reserve campus spaces (including several outdoor spaces that had not been used for events before COVID-19); set up zoom webinars; organize staff from Operations, Marketing, and Media Services; design flyers and promote events; organize the photos and videos of our students presenting, performing, publishing, speaking, exhibiting their art work; and engaging in a variety of ways in a variety of campus spaces with faculty, staff, and administration as witness. We amplified those activities via publishing photo albums, zoom recordings, short promotional videos, participant data, and social media posts.

We quite literally repeopled our college (both on-ground and virtual) and repurposed campus spaces—both the familiar and the previously unused, unseen, unknown. Our School of English and Humanities has emerged as a campus leader, and with that has come leverage for advocating for institutional resources, including new full-time faculty positions (recently we hired the college's first full-time faculty ever in music), replacing faculty in slots left open in previous years by retirements, identifying facilities and equipment needed to fully support our new AA concentrations, and intervening in initiatives that are under-resourced or implemented in ways not considerate of faculty labor. By thus recollecting the work we love—that of supporting our 2YC students as they embody the risk taking that is education—we have also been able to take on the risks of institutional thinking in this thirdspace of loss but also of possibility and change.

REFERENCES

Adams, Peter, Sarah Gearhart, Robert Miller, and Anne Roberts. 2017. "The Accelerated Learning Program: Throwing Open the Gates." In *Teaching Composition at the Two-Year College: Background Readings*, edited by Patrick Sullivan and Christie Toth, 401–18. Boston: Bedford/St. Martin's.

Bailey, Thomas R., Shanna Smith Jaggars, and Davis Jenkins. 2015. *Redesigning America's Community Colleges: A Clearer Path to Student Success*. Cambridge, MA: Harvard University Press.

Bawarshi, Anis S., and Mary Jo Reiff. 2010. *Genre: An Introduction to History, Theory, Research, and Pedagogy*. Anderson, SC: Parlor.

Bourdieu, Pierre. 1977. *Outline of a Theory of Practice*. London: Cambridge University Press.

Buzzard, Ashley, Jessica Graves, Rhonda Grego, Amy Hausser, Keith Higginbotham, Jon McCarter, Julie Nelson, and Andrea West. 2013. "FYC in Two-Year Colleges: Where Have We Been? Where Are We Going?" Paper presented at the Two-Year College Association Southeast Conference, Greenville, SC, March.

Corder, Jim. "Argument as Emergence, Rhetoric as Love." *Rhetoric Review* 4 (1): 16–32.

Council of Writing Program Administrators (WPA). 2014. "WPA Outcomes Statement (3.0)." https://wpacouncil.org/aws/CWPA/pt/sd/news_article/243055/_PARENT/layout_details/false.

Council of Writing Program Administrators (WPA), National Writing Project (NWP), and NCTE. 2011. *Framework for Success in Postsecondary Writing*. https://wpacouncil.org/aws/CWPA/asset_manager/get_file/350201?ver=7548.

Crawford, June, Susan Kippax, Jenny Onyx, Una Gault, and Pam Benton (SPUJJ Collective). 1992. *Emotion and Gender, Constructing Meaning from Memory*. London: SAGE.

Dubson, Michael. 2011. "Whose Paper Is This Anyway? Why Most Students Don't Embrace the Writing They Do for Their Writing Classes." In *What Is "College-Level" Writing?*, edited by Howard Tinberg and Patrick Sullivan, 92–109. Urbana, IL: NCTE.

Giordano, Joanne, Holly Hassel, Jennifer Heinert, and Cassandra Phillips. 2017. "The Imperative of Pedagogical and Professional Development to Support the Retention of Underprepared Students at Open-Access Institutions." In *Retention, Persistence, and Writing Programs*, edited by Todd Raeker, Dawn Shepherd, Heidi Estrem, and Beth Brunk-Chavez, 74–92. Logan: Utah State University Press.

Grego, Rhonda. 2012. "FYC at a Two-Year College in the Twenty-First Century." Paper presented at the Two-Year College Association Southeast Conference, Virginia Beach, FL, February.

Grego, Rhonda, and Nancy S. Thompson. 2008. *Teaching/Writing in Thirdspaces: The Studio Approach*. Carbondale: Southern Illinois University Press.

Griffiths, Brett. 2017. "Professional Autonomy and Teacher-Scholar-Activists in Two-Year Colleges: Preparing New Faculty to Think Institutionally." *Teaching English in the Two-Year College* 45 (3): 47–68.

Klausman, Jeffrey. 2010. "Not Just a Matter of Fairness: Adjunct Faculty and Writing Programs in Two-Year Colleges." *Teaching English in the Two-Year College* 37 (4): 363–71.

Lamos, Steven J. 2011. *Interests and Opportunities: Race, Racism, and University Writing Instruction in the Post-Civil Rights Era*. Pittsburgh: University of Pittsburgh Press.

Larson, Holly. 2018. "Epistemic Authority in Composition Studies: Tenuous Relationship between Two-Year English Faculty and Knowledge Production." *Teaching English in the Two-Year College* 46 (2): 109–36.

Lee, Melanie. 2009. "Rhetorical Roulette: Does Writing-Faculty Overload Disable Effective Response to Student Writing?" *Teaching English in the Two-Year College* 37 (2): 165–77.

Massey, Doreen. 2004. *For Space*. London: SAGE.

McGuire, Saundra Yancy. 2015. *Teach Students How to Learn*. Stylus Publishing.

Millward, Jody. 2008. "An Analysis of the National TYCA Research Initiative Survey, Section III: Technology and Pedagogy in Two-Year College English Programs." *Teaching English in the Two-Year College* 35 (4): 372–97.
National Council of Teachers of English (NCTE). 1982. "CCCC Position Statement on the Preparation and Professional Development of Teachers of Writing." Position Statements. http://www.ncte.org/cccc/resources/positions/statementonprep.
National Council of Teachers of English (NCTE). 1997. "Statement from the Conference on the Growing Use of Part-Time and Adjunct Faculty." Position Statements. http://www.ncte.org/positions/statements/useofparttimefaculty.
National Council of Teachers of English (NCTE). 1999. "More Than a Number: Why Class Size Matters."
National Council of Teachers of English (NCTE). 2008. "Twenty-First-Century Curriculum and Assessment Framework."
National Council of Teachers of English (NCTE). 2009. "Writing Assessment: A Position Statement." http://www.ncte.org/cccc/resources/positions/writingassessment.
Reason, Peter, ed. 1988. *Human Inquiry in Action: Developments in New Paradigm Research*. London: SAGE.
Reason, Peter, and John Rowan, eds. 1981. *Human Inquiry: A Sourcebook of New Paradigm Research*. Hoboken, NJ: Wiley.
Rose, Mike. 2017. "A Learning Society." In *Teaching Composition at the Two-Year College: Background Readings*, edited by Patrick Sullivan and Christie Toth, 437–41. Boston: Bedford/St. Martin's.
Soja, Edward. 2009. *Thirdspace: Journey to Los Angeles and Other Real-and-Imagined Places*. Hoboken, NJ: Wiley.
South Carolina Technical College System. N.d. *Catalog of Approved Courses*. https://www.sctechsystem.edu/pgmmanagement_cac/catalog_of_approved_courses.aspx.
Sullivan, Patrick. 2008. "An Analysis of the National TYCA Research Initiative Survey, Section II: Assessment Practices in Two-Year College English Programs." *Teaching English in the Two-Year College* 36 (1): 7–26.
Sullivan, Patrick. 2011. "An Essential Question: What Is 'College-Level' Writing?" In *What Is "College-Level" Writing?*, edited by Howard Tinberg and Patrick Sullivan, 1–28. Urbana, IL: NCTE.
Sullivan, Patrick, and Christie Toth, eds. 2017. *Teaching Composition at the Two-Year College: Background Readings*. Boston: Bedford/St. Martin's.
Sutton, Mark, and Sally Chandler, eds. 2018. *The Writing Studio Sampler: Stories About Change*. Fort Collins, CO: WAC Clearinghouse.
Swenson, Janet, Robert Rozema, Carl A. Young, Ewa McGrail, and Phyllis Whitin. 2005. "Beliefs About Technology and the Preparation of English Teachers: Beginning the Conversation." *Contemporary Issues in Technology and Teacher Education* 5 (3). http://www.citejournal.org/vol5/iss3/languagearts/article1.cfm.
Tassoni, John Paul, and Cynthia Lewiecki-Wilson. 2005. "Not Just Anywhere Anywhen: Mapping Change Through Studio Work." *Journal of Basic Writing* 24 (1): 68–92.
Tinberg, Howard, and Patrick Sullivan, eds. 2011 *What Is "College-Level" Writing?* Urbana, IL: NCTE.
Toth, Christie. 2014. "Unmeasured Engagement: Two-Year College English Faculty and Disciplinary Professional Organizations." *Teaching English in the Two-Year College* 41 (4): 335–53.
Toth, Christie, and Patrick Sullivan. 2016. "Toward Local Teacher-Scholar Communities of Practice: Findings from a National TYCA Survey." *Teaching English in the Two-Year College* 43 (3): 247–72.
Two-Year College Association (TYCA). 2004a. *Guidelines for the Academic Preparation of English Faculty at Two-Year Colleges*. http://www.ncte.org/library/NCTEFiles/Groups/TYCA/TYCAGuidelines.pdf.

Two-Year College Association (TYCA). 2004b. *Research and Scholarship in the Two-Year College.* http://www.ncte.org/library/NCTEFiles/Groups/TYCA/ResearchScholarship.pdf.

Warnke, Anthony, and Kirsten Higgins. 2018. "A Critical Time for Reform: Empowering Interventions in a Precarious Landscape." *Teaching English in the Two-Year College* 45 (4): 361–84.

Warnock, Scott. 2009. *Teaching Writing Online: How and Why.* Urbana, IL: NCTE.

Yancey, Kathleen, Andrea Lunsford, James McDonald, Charles Moran, Michael Neal, Chef Pryor, Duane Roen, and Cindy Selfe. 2004. CCCC Position Statement on Teaching, Learning, and Assessing Writing in Digital Environments. *College Composition and Communication* 55 (4): 785–90.

7
"THE PAINFUL EAGERNESS OF UNFED HOPE"
Equity-Centered Writing Assessment

Kirsten Higgins, Anthony Warnke, and Jake Frye

INTRODUCTION: REASSESSING THE STATUS QUO

Under the constraints of time, resources, and energy, two-year college faculty who participate in assessing student writing at the program or campus-wide levels often perform what we might call "good-enough" assessment. This assessment is flawed and superficial, yet it feels like the best we can manage given time constraints and demands from those in power. To meet top-down mandates, we often participate in assessment for expedience. We hope we are, at least, doing no harm. Material limitations, including meager stipends, limited institutional support, and little time, put the onus on faculty to meet institutional objectives with passable engagement. These constraints are real, and faculty members operating within them certainly have good intentions. However, the good-enough response may, ultimately, structure in and perpetuate inequities that undermine our students and profession. Furthermore, taking the managerial approach to assessment—get it done fast, without complicating large theoretical and political questions—allows the college to put the stamp of faculty autonomy on assessment projects. Constructing instructors as those who "own" and "control" the curriculum and standards encourages us to own and internalize the "failures" of their students. This logic solidifies disparate impact, especially for students of color. Consequently, it encourages the "cooling-out" effect that subtly marginalizes two-year college students (Clark 1960).

The impetus of this chapter comes from scrutinizing our own assessment practices at a two-year community college in the Seattle area. We ask to what extent our most recent program assessments have fallen short of some of the dearest values we espouse, especially those values that center on questions of equity and inclusion for students most often underserved in our service area: multilingual immigrants and refugees, students of color, low-income students, students with disabilities, and first-generation college students. We seek to uncover how an inequitable incongruity exists between the complex and diverse ecologies of two-year colleges and the traditional assessment practices bureaucratically available to us and to which we accede given institutional pressures. Last, we aim to outline dispositions and objectives for reimagining our assessment practices in progressive and just ways.

At their core, status quo assessment practices, particularly program assessment practices, rely on the logic of norming and standardization. Despite our and other faculty members' unease, these status quo processes have persisted, as have the narratives that underwrite them, especially narratives that perpetually cast students as deficient. Even well-meaning critiques of assessment that fail to offer robust alternatives act, unwittingly, as inoculation, ultimately strengthening the organism's immunity to further attack. In our experience, incremental change—often responsive to humanistic concerns about assessment—becomes easily absorbed into normative assessment practices (if they are responded to at all). Ultimately, the basic standardizing framework of assessment is left intact. Yet instructors like us struggle with a perceived lack of true alternatives compounded by a lack of resources, the result being that the good-enough status quo lives to see another day. We wonder to what extent we can move from a paradigm of assessment triage to more radical assessment reenvisioning. We can no longer abide by the ways good-enough assessment produces facile and, ultimately, unhelpful representations of our students and our service-area communities.

Outcomes are central to the issue of norming in good-enough assessment. They are posited as a device that can be used to ensure consistency across the board, course alignment, and teacher/student accountability. Outcomes, however, problematically reify fixed, immoveable, and unchanging endpoints for student learning—and many of our outcomes were written *before most of the students being assessed were even born.* As long ago as 2012, Chris Gallagher (2012) pointed out that outcomes assessment (OA) models were not built to account for unintended consequences.

> In outcomes assessment of student writing . . . we norm ourselves to read student writing "against" (read: through) the outcomes. In so doing, we close our reading selves off from what is surprising or excessive or eccentric about the writing . . . Our reading starts not with the student's text, but with the outcome, or the rubric, which conditions what we are able (and unable) to see in the text. And that is the point: in order for

a scoring session to run smoothly, unpredictability—surprising writings, rogue readings—must be minimized or removed. (46)

As he notes, "In OA, there is no such thing as an unintended outcome—but in programs and classrooms, unintended consequences are commonplace" (46). OA inherently objectifies by separating through its analytical operation and dehumanizes both its practitioners and its objects of study (ambiguously either or both the products, as in student work, or the products, as in the students themselves).

Mya Poe, Norbert Elliot, John Aloysius Cogan, and Tito G. Nurudeen (2014) move from insightful critique into a more robust fleshing out of possible strategies for enacting socially just writing program assessments. Taking up the legal lens of disparate impact as a program assessment validation tool, they argue that, particularly in the context of high-stakes assessment practices that impact students' trajectory through higher education, disproportionate burdens on students of color likely indicate invalid assessment practices. In effect, program and campus-wide practices are engines of stratification. Students, almost by design, can never fully "measure up." These assessment practices replicate a logic of deficit and reproduce narratives of failure that disproportionately affect and misrepresent our most underserved students. These assessments establish terms on which our students, and open-access institutions, will always fall short. Significantly, this model of outcomes assessment is limited in scope because it assesses the contributions of those who are on campus, neatly and silently eliding key questions of exclusion. Assessing only students who are already part of the college limits the imagined community of the service area and undermines any claims of accountability. The status quo refuses to recognize that its own facially neutral practices result in institutional consequences that disproportionately burden students who are historically underserved—the students for whom the institution itself claims a responsibility of responsiveness. Access and cultivating diversity should not just be for mission statements and promotional materials. A valid assessment framework must serve a genuine culture of access within and beyond the gates. As leaders in assessment work on many TYC campuses, English and writing departments have an ethical obligation. Developing this framework requires writing programs to take the reins to serve these ethical obligations.

TO DWELL IN POSSIBILITY

Historically, outcomes assessment has reflected accountability discourses—accountability of students, of teachers, and of institutions.

Outcomes assessment claims to objectively capture the success and seemingly inevitable failures of students and their institutions. Outcomes assessment was intended to improve access to higher education and close so-called achievement gaps by improving transparency and alignment through accountability (for an intriguing analysis of No Child Left Behind, see Jaekyung Lee and Todd Reeves 2012). However, the anxieties about underachieving students catalyzed a cyclical practice that continually produces more anxiety. Today, our institutions and our country express anxiety that our students aren't meeting academic standards; that academic standards don't align with the labor market; that, without rigorous scrutiny, the two-year college itself will fail to promote economic mobility and, in turn, further succumb to austerity policies. In short, the institutions' common response is an attempt to manage and address anxiety. However, in the anxious mode affect theorist Lauren Berlant (Berlant and Greenwald 2012) calls the obsession of our neoliberal age, outcomes assessment only exacerbates and recycles unproductive fears. Anxiety, in fact, is an outcome assessment's pathology even as it purports to be its cure. These fears lead to the push for an industrially inflected "continuous improvement" (see Madeline Murphy's 2017 critique) and a deficit logic that accompanies it—one that suggests students and institutions can never be good enough.

Two-year colleges are particularly susceptible to the neoliberal, technocratic accountability narrative that animates this anxiety and produces the narratives of outcome, accountability, and deficit (Adler-Kassner and Harrington 2010; Toth, Sullivan, and Calhoon-Dillahunt 2016). Within this narrative, students are "objectively" measured on whether they successfully convince faculty they have learned the concepts or skills as determined ahead of time by the course outcomes. The faculty, then, interpret raw data to document learning has been demonstrated to the satisfaction of the accountability narrative's stakeholders. To show just how much this form of assessment leaves out of the picture, Murphy (2017) poses the following questions, poking holes in the fictions recirculated in these narratives: "If a student takes away something we didn't anticipate, have we captured that? Does it matter? Can we agree what critical thinking looks like? Indeed, *should* we? Have we failed if students recognize and grapple with contradictions and disagreements inherent in a Western education? . . . What if learning presents itself in counterintuitive ways that quality-control models . . . of industry fail to detect?" (15).

Murphy (2017) points out complexities and ambiguities OA fails to account for and, indeed, attempts to screen out. Rather than starting on the ground level with students, student experiences, and student work, outcomes position all students against unflinching, immutable benchmarks. In doing so, goes the fiction, we can hold faculty accountable and maintain "standards." In this way, neoliberal, accountability driven decontextualization underlies current assessment practices. Such decontextualized practices prevent full representation of the complexity of students' future rhetorical situations and current practice, much less of the whole student and the ecology of the campus.

While these critiques might be convincing, they lead us to next steps: How can assessment be functionally reimagined to better serve our students? What frameworks, value systems, and scholarly resources might we draw from? What processes and models might faculty members adopt, adapt, or hack to produce valid results? Recent turns in writing assessment scholarship might offer actionable possibilities for addressing these questions. Socially just writing assessment scholarship, although often disconnected from the two-year college context, affords frameworks for repurposing in our contexts. Such scholarship attempts to shift the paradigm, with Mya Poe, Norbert Elliot, and Asao Inoue, among others, reconstituting the theoretical boundaries of validity and its role in questions of equity and disparate impact. In particular, scrutiny of the traditional assessment construct lays bare the ways material institutional support for assessment work is not sufficient (e.g., Poe and Inoue 2016; Poe, Inoue, and Elliot 2018). Josh Lederman and Nicole Warwick (2018) reformulate the problem in terms of validity and violence of assessment: "Assessment-as-normativity-check will differentially impact students/writers from socio-historical situations that are already closer to or further from those dominant norms—a clear zero-sum game in that those born into circumstances closer to the expected norms are privileged to the extent that those further from the expected norms are held down" (238).

In other words, "assessment-as-normativity" creates or extends the conditions of disparate impact, harming students and making the colleges they rely on less just. The work of assessment at the two-year college must be radically reimagined in order to treat as whole and connected students' bodies, lives, and work, and in order to, more broadly, treat community and context as a whole that cannot be divided. As instructors with some power to shape our institution's assessment processes, we see untapped potential in scholarship ranging from socially just assessment to translingual theory to critical race theory. These sources lead us to ask difficult questions we have too often ignored or diluted: To what extent does "good enough" assessment enact a "violence of assessment" on our students (Lederman and Warwick 2018)? We wonder how we can take up a responsibility to counter this violence and develop practices that align with our two-year institution's mission statement, which explicitly cites "responsiveness to diverse communities." In fact, to frame this in the more active sense, how can we, *through* assessment, structure in inclusivity so we actively expand access and hold space for our historically underserved populations? How can we use assessment to validate and reposition perpetually neglected and subjugated two-year college students? To frame this in terms of Kelly Blewett, Christina M. LaVecchia, Laura R. Micciche, and Janine Morris's (2019) call for inclusion activism, how can we be "responsible to the community that exists and the one that *could* exist if more members were shaping it" (282)? Rather than framing assessment as an institutional mandate separate from these values of inclusion, how can we harness and refashion assessment, making its validity contingent on the extent to which it serves our mission?

We start with the nonnegotiable belief that an assessment that does not actively work to increase fairness and opportunity, as Elliot, Lederman, Poe, and others repeatedly argue, is, by definition, not a valid assessment for an open-access institution (e.g., Josh Lederman 2018, 2019; Poe et al. 2014; Poe, Inoue, and Elliot 2018). Responding to these questions, therefore, calls for intentional, structural metamorphosis rather than incremental, inoculating change. Rather than comply, we urge faculty—starting with ourselves—to hold out, push, cajole, and reframe the debate. We should seize on the kairotic moment that has increasingly mainstreamed concerns for diversity and equity and show that reimagining assessment will better meet these institutional values and goals.

Yet two-year college instructors working with collaborative ecologies cannot bring about such metamorphosis on their own. How can we convince administrators and other stakeholders to walk with us in exploring these necessary changes? Fortuitously, questioning normative assessment practices has been proliferating among various stakeholders. Professional organizations as well as individual scholars have called out the gaps in understanding and weaknesses of current practices, from poor data collection to poor conceptual framing. From separate quarters, scholars and practitioners now discuss the logical limits of constructs that once seemed promising. See, for example, recent articles in *Inside Higher Ed* (2019a), the *New York Times* (Worthen, February 23, 2018), and so on.

We should not, of course, concede authority to testing companies, psychometricians, or reformers backed by Big Philanthropy who do not share our disciplinary understandings of writing as situated in social practice. Rather, we should be engaging in what our fields widely acknowledge as best practices in writing assessment, which include working as a faculty to develop local assessment processes that are validated and revised in response to changing curricula, technologies, student populations, and other institutional and community factors. The results of these processes should, then, be presented to, translated for, and, if necessary, defended against various stakeholders, such as administrators, colleagues, and students themselves.

ASSESSMENT DISPOSITIONS: DISRUPTION AND RHETORICAL ATTUNEMENT

We believe facilely replacing an outcomes framework with another, albeit more progressive, framework threatens to replicate a similar logic of universal standards and decontextualized assessment. Instead, we advocate for two assessment dispositions faculty leaders can harness and adapt to begin the work of dismantling and reorientation. We hope the following dispositions—disruption and rhetorical attunement—initiate the work of reimagining rather than providing a ready-made schema.

We understand these assessment dispositions as further contributing to what we have called "critical reform"—a concept that seeks to operationalize progressive traditions in writing studies within the two-year college (Warnke and Higgins 2019). As a move that's both pragmatic and principled, critical reform understands affecting change as dependent on, rather than separate from, deep engagement with scholarly traditions we draw inspiration from, including the pioneering work of two-year college, basic writing, and constructivist assessment scholars. Assessment is a fundamental locus for doing critical reform. Therefore, we have begun reclaiming assessment—however incrementally—on our own campus by refusing to accede to its entrenched terms. While we have not replaced these processes, we hope other faculty members can adapt and improve our tactics of disruption and our strategy for reorientation.

First, we frame disruption according to the discursive logic it usually claims in the world of business: as a passel of changes and opportunities that both signal a dramatic shift in the landscape of the sector and radically alter opportunities within that sector. Disruption seeks to denormalize processes and epistemologies that have become entrenched within programs and institutions, often asking the kinds of questions expediency and accountability disregard as overly complicated and infeasible within the status quo. When faculty members hear responses to critical questions such as "We don't have time for that" or "That's not how we do it," a disruptive disposition keeps asking "Why?" This disposition utilizes values of equity and socially just scholarship as tools for insistence, resistance, and destabilization.

Seeking to intervene in the space disruption carves out, we might apply Rebecca Lorimer Leonard's (2014) concept of rhetorical attunement to assessment. Rather than seeking to fill up that space with a more generous but still top-down assessment schematic, an assessment ethos of rhetorical attunement attempts to hold the space open for listening, observation, and inventorizing—detaching from judgment and evaluation and, instead, paying attention to what often goes overlooked or undervalued in our institutions. Rhetorically attuning ourselves to our students allows us to develop a programmatic "ear for, or a tuning toward, difference or multiplicity . . . a literate understanding that assumes multiplicity and invites the negotiation of meaning across difference" (228). If two-year colleges are, as we believe, uniquely dynamic and heterogeneous sites of identities, literacies, and material conditions, we feel it's incumbent upon us—and we speak particularly personally here, as white, middle-class, and relatively monolingual faculty members—to slow down and listen, humbling ourselves to what we don't always recognize and what our normative assessment frames don't always capture. Rhetorical attunement, we imagine, requires ongoing and long-term methods for capturing and assessing our students' literate practices that outcomes assessment, traditionally, has not employed. In the tradition of grounded theory, assessment as attunement requires beginning with what we notice first, resisting the urge to superimpose meaning and theoretical frameworks on top of a heterogeneous communicative landscape we have not, historically, sought to deeply understand.

In other words, we are advocating for English departments to take on rhetorical listening programmatically, not just between instructors and students, and to thereby advance Ellen Cushman's (2016) call to decolonize and destabilize the hierarchies present in our programs and teaching. Yet, as Cushman notes, stances of critique too often remain rooted in the very logic they intend to challenge. The pragmatic, then, is as necessary as the paradigmatic shift in assessment.

Programmatic listening could pragmatically and productively undermine dominant representations and scrutinize naturalized hierarchies that inform decision-making at the level of program and institution even as its classroom-level counterpart continually reconstructs how we think of individuals in our classrooms.

We are attempting this representational activism and race-conscious "storychanging work" at our own institution (Lamos 2011, 18) by advocating that our own department lead multilayered representational work. In a sense, those of us more firmly ensconced in the statuses privileged in the hierarchical structures bear a responsibility for holding space and cultivating an affective openness to disrupt naturalized, calcified structures. In the natural world, fires make space for renewal and growth; in departmental ecologies, orientations toward disruption and listening make space for, perhaps, the following assessment projects.

1. Large-Scale Snapshots

In "Multilinguality Is the Mainstream," Jonathan Hall (2014) outlines the Linguistic Diversity Project: A Study of Reading, Writing, and Language Background among First-Year Students, a simple, direct survey of students' language backgrounds that asks numerous questions regarding students' linguistic histories. Hall's survey emphasizes that one of the first steps for providing local representations of our student population comes from a seemingly simple question: Who are our students and what are their language backgrounds? Further, we should explore the success of these diverse students in our courses. Disparate impact, as previously described, can help us understand the efficacy of our practices for diverse individuals. Who does well in our courses? Who suffers? To what extent are any burdens that fall unevenly on historically underserved populations burdens that grow out of pedagogical necessity? Large-scale demographic data can begin to provide new lenses for understanding our students broadly but is only a first step to representation that values students' complexities.

2. Language Investments and Representations

To assess our students' goals with language, we need to know what they intend to accomplish with language and what language means to them. A dominant belief is that students want to acquire English to access various forms of capital that abide by stringent language politics—for example, writing in Standard English in a US job. However, many international students, for example, do not share this goal. By rendering a more complex picture of students' investments in English, we can begin to trouble the idea that we are preparing students for a homogeneous outside professional world that values only Standard English. We must ask such questions as, in what contexts do students plan to use their communicative skills? To what extent are those contexts English-only? What kinds of Englishes are permitted in those spaces? What are additional student aims for communication? What social identities do students feel they need to construct in the pursuit of language mastery? For us, these questions are informed by Bonny Peirce's notion of investment in languages as tied to social identities (see Peirce 1996), as well as work to take the "English-only sign" off first-year composition (Horner et al. 2011).

3. Practices and Strategies

In a move to undo a view of language as discrete, rule-based systems, translingual theory suggests returning to the multiplicity of practices to define language. A major move in translingual theory—and higher education research in general—is to understand and value resources and practices students already bring into the classroom. As Rebecca Lorimer Leonard (2014) argues, "language . . . is something we make as we move rather than something static we carry around" (232). Students construct their resources to function in the rhetorical moment. To understand what kinds of assignments, activities, and curricula to design for the translingual classroom, we must understand what practices students use outside class. We must ask questions about language use and code mixing and switching, modalities, spaces/materiality, and communication partners/networks. Practices exist beyond mere language events as well. So, we need to understand what spaces and places—metaphorically and literally—we should make available for students. How do students' practices shape the spaces in which they operate? And how do those rhetorical spaces always already privilege paradigms of linguistic deficiency? What spaces are conducive to productive and progressive communicative spaces? How do students use and reinvent language textually, verbally, and multimodally? What practices follow from their investments in language? How can these practices be reaffirmed and utilized for new meaning-making situations?

CONCLUSION

We want to acknowledge the difficulties instructors might encounter when disrupting and reimagining. There are a variety of limitations placed on this work, including the heavily skewed ratio of adjuncts to tenured instructors, scant institutional resources, heavy teaching loads, and ennui caused by discouraging experiences with previous assessment activities. There is incredible pressure to produce results and to produce them now. But asking questions can be difficult. (In our department, for instance, requests for disaggregated data have gone unfulfilled for eighteen months and more). Often, those that pose these questions may be viewed as attempting to obstruct important assessment work, or perhaps these faculty are viewed charitably, but their concerns receive responses such as "I agree with you, but right now isn't the time" or "That's one area where we can improve next time around" or "In a perfect world, that's what we would do differently." The perfectionism fallacy, frankly, fails every time. Faculty must continue to ask the tough questions, even in the face of such institutional resistance. These questions are crucial. The good-enough assessment is not merely innocuous but is also directly harmful to our most marginalized student groups. We hope this article equips disrupters and teach-scholar-activists with lines of argument and scholarship to back up potentially "troublesome" questions.

Ultimately, instructors, not administrators, must step up to the plate. Instructors should be internally incentivized by their identification with the discipline and larger social justice commitments. Yet, as strongly as possible, instructors should also demand to be externally incentivized by the institution's material commitment to instructor participation in projects that help achieve the institution's mission. We better represent our students and know their struggles, triumphs, and passions. Any attempt to subjugate faculty to assessment processes should be resisted. One way faculty are routinely subjugated is in the push to strip the classroom out of the assessment, to "screen out the noise" and to remove "biased" teachers. We argue here, however, that classroom context should be revalued as a legitimate part of the process. Writing is always contextual and contingent, always emerging, so to properly assess what our students are doing in their writing, we must understand in what conditions, environments, and ecologies they are producing their work. In doing so, we believe we may gain a more robust understanding of how students are negotiating disparate cultures and discourses, as well as how they are reimagining, remixing, and reinventing discourse tools available to them. A conventional, task-based OA analysis does not include this aspect of student work.

Such an approach would require assessors to be attentive in terms of both how language works—including how writers use rhetorical effect in a variety of ways—and how material conditions impact student writers in a local context. Such assessors would need to possess strong close reading skills. If anybody can take the lead on this form of assessment, it is the English faculty, whose expertise in close reading of difference for its rhetorical effect is paired with training in critical theory, Marxism, and so on especially useful for this sort of analysis. Looking beyond programmatic assessment work, English faculty could harness their training in close reading as a source of expertise in cross-curricular and cross-disciplinary conversations about what assessment is as they pursue the more challenging questions of localizing validity and considering it in terms of fairness rather than accuracy (Josh Lederman; Lederman and Warwick). While there is often a mismatch between faculty educational backgrounds and their perceived jobs at the TYC, this approach to assessment could be one way this unique and powerful background could be revalued. For instructors working in English and related fields, qualitative analysis of texts is one of the most important and meaningful ways of assessing what students can do and whether they have made learning gains (or whether there are bottlenecks or misconceptions that have prevented them from learning). Consequently, educators in the college English classroom are especially well positioned to pose questions and conduct analysis of those artifacts that make students' learning or nonlearning visible in ways distinct from traditional "cause-effect" and empirical approaches (Hassel 2015, 294).

We understand the rhetorical and concomitant material situation within which assessment occurs, too. Faculty must satisfy their accrediting bodies and administrators, and they may need to do so in ways that do not perfectly align with their own values. Here, too, a rhetorical attunement can be beneficial: faculty must make a strong case for the merit of this approach to assessment and how it adds value to the institution. As Susanmarie Harrington (2005) argues, "If we . . . consider assessment as a way to shape inquiry and the representation of our values and accomplishments, it becomes the foundation of all the work we do" (142). Assessment practices must be radically reframed to consider the material conditions "on the ground," so to speak. Further research and discussion about reframing assessment practices, particularly that being pioneered by Poe, Inoue, and Elliot in their latest edited collection, *Writing Assessment, Social Justice, and the Advancement of Opportunity* (2018), suggests the extent to which our fields are becoming more deeply engaged in this work. As Poe, Inoue, and Elliot write, "As a form of research, writing assessment best serves students when justice is taken as the aim of assessment; once adopted, that aim advances assessment as a principled way to create individual opportunity through identification of opportunity structures" (5). In our local context and for two-year college writing studies, disrupting status quo good-enough assessment and adopting a listening orientation are part and parcel of identifying and holding space in opportunity structures.

One area in which we have already seen progress is in placement tests. Like assessment, standardized tests assume an objective position, as if the information in the test were entirely without ideological content. And like most current assessment processes more broadly, standardized tests also prize decontextualization. Even the rhetorical situation of the test itself is stripped of context: sitting in a room full of people with whom students aren't allowed to communicate, at a computer, reading a test put together by teams and groups and corporations students will never meet and guided by those entities' cultures, values, and assumptions that are kept invisible to the students even though they become the yardstick by which student performances are measured. Yet, the neoliberalist narratives behind standardized testing—of gatekeeping, of efficiency, of monolingualism, of decontextualization, of reductive snapshots of students—were successfully interrogated on our campus, in our state, and across the country, which in turn led to real, meaningful change. This change in the end was good for our students. We believe revision of placement practices offers a template, as well as hope for real meaningful change in other areas such as assessment.

COVID CODA

This chapter was originally produced in 2019, but the pandemic and other circumstances delayed its publication. While we still believe that the ideas we laid out in this article are valid and vital for reforming our assessment practices, we'd like to take a moment to explain how our thinking has evolved and what new scholarship has emerged in the past four years.

While we maintain our advocacy in this article, we also acknowledge our own limitations and constraints. While we still believe rhetorical attunement in the name of humility is necessary, we also believe that such a practice can't fully mitigate the limitations that our white identities (im)pose. In retrospect, we would have placed bolder emphasis on two areas: (1) the need to diversify our faculty ranks and scholarly canon to make more space for BIPOC leadership and voices and (2) a more explicit link between translingual practice and antiracism. We wish, for example, we had proposed assessment practices more deeply rooted in critical race methodologies, such as counter-story. As Daniel Solórzano and Tara J. Yossa argue, "telling the stories of those people whose experiences are not often told (i.e., those on the margins of society)" is vital for "exposing, analyzing, and challenging the majoritarian stories of racial privilege" (2002, 32).

Explicit methods that link translingual assessment practice to a project of antiracism (and decolonialism) more accurately, and more strikingly, highlight our values and agenda. However, fine-tuning our language cannot replace the need for the empowerment of BIPOC faculty and scholars and the need to decenter white voices, no matter how well intentioned we might be. Truly transformative and just assessment practice depends on it. For we still believe that outcomes assessment, as it's often framed, privileges those who are closer to the dominant language standard. And such linguistic privileging reifies institutional racism, full stop.

Further, because assessment practices screen out the "noise" and "context," they often leave out the experiences and stories of students. Writing is a situated practice that occurs within a material ecology. Assessment in practice too often fails to disambiguate two disparate purposes—the purpose of assessing the college and that of assessing student learning. Assessment of the institution rarely accedes to disciplinary priorities or students' varied and important priorities. In addition, the usefulness and ethos of outcomes-based assessment of student learning has, as Doug Lederman described, come under suspicion even by those whose jobs center on assessment. Furthermore, the color-blind framing of institutional assessment processes—and the fact that color-blind assessments are incentivized in community colleges' day-to-day modes of crisis and austerity—requires further disruption. We are greatly encouraged by the ongoing scholarly endeavors to improve assessment. Of note, we see Mary K. Stewart's efforts in Antiracist Dynamic Criteria Mapping (2022), which describes how one writing program's approach took up the challenge of improving assessment practices. Jennifer Randall, writing with David Slomp, Mya Poe, and Maria Olena Oliveri (2022), takes on justice-oriented validity. Their piece builds on the work of Ellen Cushman, Asao Inoue, and others to emphasize how validation must be reframed to acknowledge and disrupt white supremacist assessment practices, and the detailed framing they offer suggests exciting ways to reshape assessment practices, including those in community college writing programs.

REFERENCES

Adler-Kassner, Linda, and Susanmarie Harrington. 2010. "Responsibility and Composition's Future in the Twenty-First Century: Reframing 'Accountability.'" *College Composition and Communication* 62 (1): 73–99.

Berlant, Lauren, and Jordan Greenwald. 2012. "Affect in the End Times: A Conversation with Lauren Berlant." *Qui Parle: Critical Humanities and Social Sciences* 20 (2): 71–89.

Blewett, Kelly, Christina M. LaVecchia, Laura R. Micciche, and Janine Morris. 2019. "Editing as Inclusion Activism." *College English* 81 (4): 273–96.

Clark, Burton R. 1960. "The 'Cooling-out' Function in Higher Education." *American Journal of Sociology* 65 (6): 569–76.

Cushman, Ellen. 2016. "Translingual and Decolonial Approaches to Meaning Making." *College English* 78 (3): 234–42.
Gallagher, Chris W. 2012. "The Trouble with Outcomes: Pragmatic Inquiry and Educational Aims." *College English* 75 (1): 42–60.
Hall, Jonathan. 2014. "Multilinguality Is the Mainstream." In *Reworking English in Rhetoric and Composition: Global Interrogations, Local Interventions*, edited by Bruce Horner and Karen Kopelson, 31–48. Carbondale: Southern Illinois University Press.
Harrington, Susanmarie. 2005. "The Place of Assessment and Reflection in Writing Program Administration." In *Discord and Direction: The Postmodern Writing Program Administrator*, edited by Sharon James McGee and Carolyn Handa, 140–57. Logan: Utah State University Press.
Hassel, Holly. 2015. "What Is Evidence of Student Learning?" *Teaching English in the Two-Year College* 42 (3): 293–96.
Horner, Bruce, Min-Zhan Lu, Jacqueline Jones Royster, and John Trimbur. 2011. "Language Difference in Writing: Toward a Translingual Approach." *College English* 73 (3): 303–21.
Lamos, Steve. 2011. *Interests and Opportunities: Race, Racism, and University Writing Instruction in the Post-Civil Rights Era*. Pittsburgh: University of Pittsburgh Press.
Lederman, Josh. 2018. "Writing Assessment Validity: Adapting Kane's Argument-Based Validation Approach to the Assessment of Writing in the Post-Process Era." *Journal of Writing Assessment* 11 (1). https://escholarship.org/uc/item/1n22m978.
Lederman, Doug. 2019. "Harsh Take on Assessment . . . From Assessment Pros." *Inside Higher Ed*, April 17. https://www.insidehighered.com/news/2019/04/17/advocates-student-learning-assessment-say-its-time-different-approach.
Lederman, Josh, and Nicole Warwick. 2018. "The Violence of Assessment: Writing Assessment, Social (In)Justice, and the Role of Validation." In *Writing Assessment, Social Justice, and the Advancement of Opportunity*, edited by Mya Poe, Asao B. Inoue, and Norbert Elliot, 229–55. Fort Collins, CO: WAC Clearinghouse.
Lee, Jaekyung, and Todd Reeves. 2012. "Revisiting the Impact of NCLB High-Stakes School Accountability, Capacity, and Resources: State NAEP 1990–2009 Reading and Math Achievement Gaps and Trends." *Educational Evaluation and Policy Analysis* 34 (2): 209–31.
Leonard, Rebecca Lorimer. 2014. "Multilingual Writing as Rhetorical Attunement." *College English* 76 (3): 227–47.
Murphy, Madeline. Fall 2017. "Beyond the Theater of Compliance?" *Intersection: A Journal at the Intersection of Assessment and Learning*, 14–16.
Peirce, Bonny Norton. 1996. "Comments on Bonny Norton Peirce's 'Social Identity, Investment, and Language Learning': A Reader Reacts." *TESOL Quarterly* 30 (2): 337–40.
Poe, Mya, Norbert Elliot, John Aloysius Cogan Jr., and Tito G. Nurudeen Jr. 2014. "The Legal and the Local: Using Disparate Impact Analysis to Understand the Consequences of Writing Assessment." *College Composition and Communication* 65 (4): 588–611.
Poe, Mya, and Asao B. Inoue. 2016. "Writing Assessment as Social Justice." Special issue, *College English* 79 (2): 119–26.
Poe, Mya, Asao B. Inoue, and Norbert Elliot. 2018. "Introduction: The End of Isolation." In *Writing Assessment, Social Justice, and the Advancement of Opportunity*, edited by Mya Poe, Asao B. Inoue, and Norbert Elliot, 3–38. Fort Collins, CO: WAC Clearinghouse.
Randall, Jennifer, David Slomp, Mya Poe, and Maria Elena Oliveri. 2022. "Disrupting White Supremacy in Assessment: Toward a Justice-Oriented, Antiracist Validity Framework," *Educational Assessment* 27 (2): 170–78. https://doi.org/10.1080/10627197.2022.2042682.
Solórzano, Daniel, and Yosso, Tara. 2002. "Critical Race Methodology: Counter-Storytelling as an Analytical Framework for Education Research." *Qualitative Inquiry* (8): 23–44. DOI: 10.1177/107780040200800103.
Stewart, Mary K. 2022. "Confronting the Ideologies of Assimilation and Neutrality in Writing Program Assessment through Antiracist Dynamic Criteria Mapping." *Journal*

of Writing Assessment. eScholarship, University of California. https://doi.org/10.5070/W4jwa.213.

Toth, Christie, Patrick Sullivan, and Carolyn Calhoon-Dillahunt. 2016. "A Dubious Method of Improving Educational Outcomes: Accountability and the Two-Year College." *Teaching English in the Two-Year College* 43 (4): 391.

Warnke, Anthony, and Kirsten Higgins. 2019. "A Critical Time for Reform: Empowering Interventions in a Precarious Landscape." *Best of the Journals in Rhetoric and Composition 2019* 45 (4): 185.

8
STRATEGIC ORGANIZING
Scaling Up Two-Year College Teacher-Scholar-Activism

Joanne Baird Giordano and Holly Hassel

On March 17, 2017, the University of Wisconsin Department of English received the CCCC Writing Program Certificate of Excellence after nearly a decade of work on the part of the coauthors and their colleagues. Six months later, a story was leaked to the *Milwaukee Journal Sentinel* announcing our statewide two-year institution would be dismantled. Thirteen open-access campuses would become branch campuses of adjacent four-year institutions to be subsumed under the programs, academic policies, and governance structures of the "parent" campus. The decision effectively dissolved the program that had garnered the CCCC award and an earlier TYCA program award for developmental education.

In the decade preceding the merger, the authors engaged in a series of increasingly more challenging teacher-scholar-activist endeavors to transform our writing program, aligning our curriculum and instruction with our institution's open-access mission. We started with studies, assessment activities, and program-development projects on our own micropolitan campus to research and then address academic barriers students faced in transitioning between writing courses and from developmental education to degree-credit coursework, completing a university transfer writing requirement, staying in good academic standing, and remaining in college to receive a degree (Hassel and Giordano 2009, 2011, 2013, 2015). We focused intensively on reforming our writing and developmental education placement methods from a stand-alone high-stakes test to a more inclusive multiple-measures placement process that decreased time to degree completion for some students and created individualized placement procedures that accounted for the widely diverse and complex literacy needs of our students within an open-admissions context (Hassel and Giordano 2011, 2015).

Through leadership positions within our statewide English Department (as a composition committee chair and program coordinator), we collaborated with colleagues to take research and program-development work from our campus to our multicampus department and online program (Phillips and Giordano 2016). We revised the writing program to create a cohesive curriculum that supported underprepared readers and writers as they transitioned between courses. We transformed our developmental English and ESL programs to align them with evidence-based practices. We engaged in time-intensive faculty-development and mentoring activities to help instructors adapt their teaching strategies to support the literacy development of two-year college students (Hassel et al. 2017).

While implementing curricular and instructional changes within our department, we worked on contingent-labor issues through scholarship (Hassel and Giordano 2017) and practical work. We provided adjunct instructors with opportunities to participate in professional-development projects and placement work (with attached compensation), developed instructional resources to address teaching-workload issues, implemented a mentoring program, changed department bylaws to be more inclusive, and created opportunities for interested instructors to participate more fully in the professional work of the department. We also worked with shared-governance leaders, through coalition building and a formal appeal through our representative governance groups to the chancellor, to advocate for and eventually eliminate a punitive compensation policy that lowered the pay per course for part-time instructors.

We share this professional history to illustrate the varied and complex work writing studies teacher-scholars can do within a program and for an institution to bring about change that improves (a) the professional lives and working conditions for instructors; (b) learning and literacy development for students; and (c) the policies, structures, and values that shape and define an institution. Individual teacher-scholars can engage in meaningful activism to create a more functional, equitable, and inclusive institution. Locally situated professional activism is an essential part of ensuring disciplinary knowledge and ethical values are accounted for in a program, department, campus, and wider institution. Our decade of intensive involvement led to departmental and institutional changes that dramatically improved the quality of our program and the professional lives of some instructors.

However, our work wasn't enough and never was going to be enough to push back against political forces that defunded higher education in Wisconsin imposed by the election of Scott Walker as governor, political gerrymandering, a legislature hostile to higher education, concentration of power in the hands of fewer political actors, and a state-system president who collaborated with these efforts (see Harris 2018). Members of our department did all we possibly could within our institution to advocate for students and develop an effective program that reflected disciplinary standards within an open-admissions context. We spent an equal number of hours taking on shared-governance leadership roles to achieve the best possible outcomes for students, faculty, and academic staff. However, in the end, our efforts were completely insufficient to combat the powerful political forces intent on reducing access to higher education for underprepared students and consolidating resources among the most selective institutions in the state system.

In this chapter, we take up three interconnected points. First, we describe how administrative and legislative mandates dictate the work of two-year college English programs in a way distinct from four-year institution programs. Next, we document the systematic dismantling of the University of Wisconsin System's two-year colleges, illustrating the sometimes-limited power individual faculty have to take action and preserve equitable access to higher education. Last, we argue that the teacher-scholar-activist paradigm for writing studies should become an animating force at the national, organizational level. While individual activism can make a difference locally (and is important to engage in), some issues facing members of our profession require an organized national response. Further, we see a need for the field of writing studies to attend to the value attached to the different components of our work, including expanding our stated social justice orientation to focus on practical ways to address significant barriers to educational access for students at underfunded two-year colleges and address the professional needs of full-time and adjunct faculty who work in those contexts.

SURVEILLANCE AND IMPOSED MANDATES: MANAGING TWO-YEAR COLLEGE ENGLISH FACULTY

Members of our profession have produced scholarship that both captures the unique professional identities of two-year college English faculty and presses us to engage more visibly in the activism and advocacy that reflect our campus missions and diverse student bodies (Hassel and Giordano 2013; Toth, Griffiths, and Thirolf 2013). In 2015, Patrick Sullivan (2015) extended Jeff Andelora's term "teacher-scholar" to "teacher-scholar-activist," calling on two-year college faculty to accept "the revolutionary and inescapably political nature of our work" (327).

Activist work within a writing program at open-access, two-year institutions is typically more complex and often more urgent than similar work at institutions with selective admissions standards and more resources. Publicly funded two-year colleges are subject to a disproportionate level of management and interference by legislators, megaphilanthropies and NGOs, and local community stakeholders (often employers or local industries). Subject to such external pressures, two-year colleges also have fewer internal resources than four-year and research campuses do; such resources, including well-prepared students, financially viable graduate programs, and connected alumni/ae, make it possible for four-year research institutions to assert agency and autonomy (see, e.g., Michael Bloomberg's $1.8 billion donation to Johns Hopkins University [Jaschik 2018]), and endowments that float institutions in leaner times help exert political influence to keep legislative interventions at bay. At the same time, two-year colleges serve the most diverse range of students in higher education, enrolling those who are excluded from higher education at other institutions.

Teacher-scholar-activist work in two-year college writing programs takes place within a context of limited resources, intensive student needs, and a high level of public accountability for student success and retention, including demand for improved performance often misaligned with the funding allotted by those who hold community college writing programs accountable for student success. Writing programs at two-year colleges have been subject to a nonstop onslaught of reforms and mandates that keep them scrambling in ways our colleagues at four-year campuses can avoid or fend off. The role of politics in dictating what happens in a writing program is based on the selectivity of the institution and its status within hierarchical structures of higher education, with the most selective research institutions having the most autonomy over their own programs and less public accountability.

COLLEGE-COMPLETION AGENDA REFORMS

Two-year college English departments are among the most monitored and legislatively controlled academic units in the country. Because reading and writing skills are required across the entire curriculum, and community colleges enroll a disproportionate percentage of students who are underprepared for college-level reading and writing, we find ourselves ever responding to new initiatives from administrators, state-level politicians, and public-policy organizations in ways less frequently encountered in higher education at other types of institutions or in other two-year college academic programs. Further, as public attention has increasingly focused on community college graduation and retention rates, pressure from external groups (Rutschow and Schneider 2011) and state legislatures (Whinnery and Pomeplia 2018) has intensified to **reduce or eliminate non-degree-credit reading and writing courses** for students who don't meet specific academic benchmarks at the time of admission (Bailey, Jaggers, and Jenkins 2015; Charles A. Dana Center 2012; Collins 2013; Neuburger, Gossen, and Barry 2013). At times, groups external to our discipline selectively apply data to suggest low rates of success progressing from developmental to degree-credit coursework are indicators that remediation itself creates failure in comparison to advocating for better placement mechanisms, curricular sequencing, instructional approaches, or innovations in student-support programming (see Hassel et al. 2015). Over the past decade, most two-year college writing programs have encountered administrative and/or legislative mandates aimed at improving college-completion rates, which can have positive benefits for students' learning and retention—and which often are rooted in disciplinary scholarship. However, these initiatives are sometimes imposed on programs without the consultation or even involvement of faculty—and sometimes are implemented in ways that stray from their research-based origins.

Acceleration is one of the most frequently mandated developmental education reform strategies and aims to reduce students' time to degree completion by eliminating one or more layers of developmental coursework. The most common model is the accelerated learning program (ALP) developed at the Community College of Baltimore County (Adams et al. 2009; Jenkins et al. 2015), which focuses on enrollment in credit-bearing first-year writing with a corequisite support course for students who would normally be placed at the highest level of developmental writing. ALP has roots in the studio model developed by Rhonda C. Grego and Nancy S. Thompson in the 1990s, which provides individualized support to student writers in a small-group learning environment outside a traditional classroom (Grego and Thompson 1995, 2007; Sutton and Chandler 2018). Another model is the stretch program developed at Arizona State University, which provides students with two semesters of first-year composition as an alternative to basic writing (Glau 1996, 2007). Other forms of acceleration focus more on placement, including lowered cut scores for first-year writing, multiple-measures placement with or without corequisite support, directed self-placement, and portfolio-challenge processes (Phillips and Giordano 2016).

Integrated reading and writing (IRW) courses are another form of acceleration that has become an increasingly used and often mandated model for teaching developmental English and reducing non-degree-credit coursework (Edgecombe et al. 2014; Saxon, Martirosyan, and Vick 2016a, 2016b). IRW courses eliminate separate developmental reading and writing courses and combine them into a single course, typically offered at the highest level of developmental education but sometimes at every level. State mandates (e.g., in Texas) and system or institutional administrative policies require campuses to offer IRW courses. These initiatives can create complex issues for English departments, as they incorporate reading instructors into a writing program, so writing instructors with no training in reading pedagogy become responsible for providing reading strategies instruction.

Most effective models for **reducing developmental coursework** and reenvisioning approaches to supporting underprepared college writers originated in writing studies as faculty-driven initiatives and typically stemmed from disciplinary knowledge of students' literacy development. However, in the age of the college-completion agenda, acceleration and other forms of restructured developmental English curricula are often imposed on two-year college faculty in ways that dilute the disciplinary roots of reform, ignore locally situated student needs, require increased faculty workload without compensation, and eliminate components of the original models that made them successful (e.g., the small corequisite support-class sizes and faculty development that accompanied the original ALP model).

For instance, our former colleagues at three of Wisconsin's small two-year campuses are now required to offer an ALP program instead of the award-winning program our former English Department developed, which focused on multiple-measures placement, individualized studio support, and reading-intensive writing courses. As part of institutional restructuring, the four-year campus imposed the ALP model on tenured faculty (along with changes to their workloads) without examining the extensive data collected and published scholarship originating from our dismantled program—and without considering that the studio model we developed in our former institution is a more cost-effective way to offer corequisite support on small rural campuses that have minimal financial resources and limited staffing. As a consequence, a program (ALP) that started as a form of writing studies teacher-scholar activism in a one-institutional context has become a mandate imposed on faculty in another context—against their will and without their input—through implementation that ignores both the material realities of teaching at underresourced rural campuses and the authority tenured faculty should normally have over curriculum and instruction.

DILUTED FACULTY AUTHORITY FOR CURRICULUM

Though by all accreditation standards, faculty are responsible for curriculum and have jurisdiction over changes to course content and pedagogical approaches, external mandates are regularly imposed on two-year colleges in ways that circumscribe the ability of faculty to make decisions that shape the curriculum. Guided Pathways is perhaps the best example of a mandate that removes decisions about curriculum from two-year college faculty. The Community College Research Center's *Redesigning Community Colleges* (Bailey, Jaggers, and Jenkins 2015) calls out the "cafeteria model" of the community college curriculum and argues for narrowing curricular offerings at community colleges, focusing students' interests into early career-focused pathways, and managing admission and advising process. Likewise, though campus mergers or closures and performance-based funding models do not on their surface seem curricular, they have implications for choices program coordinators and chairs can make to serve their students within these imposed constraints.

Disinvestment in public colleges and universities on the part of state legislatures and state governors (often accompanied by tuition freezes implemented to score political points) means many two-year colleges find themselves in a permanent state of austerity (see Kalish et al. 2019), and a not-unusual approach on the part of administrators and executives is to propose **mergers, campus closures, or system restructuring** like the one in our own state.[1] We discuss this in more detail in the following section, but we point here to the ways these seemingly solely structural or organizational decisions can influence the ability of faculty to control the curricular and pedagogical dimensions of their work. For example, a proposal to consolidate the administration of Connecticut's public colleges under a central entity was thwarted in 2018 by the New England Association of Schools and Colleges, the accrediting agency for the Connecticut State College and University system, but a year later, the president of CSCUS, Mark Ojakian, again presented his plan to move forward with the consolidation. As *Inside Higher Ed* reported April 17, 2019, faculty groups in the state are opposed to Ojakian's plan for several reasons. They fear the colleges will lose their individual cultural identities and unique academic programs. Faculty members are also concerned the colleges will be forced to deliver uniform programs whether they meet local workforce demands or not (Smith 2019).

---

1. See, for example, efforts to combine two New Jersey Colleges and mergers in Pennsylvania (Seltzer 2018a, 2018b); an effort to merger the two-year colleges in Connecticut was rejected by the system's accreditor (Smith 2019).

Reporting lines and faculty-driven processes for hiring and evaluating instructors, admitting students to programs, and assessing learning at the classroom and program level can all be affected by a restructured institution (change in location within a college or university structure, or in our case, being subsumed under an entirely new university). Consequently, institutional restructuring can prevent faculty from exercising self-determination and autonomy in making decisions that meet needs of their students and their campuses.

Another legislatively motivated mandate that disproportionately affects two-year colleges is **performance-based funding**. Though some four-year campuses find themselves subject to legislative interventions like performance-based funding, community colleges are particularly attractive targets for these kinds of efforts because of a focus on vocational training (university transfer and general education are only part of what two-year institutions do). A 2017 news story written by Paul Fain notes that thirty-five states have some component of college funding tied to metrics like graduation or retention rates; research results are mixed on whether these policies benefit students or institutions. A 2013 cosponsored report from Complete College America and the National Center for Higher Education Management Systems identified both positive outcomes and potentially unintended consequences of performance models. For example, a *Community College Review* article reported "that more aggressive forms of state-based formulas can increase public colleges' production of short-term certificates while reducing the number of associate degrees students earn" (Fain 2017).

We see other issues at work in our own institution's demise—problems that have historically affected two-year colleges but that are increasingly extended to four-year institutions, including weakening faculty oversight, and autonomy for curriculum, concentration of power in administrators (who might not have an academic background or experience in higher education), reduction or elimination of the liberal arts, and mandates to make programs career focused. Recent national news stories have highlighted the efforts, within Wisconsin specifically, to radically shift the emphasis of higher education, including gutting liberal arts major program offerings at comprehensive public universities (Flaherty 2018; Harris 2018; Meyerhofer, *Wisconsin State Journal*, December 3, 2018).

CASE STUDY: UW DISMANTLE

Even as members of our statewide English Department worked toward creating nationally recognized writing and developmental education programs, a series of statewide policies, system-level interventions, and administrative decisions created a complex set of challenges that limited equitable access to higher education for two-year campus students. The 2018 dismantling of the University of Wisconsin Colleges was the result of a long pathway away from supporting an access mission, which promised to "advanc[e] the Wisconsin Idea by bringing the resources of the University to the people of the state and the communities that provide and support its campuses" (University of Wisconsin System 2010).

Since 2010, Wisconsin has been a national testing ground for austerity measures that gutted the public university system, eventually leading to the merger of two-year campuses with four-year universities. Changes in state statutes and policies weakened tenure policies, removed collective-bargaining rights for public employees, and attempted to delete "the pursuit of truth" from the University of Wisconsin mission statement (see Strauss, *Washington Post*, February 5, 2015). A series of punishing cuts to state funding combined with years of unfunded tuition caps dramatically reduced the resources available for campuses to serve students. The recent history of the University of Wisconsin System demonstrates the negative effects of a politically motivated austerity agenda on colleges and universities. But it also highlights how higher education reform movements disproportionately affect two-year colleges in general and English programs in particular.

Over the past decade, every state budget cycle in Wisconsin reduced funding to the UW System with cuts of $100 million in 2013–2015 and $250 million more in 2015–2017 (UW System 2015). However, these cuts were most damaging to the two-year colleges, which were already operating on limited budgets with fewer state dollars and less ability to raise revenue through alumni donations, special programs, and out-of-state tuition. For instance, in fall 2017, 94.6 percent of first-year students at the two-year colleges were Wisconsin residents. In contrast, only 56.5 percent of UW–Madison students were state residents (UW System Operating 2018). Madison's tuition and fees for those nonresident students was more than $30,000 per year. Almost all two-year college students were residents who paid $2,375 a semester in tuition and less than $200 in campus-based fees. The difference in the ability of the two-year access campuses to generate tuition revenue in comparison to the R1 flagship is staggering. Further, Madison enrolls only one-fifth of UW System students and yet receives 45 percent of the UW System's state funding (UW System 2018; David, *Badger Herald*, July 12, 2017). A 2019 report by the Century Foundation confirms that inequitable funding for two-year college students is a national trend not isolated to Wisconsin:

"In fiscal year 2013, private four-year research institutions spent five times as much per full time equivalent student annually ($72,000) as did community colleges ($14,000)" and "public research universities spend 60 percent more than community colleges."

In each round of budget cuts, the University of Wisconsin System didn't take into account the inability of the UW Colleges to raise revenue and ignored an existing lack of resources (e.g., limited advising and tutoring services) for the underprepared, low-income, and first-generation students who enrolled on the two-year access campuses but who were inadmissible at other system schools. The cuts were distributed across the state with little attention to the inadequacy of services on the two-year campuses, the relatively rich sets of resources available to faculty and students at more selective campuses, and the reality that the campuses serving students with the highest academic and social needs also received less state funding to address those needs in contrast to other institutions.

The UW Colleges central administration responded to the budget cuts by creating a regionalizing leadership structure that reduced the autonomy and decision-making power of faculty while also concentrating a chunk of centralized funding into salaried positions for administrators. Over one hundred staff positions were eliminated, some full-time instructors became part-time employees, and even tenured faculty experienced forced reassignments to other campuses or to distance-education courses (UW System 2016). Most staff cuts reduced or eliminated positions traditionally viewed as an essential part of higher education. The student-per-advisor ratio became 533:1 (UW System 2016). Students could no longer access direct, in-person services for admissions, financial aid, business functions (including paying tuition, fees, and fines in person). Much of the support college students typically receive on a campus was moved to centralized or regional positions accessible only through email or phone calls, which sometimes required students to make repeated attempts over time to access help with pressing issues that affected their ability to attend and pay for college. These austerity measures had a profound effect on the ability of campuses to attract and retain students. Combined with a decline in high-school graduates and a dwindling population in some rural communities, cuts to basic campus services resulted in a steep decline in student enrollment even as the institution had an increased, dire need to generate tuition revenue.

These devastating changes to the structures that had created stable campus learning environments were especially challenging for the English Department. We spent a decade cultivating collaborative relationships with Student Affairs administrators and advisors on many of the thirteen campuses to develop local programs that reflected our open-access mission, including improving placement, developmental education advising, programs for academically at-risk students, and support for second language writers. Most of our Student Affairs partners lost their jobs or left for other institutions before their positions were eliminated, and those who remained faced increased workloads and reduced autonomy, which prevented them from continuing many of our previously successful collaborations.

At the same time, regional administrators had more concentrated power, and they were less inclined than many of the former campus leaders to consult with faculty, pay attention to our program assessment data on student success, and make evidence-based decisions. They ignored the years of peer-reviewed scholarship members of our department had produced about students' transitions to college-level reading and writing. Over time, administrators attempted to dismantle our corequisite writing studio support program, reduced writing center support, and eventually eliminated our multiple-measures placement process without providing a suitable replacement (Phillips and Giordano 2016). Elimination of what had previously been essential student support services also increased both the workload and emotional labor of English instructors, who increasingly but often futilely spent more of their time attempting to fill in gaps in missing services for their own students by serving as unofficial advisors and doing other uncompensated work (Kalish et al. 2019).

On some campuses, administrators refused to offer ESL and reading courses, or they eliminated spring sections of developmental writing even though they continued to admit students who did not meet the prerequisites for first-year writing were significantly underprepared for college. In theory, there should have been enough money on most campuses to continue funding eliminated courses and writing center support because the state of Wisconsin does not pay for developmental education, which is self-funded through tuition. In turn, the UW System normally requires campuses to reserve excess developmental education revenue for courses and support for students enrolled in the program. However, in the UW Colleges, the institution as a whole and individual campuses used funds to balance other areas of the budget, which meant fully enrolled fall courses could no longer generate enough money on some campuses to fund smaller spring classes, professional writing center staffing, or corequisite writing support. English instructors paid a heavy price for these program cuts. The intensive workload of supporting underprepared college readers and writers gradually shifted away from compensated disciplinary work toward writing classrooms, even as many of those same instructors faced employment instability, reduced teaching loads, and perpetual uncertainty about their futures as members of the profession (see Kalish et al. [2019] for an overview of instructor concerns and the effects of austerity).

These examples are just a few of multiple ways budget cuts and the erosion of faculty authority had a profound and negative impact on Wisconsin's two-year college students. They also illustrate that politically motivated austerity policies can (a) have a significant impact on the sustainability of a writing program, (b) disproportionately increase the workload and emotional labor for writing and developmental English instructors, and (c) eliminate ethical and equitable access to college education. Although the elimination of collective bargaining, tenure protections, and liberal arts programs in Wisconsin have perhaps gained more attention than the budget cuts and eventual dissolution of the two-year institution, members of our profession at any type of institution should be alarmed by how Wisconsin has been used as a testing ground for policies intended to reshape public higher education. More important, our experience in Wisconsin illustrates that, while individual activism can make a difference at the local level, some issues facing members of the profession require an organized response at the national level.

A TYCA NATIONAL ADVOCACY AGENDA

What stands out to us not just in our own local context but in conversations with TYCA colleagues is the necessity of a coordinated, national-level response. It can be difficult to arrive at consensus on what that response would look like, in part because any national group must respond to an array of competing pressures and perspectives that may simply not reflect the view of every constituency. Nevertheless, we see a need for TYCA to press forward with scaling up local teacher-scholar-activist work and developing a national agenda, one that takes an *organizational* position on the wide range of issues that face most two-year college students and their instructors. NCTE and CCCC have effectively responded to issues that affect K–12 education (e.g., legislative education policies and censorship) and postsecondary English in general (e.g., labor equity and social justice). Our disciplinary organizations have mostly been silent on legislative and administrative initiatives that have fundamentally changed curriculum, instruction, and faculty authority in many two-year college writing programs.

We call for a coordinated national effort because individual activism is inadequate, and local ecologies have limits and constraints that can prevent individual faculty, departments, or other groups from influencing the outcomes of an externally imposed mandate or legislative fiat. We strongly support the assertions of Christie Toth, Patrick Sullivan, and Carolyn Calhoon-Dillahunt in "A Dubious Method of Improving Educational Outcomes" (2016): "It has become increasingly clear that the work we do—or don't do—outside the classroom affects the work we do inside the classroom in profound ways" (405). We must become what Anthony Warnke and Kirsten Higgins (2018) call "critical reformers" and "move from an ad hoc, defensive posture to a consistent, offensive position with a reliable framework and value system" (363) but do so by organizing nationally to engage in teacher-scholar-activist work that preserves the open-access mission of two-year colleges. Likewise, Brett Griffith's (2017) calls for better preparing new instructors in two-year colleges as "autonomous teacher-advocates," which she contrasts with "independent contractor" models, the former of which work to "collaborate with departmental colleagues to define and modify department curriculum, as well as institutional outcomes" versus faculty who operate independently, exerting influence over their classroom practice but not necessarily through larger departmental service work (55). We extend that call to include service, colleague collaborations, and advocacy work at the national level that will improve outcomes for two-year colleges and the students they serve.

As TYCA continues to evolve from a largely regional to a national presence, members of our profession need resources that bring evidence-based practices and research to nonspecialist policy-making audiences. White papers such as the "TYCA White Paper on Placement Reform" (Klausman et al. 2016) and the "White Paper on Developmental Education Reform" (Hassel et al. 2015) are useful resources because they assemble disciplinary knowledge in an accessible and organized way two-year college faculty can use to make program decisions and potentially respond to imposed mandates. However, more forceful positions and policy statements are also needed. For example, the Council of Learning Assistance and Developmental Education Associations provides a series of policy statements on topics often under threat in imposed environments of austerity and as external mandates are imposed on public institutions most likely to serve vulnerable, structurally disadvantaged, and marginalized student populations: learning assistance, developmental education, and access. Their policy statement on college access takes a firm stance on what ethical and evidence-based approaches to college success look like, and end with a resolution:

Organizations representing faculty and staff affiliated with learning assistance in higher education support common sense in funding decisions related to learning assistance programs, continued research into the efficacy of learning support models to fully embrace the goal of equal access, and all legislation that protects the equal access directive in higher education. (n.d.a)

We also imagine the value of resources, whether that's advocacy toolkits, workshops, training, documents, or other materials that give two-year college faculty the ability to address imposed mandates in ways that can limit harm to instructors, students, and their communities.

With the advent of the first national TYCA conference in March 2019, we see an important opportunity concurrently emerging to move the profession for two-year college English forward, one that requires a collaborative partnership between scholars in the field and national governance leadership. For TYCA, that means examining and potentially proposing changes to the organizational architecture of its past structures. The regional model so central to TYCA's identity historically may need to make way for a national approach, one that allows its members to bring forward issues for position statements, resolutions, and activist priorities. TYCA has long been an affiliate (or a kind of protectorate) of the larger NCTE organization; this has allowed it to become established and to grow. But the next steps require TYCA's autonomous self-determination and advocacy to address not just the pressing issues that face two-year colleges but the agendas and attacks from external forces that are limiting access to higher education in the United States.

REFERENCES

Adams, Peter, Sarah Gearhart, Robert Miller, and Anne Roberts. 2009. "The Accelerated Learning Program: Throwing Open the Gates." *Journal of Basic Writing* 28 (2): 50–69.

Andelora, Jeff. 2008. "Forging a National Identity: TYCA and the Teacher/Scholar." *Teaching English in the Two-Year College* 35 (4): 350–62.

Bailey, Thomas R., Shanna Smith Jaggers, and Davis Jenkins. 2015. *Redesigning America's Community Colleges: A Clearer Path to Student Success.* Cambridge, MA: Harvard University Press.

Century Foundation Working Group on Community College Financial Resources. 2019. "Recommendations for Providing Community Colleges with the Resources They Need." https://productiontcf.imgix.net/app/uploads/2019/04/25171942/recommendation_commcollege_2019.pdf.

Charles A. Dana Center, Complete College America, Education Commission of the States, and Jobs for the Future. 2012. *Core Principles for Transforming Remediation: A Joint Statement.* https://www.csun.edu/sites/default/files/core_principles_2012.pdf.

Council of Learning Assistance and Developmental Education Associations (CLADEA). N.d.a. *Policy Statement on College Access.* CLADEA. https://cladea.info/resources/CLADEA_policy_CA.pdf.

Council of Learning Assistance and Developmental Education Associations (CLADEA). N.d.b. *Policy Statement on Developmental Education.* CLADEA. https://cladea.info/resources/CLADEA_policy_DE.pdf.

Council of Learning Assistance and Developmental Education Associations (CLADEA). N.d.c. *Policy Statement on Learning Assistance.* CLADEA. https://cladea.info/resources/CLADEA_policy_LA.pdf.

Collins, Michael Lawrence. 2013. "Discussion of the Joint Statement of Core Principles for Transforming Remedial Education." *Journal of College Reading and Learning* 44 (1): 84–94.

Edgecombe, Nikki, Shanna Smith Jaggars, Di Xu, and Melissa Barragan. 2014. "Accelerating the Integrated Instruction of Developmental Reading and Writing at Chabot College." CCRC Working Paper 71, Community College Research Center, Teachers College, Colombia University, New York.

Fain, Paul. "Negative Findings on Performance-Based Funding." 2017. *Inside Higher Ed*, December 18. https://www.insidehighered.com/quicktakes/2017/12/18/negative-findings-performance-based-funding.

Flaherty, Colleen. 2018. "Wisconsin's Controversial Proposal on Program Elimination." *Inside Higher Ed*, December 4. https://www.insidehighered.com/quicktakes/2018/12/04/wisconsins-controversial-proposal-program-elimination.

Glau, Greg. 1996. "The 'Stretch Program': Arizona State University's New Model of University-Level Basic Writing Instruction." *WPA: Writing Program Administration* 20 (1): 79–91.

Glau, Greg. 2007. "Stretch at 10: A Program Report on Arizona State University's Stretch Program." *Journal of Basic Writing* 26 (2): 30–48. https://profession.mla.org/demand-for-new-faculty-members-1995-2016/.

Grego, Rhonda C., and Nancy S. Thompson. 1995. "The Writing Studio Program: Reconfiguring Basic Writing/ Freshman Composition." *WPA: Writing Program Administration* 19 (1): 66–79.

Grego, Rhonda C., and Nancy S. Thompson. 2007. *Teaching/Writing in Thirdspaces: The Studio Approach.* Carbondale: Southern Illinois University Press.

Griffiths, Brett. 2017. "Professional Autonomy and Teacher-Scholar-Activists in Two-Year Colleges: Preparing New Faculty to Think Institutionally." *Teaching English in the Two-Year College* 45 (1): 47–68.

Harris, Adam. 2018. "The Liberal Arts May Not Survive the Twenty-First Century." *Atlantic*, December 12. https://www.theatlantic.com/education/archive/2018/12/the-liberal-arts-may-not-survive-the-21st-century/.

Hassel, Holly, and Joanne Baird Giordano. 2009. "Transfer Institutions, Transfer of Knowledge: The Development of Rhetorical Adaptability and Underprepared Writers." *Teaching English in the Two-Year College* 37 (1): 24–40.

Hassel, Holly, and Joanne Baird Giordano. 2011. "FYC Placement at Open-Admission, Two-Year Campuses: Changing Campus Culture, Institutional Practice, and Student Success." *Open Words: Access and English Studies* 5 (2): 29–59.

Hassel, Holly, and Joanne Baird Giordano. 2013. "Occupy Writing Studies: Rethinking College Composition for the Needs of the Teaching Majority." *College Composition and Communication* 65 (1): 117–39.

Hassel, Holly, and Joanne Baird Giordano. 2015. "The Blurry Borders of College Writing: Remediation and the Assessment of Student Readiness." *College English* 78 (1): 56–80.

Hassel, Holly, and Joanne Baird Giordano. 2017. "Contingency, Access, and the Material Conditions of Teaching and Learning in the 'Statement of Principles.'" In *Labored: The State(ment) and Future of Work in Composition*, edited by Randall McClure, Dayna V. Goldstein, and Michael A. Pemberton, 147–67. Anderson, SC: Parlor.

Hassel, Holly, Joanne Baird Giordano, Jennifer Heinert, and Cassie Phillips. 2017. "Student Retention and Professional Development in Two-Year College English Departments."

In *Retention, Persistence, and Writing Programs*, edited by Todd Ruecker, Dawn Shepherd, Heidi Estrem, and Beth Brunk Chavez, 74–92. Logan: Utah State University Press.

Hassel, Holly, Jeffrey Klausman, Joanne Baird Giordano, Margaret O'Rourke, Leslie Roberts, Patrick Sullivan, and Christie Toth. 2015. "TYCA White Paper on Developmental Education Reforms." *Teaching English in the Two-Year College* 43 (3): 227–43.

Jaschik, Scott. 2018. "$1.8 Billion to Make Johns Hopkins Need-Blind." *Inside Higher Ed*, November 19. https://www.insidehighered.com/admissions/article/.

Jenkins, Davis, Cecilia Speroni, Clive Belfield, Shanna Smith Jaggars, and Nikki Edgecombe. 2010. "A Model for Accelerating Academic Success of Community College Remedial English Students: Is the Accelerated Learning Program (ALP) Effective and Affordable?" CCRC Working Paper 21, Community College Research Center, Teachers College, Columbia University. https://ccrc.tc.columbia.edu/media/k2/attachments/remedial-english-alp-effective-affordable.pdf.

Kalish, Katie, Holly Hassel, Cassie Phillips, Jennifer Heinert, and Joanne Giordano. 2019. "Inequitable Austerity: Pedagogies of Resilience and Resistance in Composition." *Pedagogy: Critical Approaches to Teaching Literature, Language, Composition, and Culture* 19 (2): 261–81.

Klausman, Jeffrey, et al. 2016. "TYCA White Paper on Placement Reform." *Teaching English in the Two-Year College* 44 (2): 135–57.

Neuburger, Jane, Rebecca Gossen, and William J. Barry. 2013. "Developmental Education Policy and Practice: Claiming Our Seat—and Voice—at the Table." *Journal of College Reading and Learning* 44 (1): 72–83.

Phillips, Cassandra, and Joanne Baird Giordano. 2016. "Developing a Cohesive Academic Literacy Program for Underprepared Students." *Teaching English in the Two-Year College* 44 (1): 79–89.

Rutschow, Elizabeth Zachry, and Emily Schneider. 2011. *Unlocking the Gate: What We Know about Improving Developmental Education.* MDRC, June. https://www.mdrc.org/sites/default/files/full_595.pdf.

Saxon, D. Patrick, Nara M. Martirosyan, and Nicholas T. Vick. 2016a. "NADE Members Respond: Best Practices in Integrated Reading and Writing, Part I." *Journal of Developmental Education* 39 (2): 32–34.

Saxon, D. Patrick, Nara M. Martirosyan, and Nicholas T. Vick. 2016b. "NADE Members Respond: Best Practices in Integrated Reading and Writing, Part 2." *Journal of Developmental Education* 39 (3): 32–34.

Seltzer, Rick. 2018a. "New Jersey 2-Year Colleges Pursue Merger." *Inside Higher Ed*, September 7. https://www.insidehighered.com/quicktakes/2018/09/07/new-jersey-2-year-colleges-pursue-merger.

Seltzer, Rick. 2018b. "New Report Recommends Mergers in Pennsylvania." *Inside Higher Ed*, April 26. https://www.insidehighered.com/quicktakes/2018/04/26/new-report-recommends-mergers-pennsylvania.

Smith, Ashley. 2019. "Connecticut Moves to Consolidate Community Colleges Amid Faculty Opposition." *Inside Higher Ed*, April 17. https://www.insidehighered.com/news/2019/04/17/connecticut-community-colleges-faculty-and-administration-odds-over-proposed.

Sullivan, Patrick. 2015. "The Two-Year College Teacher-Scholar-Activist." *Teaching English in the Two-Year College* 42 (4): 327–50.

Sutton, Mark, and Sally Chandler, eds. 2018. *The Writing Studio Sampler: Stories About Change.* Fort Collins, CO: WAC Clearinghouse https://wac.colostate.edu/books/perspectives/studio/.

Toth, Christie, Brett Griffiths, and Kathryn Thirolf. 2013. "'Distinct and Significant': Professional Identities of Two-Year College English Faculty." *College Composition and Communication* 65 (1): 90–116.

Toth, Christie, Patrick Sullivan, and Carolyn Calhoon-Dillahunt. 2016. "A Dubious Method of Improving Educational Outcomes: Accountability and the Two-Year College." *Teaching English in the Two-Year College* 43 (4): 391–410.
University of Wisconsin Colleges. "UW Colleges Mission and Goals." April 2010. http://www.uwc.edu/catalog/about/mission.
University of Wisconsin System. 2016. "Campus Summaries Describing Impact of State Budget Cuts." Madison.com, April. http://host.madison.com/campus-summaries-descri bing-impact-of-state-budget-cuts/pdf_3c41eadd-cb0e-5935-b3b0-fb4f9b84a24e.html.
University of Wisconsin System. "Operating Budget and Fees Schedule." July 2017. https://www.wisconsin.edu/budget-planning/download/budget_documents/annual _budget_documents/2017-18-Annual-Budget.pdf.
University of Wisconsin System. Student Statistics. "Headcount Enrollment—Undergraduate Students by Institution, Fall 2017 to 2018." Retrieved December 19, 2018. https://www .wisconsin.edu/education-reports-statistics/student-statistics/.
University of Wisconsin System. "Remedial Education Policy." Regent Policy Document 4–8. Revised November 11, 2018. https://www.wisconsin.edu/regents/policies/reme dial-education-policy/.
University of Wisconsin System. "UW Regents Approve 2015–16 Annual Operating Budget." UW System News Release. July 9, 2015. https://www.wisconsin.edu/news /archive/uw-regents-approve-2015-16-annual-operating-budget-news-summary/.
University of Wisconsin System. 2017. "The New Freshman Class: Fall 2017." Informational Memorandum. https://www.wisconsin.edu/education-reports-statistics/download/edu cational_statistics/informational_memoranda/The-New-Freshman-Class,-Fall-2017 .pdf.
Warnke, Anthony, and Kirsten Higgins. 2018. A Critical Time for Reform: Empowering Interventions in a Precarious Landscape. *Teaching English in the Two-Year College* 45 (4): 361–84.
Whinnery, Erin, and Vilan Odekar. 2021. "50-State Comparison: Developmental Education Policies." Education Commission of the States, April 25. https://www.ecs.org/50 -state-comparison-developmental-education-policies/?fbclid=IwAR0PtWtTt8i1gToFG nOobAvZ1uY49Xc_y1j7VMDxrLqs8l1bo_sL9vNwyTo.

Afterword
CONSIDERING THE CONVERSATION

Darin Jensen and Brett Griffiths

Like many books in our field, this anthology began as a conversation in the lobby of a hotel at the closing of a CCCC conference. We (Darin and Brett) discussed the highlights of our conference experience with trusted colleagues from two-year colleges. We sought to extend our conversations from that lobby and respond to the contributions—and gaps—we witnessed in the overall presentation of two-year college pedagogies at the conference. We envisioned a book that would continue the conversations begun in three edited collections: Mark Reynolds's *Two-Year College English* (1994), Barry Alford and Keith Kroll's *The Politics of Writing in the Two-Year College* (2003), and Mark Reynolds and Sylvia Halliday-Hicks's *The Profession of English in the Two-Year College* (2005).

These collections had spent a lot of time on our desks. The voices and experiences recorded in them fostered the professional observations and reflections that became our scholarly inquiries and our life's work. They shaped the fabric of our nascent professional identities and, we have come to find, the identities of many of our colleagues, too. These collections showcased professional narratives about the institutions we most valued—narratives that were almost always neglected in the core curricula of our graduate education and that of our peers (Jensen and Toth 2017; Toth and Jensen 2017). We wondered, How can fundamental questions of educational equity and access be taken up in writing studies if not through scholarly attention to America's democratic colleges? We had ruminated on this question individually and with the voices in these books long before we met. The histories and voices recorded in those volumes offered a trail of breadcrumbs to our collegial past and to the work of the teacher-scholar-activists who continue to shape our thoughts and shared profession today.

We see these conversations as a set of counternarratives threading through our discipline and cuffing at the margins of our professions. These counternarratives, what Nancy Fraser (1990) has called "subaltern counter publics" and "parallel discursive arenas," afford teacher-scholar-activists the opportunity to "formulate oppositional interpretations of [the] identities, interests, and needs" (67) of two-year college writing studies—the concerns of nearly half the field of writing instructional professionals in higher education—as a way of observing, organizing, and advocating for both the value of our work and its long-term sustainability. They conceive of two-year college English teaching as a distinct and significant profession (Reynolds and Holladay-Hicks 2005), one that is at the center of composition and rhetoric and comprises the majority of labor and teaching (Calhoon-Dillahunt 2018; Hassel and Giordano 2013). Taken as a series, they witness and highlight the histories of the pedagogical, political, material, and institutional conditions that make us distinct. Like all counternarratives, they function as spaces of withdrawal and resistance, ways of hailing one another from within our margins and of dialoguing with our partners in the wider field of writing studies. They are both the genesis and the extension of John Lovas's rallying call in his chair's address at CCCC in 2002. This address became the *CCC* article "All Good Writing Develops at the Edge of Risk," which argues,

> While it's easy to see this issue as political—junior professors in universities need publications and citations to gain tenure and community college professors do not—I see it as a scholarly and intellectual failing. (276)

Lovas's (2002) call, and the moment it described, formed the exigence for a decade of new scholarship on teaching and learning specific to English classrooms in the two-year college. Important, these conversations have included academic discussions about the preparation of two-year college English faculty, as well as public discussions about the state and purpose of our profession as it should be (see Klausman 2018, 2019). For many of the writers in this volume, these documents have been both inspirational and communal; they have helped us find one another. Nevertheless, a lack of disciplinary visibility and professional recognition from our peers at four-year institutions can complicate and confound the reach of the inclusive, antiracist, anticlassist teaching practices evolving in our classrooms where access and inclusion have been foundational to our missions. This invisibility and, frankly, the ill-conceived hierarchy that maintains it, helps erode both the status and the position of our profession. This erosion directly impacts and impedes student access and inclusion because as long as the status of institutions and instructors at two-year colleges remains provisional within our professional circles, so too do our students hold provisional status within our scholarship, our classrooms, our pedagogies.

Likely, this erosion results from a disconnect between teacher-scholar-activists at different kinds of institutions and our overwhelming invisibility and neglect of one another (Griffiths 2020). We suspect it is fomented by a lack of engagement in graduate school between graduate programs and the disciplinary and intellectual inquiries of open-access, two-year college pedagogies. A more insidious breach comes from implicit messages of NOKD—"not our kind, dear"—graduate students who have pursued interest in two-year college scholarship report from their programs (Jensen 2017). In absence of formal pathways for professionalization—or lack of awareness from mentors and advisors that such pathways exist—future teacher-scholar-activists are left to forge their own intellectual journeys, to self-professionalize in a wilderness.

The erosion reflects a community of two-year college instructors who—once engaged—have often become disenfranchised from the academic work of neighboring universities where interest in research projects is high but interest in students is short-lived. And it is in part because community college administrations and boards are often not educated or invested in the expertise and professionalization of faculty, which is to say, no element of institutional accreditation or program evaluation for the liberal arts, for example, calls for documentation of professional engagement among teachers of writing or literature. These factors and others form a disconnect between two-year college writing instructional practitioners and teacher-scholar-activists like the authors in this book.

Finally, we acknowledge that some disengagement reflects a simple lack of interest, curiosity, or sustained professional commitment in the work of open-access, inclusive, antiracist, anticlassist teaching and faculty's roles in it. This disengagement has been dubbed the "fossilization" of professional identities (Toth and Sullivan 2016; Suh and Jensen 2020), and can be found on all kinds of education campuses. Within our own community of two-year college teachers, we have known such fossilized coworkers—fellow faculty members, even friends—who are disengaged (or disenfranchised) from the literature of our field. This kind of disengagement is sometimes performatively nostalgic, shifting the onus of educational expertise to abstract frameworks of blame and shame. Its keepers may harken back to "good ol' days" of students from the past while wagging their fingers about students, administrators, or teachers today. This disengagement may reflect extended burnout from exploitation, the result of the enormous strain of teaching four, five, or six courses every semester and the commensurate preparation, grading, and emotional labor that comes with teaching 80–120 differently prepared students. Likely it is informed by the perpetual call to adapt to education reforms that focus on effects rather than causes and that foster a manufactured sense of "crisis" about the education of our students. This ongoing crisis is concomitant with a compensatory call to do more with less to shore up "temporary" conditions (see, e.g., Soliday 2002). Whatever the causes, we know this situation is not sound pedagogy, nor is it sustainable. And that may be the most difficult condition of our work—because as those of us engaged in the field fight for the visibility of our work and the conditions necessary to support our students, we heft not only the weight of structural inequities and decades of poor education policy but also the burden of the neglect and apathy of our better-resourced colleagues.

ARTICULATING A VISION

It doesn't have to be this way. The way forward depends on intentional, inclusive, and connective recentering of the work of our discipline as emancipatory, both for our students and ourselves, to cast off the effects of our too-narrow choices, those institutional bargains we have made for one specialized program or another. We must see each other and be seen for the work we all do to locate the learning of language and writing at the center of student inclusion and uplift.

Even so, if we point a finger at how graduate education and universities fail two-year college writing studies, we must look inward at the work deeply engaged teacher-scholar-activists must do, too. Readers may notice this book is written by eight women and four men. This representation is similar to the demographic composition of respondents to the TYCA 2019 labor task force survey (Suh et al. 2021), 73 percent of whom self-identified as female, 21 percent as male, and 6 percent as nonbinary or "prefer not to say." Readers may notice that only three of the twelve authors in this book are people of color—two of whom teach at universities. This number is consistent with the demographic representation in the same survey, for which 81 percent of respondents self-identified as white, 4 percent Latinx, 2 percent African American, 2 percent Asian or Pacific Islander, and roughly 10 percent "other": Native American, multiracial, or "prefer not to say." While the demographic composition of respondents to the labor task force survey is not a perfect proxy for our field, it likely mirrors, or is a close reflection, of our overall composition. At the time of this writing, the TYCA is undertaking a national survey to understand who our teachers are, how they are prepared, and what they need a national professional organization to be. Given what we can observe, it is fair to say the professional organization of two-year college English is overwhelmingly white—far whiter than our student body nationally. This discrepancy contributes to continued white language supremacy and the ways our own complicity remains so often invisible to us.

While this book reflects that existing demographic, we note here that we actively solicited authors from diverse groups, those beyond the TYCA listserv and the CCC conference. We know faculty who represent BIPOC communities often carry disproportionate service loads at their institutions. Beyond and in addition to the heavy teaching loads all two-year college faculty balance, BIPOC faculty are often called on by their institutions or their consciences to serve on additional DEI initiatives, with student identity groups, and on faculty labor-resolution panels, which attempt to respond to and improve working and learning conditions experienced by staff and students. In recognizing this imbalance, we are naming work that must be done, work we have been unable to do in this collection—work to invite, include, and unburden the many professionals in our field, in our discipline, and within our institutions, to recognize and amplify their voices regularly and powerfully. There is a call to support the work already being done and that which has not begun, and to do so in ways our colleagues of color identify as supportive and purposeful. This book isn't about graduate preparation or how BIPOC people are brought into the field, but we sincerely hope that—in writing this book—we call that book into being, and that you, the person reading this book and asking these questions along with us, will write it.

Further, there are problems in two-year college writing studies we don't address in this volume. The contingent labor crisis is nothing short of a catastrophe. Some estimates of part-time instruction in two-year college English departments are as high as 80 percent (Hurlburt and McGarrah n.d.; McNaughtan, García, and Nehls 2017). Rhonda Grego's chapter in this collection touches briefly on labor and finding a space for part-time professionals who have been disenfranchised and whose work has been delegitimized through our institutional processes. Unfortunately, adjunct labor is often part of what Seth Kahn (2015) in "Towards an Ecology of Sustainable Labor in Writing Programs (and Other Places)" calls a narrative of propaganda in which adjuncts labor for love and are positioned as "morally bankrupt" when they seek fair compensation (110). Like the escalated propaganda labeling our education system writ large a failure during the COVID-19 pandemic while calling teachers to return to their schools in person without vaccines if they truly loved our children, this polemic is trite and sentimental. It is the epitome of deprofessionalization, devaluing the meaningful professional preparation and engagement required for sustained and quality instruction and substituting for it a handful of warm fuzzies and an invitation to dance. We agree with Kahn, who argues that "any conversation about labor equity probably has to contend with propaganda like this story" (110). Like our colleagues in public primary and secondary schools, this is certainly an issue faculty at two-year colleges more broadly—and in two-year college writing studies specifically—will have to contend with in the aftermath of COVID-19, as the great resignation has brought to the forefront of conversations questions about labor equity, intrinsic value, and earned rewards. Most people want a satisfying job with wages and benefits (Cook 2021). This book does not pay enough attention to the crisis of academic labor and how it plays into deprofessionalization. Perhaps that is our or a reader's future work.

It is easy to lose site of the notion that community college education is supposed to uplift communities socially and civically, to focus on the day-to-day work of teaching and research while assuming the system will chug along more or less as it has for a few decades. However, if these last few years have highlighted anything, it is just how fragile our democracy is and how robust our supports for education must be to sustain it. With this in mind, we echo Patrick Sullivan in his chapter as we point to takeaways and applications we might all consider as we develop our own practices, sustain our communities, and advance our discipline.

TAKEAWAYS FROM THIS BOOK

This book begins with Sullivan's chapter, which helps establish why this work is important. Sullivan has long taken the position that the Truman Commission's call for democratic two-year colleges should form the core of our mission. His chapter, in a way, is the ethos underneath the disciplinary and professional practices of two-year college writing studies. It is a distinct and significant profession that has a deep well of disciplinary knowledge and best practices, and it is in service to a vision of equitable democratic education—a more perfect union. Sullivan's optimism is important in sustaining our work in hard times.

The three chapters following Sullivan's demonstrate what is possible in the two-year writing classroom. Bernice Olivas, Emily Suh, and Jamila Kareem point to

- the kinds of curriculum that empower learners,
- the work we must do as identity agents in the classroom, and
- the raciolinguistic work necessary in two-year writing studies.

Taken together, these three chapters point to how we can combat white language supremacy, bring all students into the classroom, and help the students negotiate their interactions with higher education. These are the pedagogical aims of two-year college writing studies, and the goal of these chapters is to serve and champion the linguistic diversity of students while helping them gain powerful literacies that serve their own. Our vision of two-year writing studies is an education in the tradition of bell hooks and Paulo Freire (Freire 2005; Freire and Macedo 2005; hooks 2014). These chapters outline important best practices for two-year colleges—the most diverse colleges in the United States.

The next three chapters of the book lay out schemes for the programmatic and institutional work of two-year college writing studies. Kirsten Higgins, Anthony Warnke, and Jake Frye point out a model for critical and authentic assessment, Grego describes the fostering of a thirdspace to create programmatic and departmental growth, and Joanne Giordano and Holly Hassell point to the perils of neoliberal institutional overreach and just how damaging that model is. Let us be clear, two-year writing studies is a discipline and a profession. It is a discipline because it is a specialized set of academic knowledge, and it is a profession because it enacts that knowledge in a particular institutional space. These chapters make the case that the enactment and strengthening of the profession are vital for doing the social justice and democratic work of two-year colleges.

In the 2018 CCCC chair's address, Carolyn Calhoon-Dillahunt calls for composition scholars and teachers to seize our current moment, to recognize the kairos of this moment in writing studies by returning "to our disciplinary and organizational roots" (274). This collection heeds her call. She encouraged those of us in the field to envision our enterprise widely, "referring to the whole support network around First-Year Writing, which may include developmental coursework, ESL courses, writing centers, and writing programs" (277). The authors in this collection have taken up the work of composition from its epicenter—the students in their classrooms. From there, they have drawn on writing studies scholarship to name those students' writing goals and needs, the language and learning barriers faced, as well as the institutional and structural reforms necessary for us to meet our democratic goals.

The chapters in the book offer a glimmer of what is possible—what is happening around the country with teachers who have each taken on their own professionalization, who have helped professionalize their colleagues and peers through informal and formal avenues (such as TYCA) despite barriers and obstacles. But if these chapters offer hope, they also offer a cautionary tale of what reform-minded efforts, disconnected from embodied and scholarly understanding of our students, our histories, and our disciplinary pedagogies, can do to undermine, immobilize, and destroy the promise of democratic higher education. Specifically, Giordano and Hassel highlight how broad, top-down initiatives—however well meaning they may have begun—can decimate educational access, especially for those of highest need, including rural and urban satellite campuses. They can also silence and ultimately excommunicate educators from policy and reform. With these challenges in mind, we hope the calls from this anthology—improved graduate education and political advocacy from within the family of writing studies disciplines, as well as among and between professionals in writing studies—can hinder or prevent such losses in the future.

To be clear, we are not writing from a sea of despair. We are, in the words of John Lewis, seeking to "be bold, be courageous." Our job is to report from the field—a field of professionals often ignored in their own discipline—to tell the story of our teachers and the dreams of our students, both voices often silenced or tokenized in the very scholarship of activism we seek to uphold through our daily praxis. This volume, which centers community college writing studies, is a rhetorical predication of hope—both against and in response to this backdrop of curdling oppression. It is a manifesto of what is possible, even in the face of pervasive neoliberal rhetorics, an adjunct crisis of manufactured scarcity, teacher exploitation, valorization of credentialism over learning and of instrumentalism over character. All these circumstances have been compounded by a national pandemic and an attached economic reckoning we have yet to comprehend. We must be hopeful because our work—the work of democracy in open-access two-year colleges—holds the potential for democratic and liberatory education. We must be hopeful because it is our charge to bend the stubborn arc that will wear the future moniker of *history*. Education toward a just world may seem out of place in our current politics, naïve even, but it is the point on the horizon at which this book aims.

WHAT'S NEXT FOR COMMUNITY COLLEGES?

As we progress into the third decade of the twenty-first century, much about the assumptions and routines of teaching and learning from the past have been upended by a pandemic—just how much, we do not yet know. A resulting shift to predominantly remote and/or virtual modes of learning and working invite speculation about what instruction will look like at open-access, public two-year colleges in the future. To what extent does remote and virtual access enable and empower access? At what point do the learning curves for new technology and cracks on our digital infrastructure obstruct any advantages offered through access? Meanwhile, the workforce is experiencing a parallel reckoning in which employees in all fields are stopping to ask a question long on their minds—"What's in it for me?"—concerning the conditions of their employment, the reciprocal loyalties of their employers. These reflections have triggered employees to walk away from their jobs in record-breaking numbers in 2021, a harbinger of a reckoning in our economic and employment relationships that may bring permanent changes to our workforce (Thompson 2021). Among the changes this moment, dubbed "The Great Resignation," is likely to foster are shifts to remote work, a responsive shrinkage of the overall physical footprint of corporate offices, and a shift in what and how students prepare to enter the virtual and physical spaces of their intellectual futures and professions (Fox 2021).

Meanwhile, small shifts in the political temperature of our country show that the prospect of free college for all—or at least free community college—remains a popular bartering chip among progressives who, quick to raise the need for policy changes in higher education, are also quick to sacrifice higher education access in negotiations for political gains they hold closer to their chest. In 2021, Michigan joined nineteen other states, including Tennessee, Arkansas, Indiana, Kentucky, Louisiana, Delaware, and Massachusetts, in creating targeted legislation making two-year college tuition free for students with designated criteria (Bisht 2021). And even though these "last-dollar" options frontload economic plans with scholarships and Pell grants, they point to a subtle shifting of the burden of higher education from a private good to a public good—notably even in "red states"—a glimmer of recognition that access to higher education and successful learning experiences with it contribute overall to the well-being of communities. Michigan's legislation, passed in the spring of 2021 and enacted with precarious funding and even more mercurial legislative support, specifically targets "essential workers" who kept the state's economy open during the early months of the pandemic. It is funded through the Futures for Frontliners initiative ("Governor Whitmer" 2020; Associated Press 2021), and it offers incentives for anyone over twenty-five with a GED (and without a college degree) to attend college ("Gov. Whitmer" 2021). With notable limitations in the early enactment, including reduced access for residents living in counties where no community college is present, the legislation shifts the rhetorical framing from one about the merits of free college to the criteria for free college.

Important in the Michigan legislation is a focus on the criteria institutions must demonstrate to qualify for those tuition dollars. Among them are a list of interventions intended to support student success in their gateway math and English courses. These interventions include:

- default placement into college-level courses,
- the use of multiple measures for course placement with a prioritizing of GPA,
- a decentering of computer-based placement, such as Accuplacer, which has maintained preferential status at many colleges across the state,
- implementation of guided self-placement/directed self-placement measures into the placement and appeals process,
- inclusion of K–12 teachers and college faculty on state work forces to develop and expand placement practices and professional development appropriate to enact them.

Further, the legislation and associated documentation of its enactment call for material support and resources for "faculty and staff to design, implement, and continuously improve evidence-based practices" (Michigan Community College Association 2022). This call for resources is among five kinds of material support for faculty specified in the developing documentation from the state of Michigan regarding the development and implementation of the new legislation. And while it remains unclear whose evidence this legislation hails, the central role faculty occupy in the call for professional development and placement practices is promising. What's more, some of the language of the developing documentation seems to echo calls from the TYCA "White Paper on Placement"—specifically deemphasizing computer-based assessment (AWE) and emphasizing performance over time —as well as some from the "White Paper on Developmental Education" (Hassel et al. 2015), including supported collaboration between K–12 teachers and college faculty, ongoing professional development, and the development and implementation of locally responsive measures designed and enacted by faculty.

While these legislative calls do not name the TYCA recommendations and fall, in some places, short of the mark (there is, notably, no direct call for incorporating students' real writing), they do position faculty to design and enact changes in their institutions and emphasize the need for material support for professional development. Left wanting, as well, is specification about how such professional development will be conducted, except to call for the formation of a working group of high-school teachers, college faculty members, staff, and administrators to convene and determine these specifics. But if much is left unsaid, what is clear in the moves in Michigan—and in the nineteen other states—is that the notion of free two-year college has begun moving from the fringe to the center of moderate political conversations—and, to our focus here, English faculty and our colleagues in mathematics will be at the center of those conversations. If we choose to be. If we leverage the knowledge and experience of our scholarly and disciplinary communities to bear meaningfully on these conversations, we may be well positioned to make the kinds of curricula-altering, student-changing policies Warnke, Higgins, and Frye describe in this volume. We may be positioned to make more visible the distinctive and layered identities of learners in our classrooms, to advocate for their space at the table as well as our own, and to expand the kinds of classroom approaches exemplified by Kareem and Olivas in this collection into the cultural interactional norms for our institutions. And we may help stave off terrible and destructive policy decisions, such as those outlined by Giordano and Hassel.

We can be sure community colleges—the oft-advertised prop of social change and labor revisions—will play a role in these conversations. Ultimately, we believe as Mike Rose did, and as Sullivan describes in his chapter in this volume, that the community college has enormous democratic potential—including potential for supporting a pluralistic, diverse citizenry.

However, that potential can only be realized when we position students as agents in rather than recipients of their education, when we recognize our roles in scaffolding their pathways rather than assigning a narrow functionalist path. We must see students as human beings with inherent abilities, tools, and interests to drive their learning, not as mere cogs to insert into the rusted-out engine of late capitalism to keep the United States' economy chugging for one more generation. The challenges are daunting. Rose, in *Back to School* (2012), maintains that "there is a complex web of traditions, turf, and status dynamics, and beliefs about institutional mission, the purpose of education, and the abilities of students" that make community college work especially difficult (12). This complexity is confirmed in this volume. Nonetheless, the distinct and significant profession of two-year college writing studies has much to offer to students and to the democratic potential of community colleges. In response to austerity, authoritarianism, a global pandemic, structural racism and classism, and a narrowing of education, we have no choice but to identify and seize this kairotic moment for our profession, for our students, and for our democratic future. That work continues today, and the next move begins with our readers.

REFERENCES

Alford, Barry, and Keith Kroll, eds. 2003. *The Politics of Writing in the Two-Year College*. Portsmouth, NH: Boynton/Cook.
Associated Press. n.d. "Whitmer: Expand Tuition Aid to 22K More Frontline Workers." US News and World Report. Accessed November 2, 2021. https://www.usnews.com/news/best-states/michigan/articles/2021-06-22/whitmer-expand-tuition-aid-to-22k-more-frontline-workers.
Bisht, Inder Singh. 2021. "Is Community College Free? In These 19 States, Yes." College Post, June 15. https://thecollegepost.com/free-community-college-states/.
Calhoon-Dillahunt, Carolyn. 2018. "2018 CCCC Chair's Address: Returning to Our Roots: Creating the Conditions and Capacity for Change." *College Composition and Communication* 70 (2) 273–93.
Cook, Ian. 2021. "Who Is Driving the Great Resignation?" *Harvard Business Review*, September 15. https://hbr.org/2021/09/who-is-driving-the-great-resignation.
Fox, Michelle. 2021. "The 'Great Resignation' Is Altering the Workforce Dynamic—Maybe for Good." CNBC, November 1. https://www.cnbc.com/2021/11/01/great-resignation-may-be-altering-workforce-dynamic-for-good.html.
Fraser, Nancy. 1990. "Rethinking the Public Sphere: A Contribution to the Critique of Actually Existing Democracy." *Social Text* 25/26: 56–80.
Freire, Paolo. 2005. *Pedagogy of the Oppressed*. 30th ann. ed. New York: Continuum.
Freire, Paulo, and Donaldo Macedo. 2005. *Literacy: Reading the Word and the World*. New York: Routledge.
"Gov. Whitmer Launches Bipartisan $30M Michigan Reconnect Program." 2021. Labor and Economic Opportunity, February 2. https://www.michigan.gov/leo/News/2021/02/02/gov–whitmer-launches-bipartisan-30m-michigan-reconnect-program.
"Governor Whitmer Announces New 'Futures for Frontliners' Initiative." 2020. WLUC. https://www.uppermichiganssource.com/2020/09/11/governor-whitmer-announces-new-futures-for-frontliners-initiative/.
"Gov. Whitmer Launches Bipartisan $30M Michigan Reconnect Program." 2021. Labor and Economic Opportunity, February 2. https://www.michigan.gov/leo/News/2021/02/02/gov–whitmer-launches-bipartisan-30m-michigan-reconnect-program.
Griffiths, Brett M. 2020. "Reinventing the Spiel: The Context and Case for Interinstitutional Collaboration in an Era of Education Austerity." *WPA: Writing Program Administration* 43 (3): 88–106.
Hassel, Holly, and Joanne Baird Giordano. 2013. "Occupy Writing Studies: Rethinking College Composition for the Needs of the Teaching Majority." *College Composition and Communication* 65 (1): 117–39.
Hassel, Holly, Jeff Klausman, Joanne Baird Giordano, Margaret O'Rourke, Leslie Roberts, Patrick Sullivan, and Christie Toth. 2015. "TYCA White Paper on Developmental Education Reforms." *Teaching English in the Two-Year College* 42 (3): 227–43.
hooks, bell. 2014. *Teaching to Transgress*. New York Routledge.
Hurlburt, Steve, and Michael McGarrah. n.d. *The Shifting Academic Workforce: Where Are the Contingent Faculty?* TIAA Institute. https://www.air.org/sites/default/files/downloads/report/Shifting-Academic-Workforce-November-2016.pdf.
Jensen, Darin Lee. 2017. "Tilting at Windmills: Refiguring Graduate Education in English to Prepare Future Two-Year College Professionals." PhD diss., University of Nebraska–Lincoln.

Jensen, Darin L., and Christie Toth. 2017. "Unknown Knowns: The Past, Present, and Future of Graduate Preparation for Two-Year College English Faculty." *College English* 79 (6): 561–92.

Kahn, Seth. 2015. "Towards an Ecology of Sustainable Labor in Writing Programs (and Other Places)." *WPA: Writing Program Administration* 39 (1): 109–21.

Klausman, Jeffrey. 2018. "The Two-Year College Writing Program and Academic Freedom: Labor, Scholarship, and Compassion." *Teaching English in the Two-Year College* 45 (4): 385–405.

Klausman, Jeffrey. 2019. "That's an Ugly Quote: Some Thoughts on Fear, Identity, and Indirect Activism." Teacher-Scholar-Activist, February 27. https://teacher-scholar-activist.org/2019/02/27/thats-an-ugly-quote-some-thoughts-on-fear-identity-and-indirect-activism/.

Lovas, John C. 2002. "All Good Writing Develops at the Edge of Risk." *College Composition and Communication* 54 (1) 264–88.

McNaughtan, Jon, Hugo A. García, and Kim Nehls. 2017. "Understanding the Growth of Contingent Faculty." *New Directions for Institutional Research* 2017 (176): 9–26.

Michigan Community College Association. 2022. "Michigan Developmental Education and Placement Recommendations." Initiatives and Resources. May 15, 2022. https://www.mcca.org/uploads/ckeditor/files/Final%20MI%20Developmental%20Education%20Recommendations6_30_21.pdf.

Reynolds, Mark. 1994. *Two-Year College English: Essays for a New Century*. Urbana, IL: NCTE.

Reynolds, Mark, and Sylvia Holladay-Hicks. 2005. *The Profession of English in the Two-Year College*. Portsmouth, NH: Boynton/Cook.

Rose, Michael. 2012. *Back to School: Why Everyone Deserves a Second Chance at Education*. New York: New Press.

Rose, Mike. 2014. *Why School? Reclaiming Education for All of Us*. New York: New Press.

Soliday, Mary. 2002. *The Politics of Remediation: Institutional and Student Needs in Higher Education*. Pittsburgh: University of Pittsburgh Press.

Suh, Emily, Joanne Baird Giordano, Brett Griffiths, Holly Hassel, and Jeffrey Klausman. 2021. "The Profession of Teaching English in the Two-Year College: Findings from the 2019 TYCA Workload Survey." *Teaching English in the Two-Year College* 48 (3): 332–49.

Suh, Emily, and Darin Jensen. 2020. "Examining Communities of Practice: Transdisciplinarity, Resilience, and Professional Identity." *Journal of Basic Writing* 39 (2): 33–59.

Thompson, Derek. 2021. "The Great Resignation Is Accelerating." *Atlantic*, October 15. https://www.theatlantic.com/ideas/archive/2021/10/great-resignation-accelerating/620382/.

Toth, Christie, and Darin Jensen. 2017. "Responses to the TYCA Guidelines for Preparing Teachers of English in the Two-Year College." *Teaching English in the Two-Year College* 45 (1): 29.

Toth, Christie, and Patrick Sullivan. 2016. "Toward Local Teacher-Scholar Communities of Practice: Findings from a National TYCA Survey." *Teaching English in the Two-Year College* 43 (3): 247.

INDEX

absent present of race in composition studies, 82
academic capital, 66, 68, 70–72
Academic Cultural Language Statement, 93–94
academic identity: community membership, 55–56, 64; critical thinking, 52, 55–56, 132; field/discipline, 54–56; first-generation students, 53; immigrants/refugees, 56, 63, 64, 68–70, 72; LGBTQA+, 52–53; literacy sponsors, 52, 55; negotiation, 73; non-traditional students, 47–48, 55–56; persistence, 71–72; reflection, 52, 55–56; retention rates, 37, 49, 149; role identity, 50, 55–56; self-awareness, 76, 92; Students' Right to Their Own Language (SRTOL), 36, 61, 85–86, 92; support networks, 49; symbolic power, 65; writing projects, 55–58, 59, 74, 75
academic language in the classroom, 91
academic literacy skills, 49
academic transfer paths, 4, 33
accelerated learning programs (ALPs), 109, 149, 150
access to higher education, 13, 16, 27–29, 55, 102, 147, 153, 170
accountability, neoliberal policies, 131–33, 148
accreditation, two-year colleges, 104
Accuplacer, 171
Ackerman, John M., 6
activism, 29, 90, 134
Adams, Peter, 109
adjunct faculty, 15, 32, 33, 166; compensation, 146; lack of institutional support, 35; placement work 146; professional development, 118, 120, 121; two-year colleges, 32, 33; workload, 35, 111, 120
Adler-Kassner, Linda, 98
administrative mandates on two-year college English programs, 147–51
adult English as a Second Language (ESL). *See* English as a Second Language (ESL)

adult immigrant learners. *See* Generation 1 learners; immigrant students; refugee students
advocacy initiatives, Two-Year College Association (TYCA), 156–58
affordability, two-year colleges, 27–28
African American students. *See* Black students
Alford, Barry, 162
Alim, H. Samy, 98
allyship, identity agents, 53
alphabetic modalities, 97
American exceptionalism, 4
Andelora, Jeff, 22, 147
andragogy, 18, 64
antiracism pedagogies: composition studies, 11, 85; first-year writing curriculum, 93–94; linguistic racism, 91; writing assessments, 32, 36, 141–42
anxious mode effect, 132
Anyon, Jean, 14, 15, 33
"Argument as Emergence: Rhetoric as Love," 22–23
Arizona State University, 149
Armour Institute, 13
Asian/Pacific Islander students, 3, 30, 31, 165. *See also* students of color
assessments: access institutions, 103; best practices, 20, 134–35; code switching, 87, 89; critical thinking skills, 59; cross-curricular/cross-disciplinary, 140; curriculum development, 145, 146, 168; data research and scholarship, 19; equity/inequity, 32, 61, 90–91, 136; first-year writing courses, 83; good enough, 130, 133–34, 139; grading equity, 36–37, 136; in-house writing placement tests, 121; institutional resources, 138, 139; literacy narratives, 59; misconceptions about writing, 58–59; multilingual students, 61; outcomes assessment (OA) models, 130–31; rhetorical attunement, 135, 136, 140; scholarship at two-year colleges, 7; socially just, 131; standardized testing, 36, 121, 130, 141; student

INDEX

learning outcomes (SLO), 110, 112–16, 129; Students' Right to Their Own Language (SRTOL), 36, 61, 85–86, 92; translingual, 141–42
audience, student writing, 52–53, 116–17
austerity measures, two-year colleges, 15, 33–35, 151, 153, 154, 172
authoritarianism, 172
autonomy, faculty, 106, 148, 152, 154

Baca, Damián, 95
Back to School, 103, 172
Baker-Bell, April, 36
Balester, Valerie, 89
Baltimore County, Community College, 149
Barrett, Rusty, 97
Bawarshi, Anis, 122
benchmarks. *See* assessments
Berlant, Lauren, 132
best practices, curriculum design, 114, 117, 134–35
Biden, Jill, 12
bildungsroman, 65–66
Biondi, Martha, 29
BIPOC faculty, 9, 166
Black Lives Matter, 90
Black students: academic identity, 81–82; activism, 29, 30; code switching, 91; enrollment, 29–31; life experiences, 90; racial narrative, 89–91; racial violence, 3; rhetorical traditions, 19, 94–95; Students' Right to Their Own Language (SRTOL), 18, 36–37, 83–86, 92. *See also* students of color
Blewett, Kelly, 134
Bloom, Lynn Z., 84
bootcamp writing courses, 116
border rhetorics, 95
Bourdieu, Pierre, 18, 63, 64, 65, 69, 74
Brandt, Deborah, 17, 52
Bridges Writing Program, 108–9
Bridging Lab (B-Lab), 70–72
budgets, writing courses, 7, 104, 154, 156
Burke, Peter, 49, 50
burnout, faculty, 16, 164
Bush, George W., 12
Buzzard, Ashley, 122

Calhoon-Dillahunt, Carolyn, 157, 168
call-and-response, 94
campus mergers/closures, 151, 152, 153
Canagarajah, A. Suresh, 80, 85, 92
Cardona, Miguel, 38
cause/effect, educational reforms, 165
CCCC. *See* Conference on College Composition and Communication

Center for American Progress, 39
certification, professional, 14–15
Chandler, Sally, 109
changes in the purpose of higher education, 55
changing racial narratives, 81, 82, 83, 84, 85, 97
Chicanx-identifying students, 95–96. *See also* Latinx students; students of color
circumstantial barriers for students, 17, 37
civil rights movement in higher education, 29
Clark, Burton R., 14
classism in higher education, 4, 5, 9, 12, 13, 16, 27–28, 33–34, 84–85, 172
classroom design. *See* curriculum design
classroom experience for students, 17, 55–56, 71, 74, 76, 87, 92–93
closures of campuses, austerity measures, 151, 152
code meshing, 95
code switching, 87, 89, 91
codex rhetorics, 95
Cogan, John Aloysius, 131
collaborative learning, 51, 107
collective bargaining, 153, 156
collective identity, 50
college-completion rate initiatives, 37, 149
College Redesign movement, 15
college-student identity. *See* academic identity
college success, symbolic capital, 63–64
color, students of, 61
communication literacy, 117
community colleges. *See* two-year colleges
community identity, 13, 14, 55–56, 64, 72, 82
compensation policies for faculty, 146
composition studies: absent present of race, 82; academic identity, 49, 55–56, 98; antiracism pedagogies, 11, 19, 85, 93–94; audience, 52–53; critical race theory (CRT), 18, 61, 91–92, 98, 133–34; current-traditional (CTR), 103; Eurocentric, 19, 97; faculty, 32, 33, 113, 163; graduate students, 6–9; history, 81–82; linguistic hierarchy, 18, 36, 80, 83–85; origins, 16; peer-reviewed scholarship, 6; reading instructors, 150; rhetorical analysis, 57; structural inequities, 37, 48–49, 136; students of color, 8, 19; teacher-scholar-activist paradigm, 147; teaching practices, 163; two-year colleges, 162; value, 10–11; writing assignments, 56, 58–59. *See also* first-year composition (FYC)

Conference on College Composition and Communication (CCCC): Statement on Second Language Writing and Multilingual Writers (SOSL), 88–89, 90; Students' Right to Their Own Language (SRTOL), 61, 85–86, 92; Studio+ Special Interest Group, 109; Two-Year English Association, 22
conferences for faculty professional development, 6, 11, 105, 117
Connecticut State College and University system, 151
connections between curriculum development and professional development, 115
context, student writing assignments, 117
contingent writing instructors, 8
continuing-generation students, 37, 49, 149
controlled experiment approach, 107
Corder, Jim, 22–23, 102
cost. *See* tuition
counternarratives, 162–63
course committees, student learning outcomes (SLOs), 113–16
course design. *See* curriculum design
course placement, 171
course releases, 113
COVID-19, 3, 124
Cox, Michelle, 76
creative thinking skills, 51
credentialing, 4
credit-bearing first-year writing, 149
critical consciousness (conscientização), 58
critical language awareness, 36–37
critical pedagogy, 57–58
critical race English education (CREE), 82, 133–34
critical race theory (CRT): assessments, 133–34, 141; composition studies, 91–92; first-year writing, 98; linguistic hierarchy, 18, 80, 81, 133–34; racial narratives, 18, 81, 84; social factors, 18, 80; Students' Right to Their Own Language (SRTOL), 86–87, 92; writing studies, 18, 61, 80, 91–92
critical reform, 103, 135
critical thinking skills, 4, 51, 52, 55–57, 59, 132
cross-curricular/cross-disciplinary assessment, 140
cultural arbitraries, 69, 71
cultural capital, 75
Culturally Dominant English, 93
CUNY Accelerated Study in Associate Programs (ASAP), 37

current-traditional rhetoric (CTR), 103
curriculum design: autonomy, 152; bootcamp writing courses, 116; cafeteria model, 151; connection with professional development, 115; critical language awareness, 36–37; critical race English education (CREE), 82, 133–34; diversity, 32; Eurocentric ideologies, 92, 95, 97; evidence-based practices, 171; first-year composition, 110–11, 117; identity-conscious framework, 17, 48–49, 55–56; multicultural rhetorical traditions, 91–93, 94–96; open-admissions policies, 145; performance measures, 114, 115, 116; raciolinguistics, 36–37, 82–83; research and scholarship, 48; Statement on Second Language Writing and Multilingual Writers (SOSL), 88–89, 90; student learning outcomes (SLO), 110–14; student retention, 37, 48, 149, 167; translingual theory, 138; writing instructors, 19; writing programs, 146
Cushman, Ellen, 136, 142

D2L teacher resource sites, 115
data collection, research, 67, 114
Davis, Jeff, 48, 49
decision-making power, faculty, 154
decontextual writing, 97, 133
deficit models of education, 17, 20, 130, 131, 132
defunding/funding of two-year colleges, 33, 146–47, 153
degree-credit coursework, transition from developmental education, 145
democratic ideal of higher education, 16, 28–30, 32, 34, 37, 38, 172–73
demographics of faculty, 54–55, 165–66
departmental cultures, 105–6
descriptions, faculty positions, 103
devalue, two-year college writing instructors, 10–11
development of academic identity, 50, 55–56
developmental education: acceleration, 149; coursework, 65, 103, 156, 168; elimination/reduction, 149–50, 155; faculty, 33, 35, 62; Generation 1 learners, 67, 69, 71, 75; graduate programs, 8; placement methods, 145; reform, 157
deviation from main topic, 95
dialect switching, 87, 89
dialogue, identity agents, 53
difference-centered ideological approaches, 84–85

disabilities, students with, 4, 8, 27, 130
disciplinary identity, 5–6, 102
disciplinary knowledge, 7, 10
discourse features, 94
discussion, critical pedagogy, 56–58
disenfranchisement, 4, 33
disengagement, faculty development, 164–65
disruption assessment disposition, 135
diversity initiatives: curriculum design, 32, 172; faculty, 30–32, 141; raciolinguistic, 61, 98; responsiveness, 134; students, 7, 8, 86, 92, 148
domestic violence, 8, 12
dominant social group, linguistic hierarchy, 18, 36, 81, 82, 83, 84, 85, 97
Dubson, Michael, 121

education: access, 14, 27; efficiency, 12; neoliberal policies, 103; reform initiatives, 4, 104, 149, 165; research and scholarship, 107; resources, 69
elaborative structure writing, 95
elimination of college coursework, 149, 150, 152, 155
elitism in higher education, 27–28
Elliot, Norbert, 131, 133, 134, 140
emergence of university systems, 55
emotional distance writing, 97
emotional labor of faculty, 34–35, 121, 155, 156
English as a Second Language (ESL): elimination of available courses, 155; evidence-based practices, 146; language learners support, 66–67; life experiences, 64; transition to college credit courses, 62–63
English departments: administrative/legislative mandates, 55, 147, 148, 149, 151, 170–71; curriculum design, 82, 117; diversity, increasing, 31–32; emotional labor, 34–35; faculty of color, 90; institutional resources, 125; programmatic listening, 136–37; research and scholarship, 163; rhetoric assignments, 117; standardization of racist ideologies, 18, 80, 85; workload, 155–56
English-dominant second-generation students, 66
enrollment rates, students, 15–16, 29, 66, 154
equity initiatives: affordability of college, 27–28, 38, 90–91, 136; grading, 32, 36–37, 136; graduate programs, 9, 32, 38, 90–91, 136; higher education, 37, 38, 90–91, 136, 146; pedagogy, 12, 32,

38, 90–91, 136; social uplift, 14, 32, 34, 38, 90–91, 136; teaching ideologies, 9, 32, 38, 90–91, 136; Truman Commission Report, 27–29, 167; writing assessments, 20, 90–91, 131, 133
ESL. *See* English as a Second Language (ESL)
ethical responsibilities, 14
ethnic identity, 47–48, 55–56
ethnographic case study, 62
ethnolinguistic idioms, 94
ethos, 52–53
Eurocentric American rhetorical traditions, 19, 92, 94, 95, 97
evidence-based practices, curriculum design, 19, 146, 171
explicit raciolinguistic instruction, 19

faculty: adjunct, 15, 32, 33, 166; BIPOC, 30–31, 81–82, 141, 165–66; compensation policies, 146; curriculum design, 151; decision-making power, 106, 152, 154–55; departmental cultures, 105–6; emotional labor, 34–35; first-generation students, 33, 38, 48, 149; first-year composition, 111; fossilization, 164; full-time, 125; governance, 55, 104, 170–71; identity agents, 32, 33, 51, 55–56, 63, 64, 67, 73–74; information-sharing discussions, 105; interactional inquiry, 113; isolation, 103; labor equity, 167; lack of institutional support, 35; metadiscourse, 110; non-tenured, 33; recruitment, 31–32; recognition, 163; teacher-scholar-activist, 35; transfer of knowledge, 63; values-driven change, 75–76; workload issues, 33, 35, 111, 119, 123, 146, 164–65; writing studio programs, 113
faculty development, 115; disengagement, 164–65; funding, 171; impact on student learning, 118–20; mentoring, 35, 146; professional organizations, 20, 106, 112, 123; support networks, 108, 121
Fain, Paul, 152
fast-track writing courses, 116
female students, 27
feminist standpoint theory, 106, 108
fiction/nonfiction in writing studies, 112, 115, 122
field/discipline, 54–56
first-generation students, 8; academic identity, 53; graduate students, 9; identity control theory (ITC), 50–51; learning needs, 17–18; literacy skills, 49; representation, 4; retention rates,

37, 38, 48, 149; self-perception, 49, 92; writing assessments, 130
first-year composition (FYC): classism, 84–85; credit-bearing, 149; curriculum design, 110–11; difference-centered ideological approaches, 84–85; emotional labor, 121; fiction/nonfiction, 112; grading assessments, 83; implicit whiteness rhetoric, 84–85; lack of student support, 38, 84; language-diversity ideologies, 17, 18, 80; persuasive writing, 97; professional development for faculty, 121; raciolinguistic diversity, 98; student interaction, 108; support networks, 168. *See also* composition studies
5/5 teaching workload, 35–36, 110, 119, 120
Flores, Nelson, 92
fossilization, professional identities, 164
Fought, Carmen, 83, 84, 98
4/4 teaching workload, 36, 38
four-year colleges: administrative structures, 7–8; autonomy, 148; English studies, 20; spending per student, 153–54; tenure-track positions, 123; transfer from two-year colleges, 14, 33
Fraser, Nancy, 162–63
Freire, Paolo, 17, 56, 57, 58, 168
Frye, Jake, 20, 21, 168, 172
full-time faculty, 33, 38, 110, 111, 118, 125
Fund for the Improvement of Post-Secondary Education (FIPSE), 108
funding for higher education, 10, 33, 39, 110, 151–54, 171
Futures for Frontliners, 170–71

Gallagher, Chris, 130
gender identity construct, 52
Generation 1 learners: academic identity, 55–56, 63, 66, 68–70; class placement, 67; cultural capital, 75; developmental English courses, 67; social capital, 68; symbolic capital, 62–65, 67, 69, 75; symbolic power, 73; transfer of knowledge, 63. *See also* immigrant students; refugee students
Generation 1.5 students, 66
generational identity, 47–48, 55–56
Giffen, Robyn, 95
Gilyard, Keith, 94
Giordano, Joanne Baird, 21, 22, 33, 38, 103, 109, 122, 168, 169, 172
Gonçalves, Zan Meyer, 52
good-enough assessment practices, 129, 130, 133–34, 139
grading practices, 32, 36–37, 83, 136

graduate studies, 80, 85; equity initiatives, 9, 32, 38, 90–91, 136; resistance to two-year colleges, 7–9; seminars, 108
graduation rates initiatives, 5, 37, 148–49, 152
Graves, Jessica, 122
"The Great Resignation," 167, 170
Grego, Rhonda C., 19–20, 107, 149, 166, 168
Griffiths, Brett, 32–34, 103, 104, 106, 157
Guided Pathways Model, 123–24, 151

habits of persisting, 75
Hairston, Maxine, 84
Hall, Jonathan, 137
Halliday-Hicks, Sally, 162
Harrell-Levy, Marinda K., 51, 56
Harrington, Susanmarie, 140
Hassel, Holly, 21, 22, 33, 38, 103, 109, 168, 169, 172
Hausser, Amy, 122
HBCUs (Historically Black Colleges and Universities), 29, 38
Heinert, Jennifer, 103
hidden curriculum, 15
Higginbotham, Keith, 122
Higgins, Kirsten, 20, 21, 103, 104, 157, 168, 172
Higher Education for American Democracy (1947), 27–29
higher education: accessibility, 13, 16, 27–29, 55, 147; civil rights movement, 29; classism, 13, 16, 27–28, 33–34, 85; defunding, 146–47, 153; democratic ideal, 32, 34, 172–73; dominant social groups, 81, 82, 83, 84, 85, 97; education reform, 104; elitism, 27–28; equity, 37, 38, 90–91, 136, 146; non-traditional students, 29, 47; purpose, 55; racism, 13, 16, 18, 27–28, 80, 85; religious discrimination, 27; rural campuses, 150; space, 102
Hispanic students, 29, 38, 95–96. *See also* Latinx students
Historically Black Colleges and Universities (HBCUs), 29, 38
history and mission: two-year colleges, 29, 34, 102, 134
home languages, non-white students, 83–84, 89
hooks, bell, 168
hybrid teaching, 3
hyperindividualist writing, 97

identity agents: allyship, 53; classroom interaction, 55–57, 98, 167, 172; dialogue, 53; faculty, 17, 19, 47, 51,

64; judgments/observations, 53; LGBTQA+, 52; literacy sponsors, 52; positive reinforcement, 50, 55–56; reflective method of research, 51; rhetorical analysis, 57; self-reflection, 53, 55–56; student demographics, 54–55; teaching practices, 51, 74–76
identity-conscious frameworks, 17, 48–49, 55–56
identity control theory (ICT), 17, 49, 50–51
identity development: academic, 47, 50, 55–56; community membership, 55–56, 64; Generation 1 students, 55–56, 63, 68; investment theory, 64; performance, 52–53; self-awareness, 53, 55–57, 92; student negotiation, 73–74; Students' Right to Their Own Language (SRTOL), 36, 61, 85–86, 92; symbolic power, 65
identity-neutral frameworks, 47–48
image making, 94
immigrant students: academic capital, 68–69; cultural arbitraries, 69, 71; educational resources, 69; non-traditional students, 61; second-language writing, 88; social capital, 68–70; symbolic capital, 65, 74; visa programs, 68; writing assessments, 129. *See also* Generation 1 learners; refugee students
implicit whiteness rhetoric, 84–85
inclusion in higher education, 11–12, 74, 134, 146
income gaps, 14–15
Indigenous American rhetorical traditions, 81–82, 94, 96
inequalities in higher education, 31, 33–34, 37, 75–76, 90–91, 130, 136
information literacy, 111, 113, 114, 117, 121
information-sharing discussion, 105
Inoue, Asao, 9, 133, 140, 142
institutional knowledge, 50
institutional thinking: assessment accountability, 131–32, 138, 139; classism, 12, 13, 16, 33–34, 85; faculty, 35, 73, 102, 104, 105, 125; interactional inquiry, 123; mission, 29, 34, 134, 146, 172; objectives, 129; values-driven change, 75–76
instructors. *See* faculty
integrated reading and writing (IRW) program, 149–50
intentionality, identity agents, 51
interactional inquiry, 67, 108, 115, 113, 123
investment theory, 18, 64, 72–73
Iredell, Nancy J., 87–88
isolation, faculty, 103

Jensen, Darin, 6, 32–34, 103
Johnson, Lamar L., 82, 90
Joliet Junior College, 13
jubilee/tragic undertone, 94
judgments/observations, identity agents, 53
just-teaching mythology, 6–7

K-12 instructors, 7–8
Kahlenberg, Richard, 38
Kahn, Seth, 166–67
Kareem, Jamila, 17, 18, 19, 167, 172
Kei Matsuda, Paul, 97, 98
Kendi, Ibram X., 29
Kerpelman, Jennifer L., 51, 56
Kezar, Adrianna, 32–33
Kinloch, Valerie, 85
Knowles, Malcolm, 18, 64
Kroll, Keith, 162
Kynard, Carmen, 29, 85

labels, disciplinary identities, 102
labor equity, 167
language-learning experiences, 18, 55–56, 64, 68–69, 80, 137
Larson, Holly, 106
Latinx faculty, 81–82
Latinx students, 19, 29, 30, 31, 36, 55, 83, 85–86, 92, 94–96. *See also* students of color
LaVecchia, Christina M., 134
Layton, Marilyn Smith, 16
learning development, 4, 5, 17–18, 146, 132, 172
Lederman, Doug, 142
Lederman, Josh, 133
legislative mandates, two-year colleges, 55, 147, 148, 149, 151, 170–71
Leonard, Rebecca Lorimer, 136, 138
Lewis, John, 169
LGBTQA+ students, 31, 52–53
liberal arts programs, 152
Liewecki-Wilson, Cynthia, 109
life experiences: Black students, 90; English as a Second Language (ESL), 64; immigrants, 66–69; instructors' perceptions, 73; middle-class students, 58; refugee students, 70, 72; students, 15, 18, 55, 57, 62–63, 74; writing topics, 59. *See also* social capital
limitations, outcomes assessment (OA) model, 131, 133
limited teaching resources, 148
linear argument structure, 97
linguistic diversity: African American students, 36–37, 83–84, 90, 91; criti-

cal race theory (CRT), 18, 81, 133–34; dominant social groups, 18, 36, 80, 81, 82, 83, 84, 85, 97; raciolinguistic social systems, 61, 83, 84–85; Students' Right to Their Own Language (SRTOL), 86, 92; white-dominated spaces, 83–84, 89
Lippi-Green, Rosina, 97
literacy development, 51, 52, 146
literacy narratives, 18, 59, 80, 85, 90, 97
Looker-Koenig, Samantha, 98
Lovas, John, 5, 163
Love, Bettina L., 36
low-income students, 38, 57–58, 130

Macedo, Donaldo, 56, 57
mainstream discourses: African American faculty, 81–82; dominant social groups, 81–84, 97; Indigenous faculty, 81–82; Latinx faculty, 81–82
marginalized literacy narratives, 58, 82, 85
Massey, Doreen, 106
Maxey, Daniel, 32–33
McCarter, Jon, 122
McGuire, Saundra, 121
McIntosh, Peggy, 54
McKay, Sandra Lee, 73
memberships in professional organizations, 10
mental health issues: students, 124
mentoring programs for professional development, 35, 146
mergers/closures: campuses, 145, 151, 152, 153
metacognition, 121
Miami University-Middletown, 109
Micciche, Laura R., 134
Michigan, two-year colleges, 170–72
middle-class students, 57–58, 84–85
mimicking, 53, 94
minority-serving institutions (MSIs), 38
misrecognition, student identity negotiations, 73–74
mission and purpose of two-year colleges, 13, 14, 29, 34, 134, 153
modeling, 53
Morris, Janine, 134
motivation for identity development, 55–56, 64
multicultural curriculum design, 48, 88–89, 91–93
multilanguage writing, 32, 61, 88–90, 92–94, 136
multiple-measures placement, 150
Murphy, Madeline, 132–33
Myers Zawacki, Terry, 97

narrativizing, 94
national advocacy initiatives, Two-Year College English Association (TYCA), 156–58
National Center for Education Statistics, 66
national conferences attendance, 6, 10, 11
National Council of Teachers of English (NCTE):1999 position statement, 86, 111, 119
Native American students, 30, 31, 36, 85–86, 92, 94, 96. *See also* students of color
Naynaha, Siskanna, 83
negotiation, academic identity, 73–74
Nelson, Julie, 116, 122
neoliberal policies, two-year colleges, 10, 13–15, 20, 33–34, 103, 132–33, 141
No Frills annual meeting, 105
non-CDE (Culturally Dominant English) students, 71, 87, 92–93
non-degree-credit coursework, 149, 150
nonfiction/fiction, 112, 115, 122
non-tenured faculty, 33
non-traditional students, 12, 29, 47–48, 61
non-white students, home languages, 83–84, 89
Norton, Bonny, 18, 64
Nurudeen, Tito G., 131

Obama, Barack, 12–13
Okajian, Mark, 151
Olivas, Bernice, 17, 18, 19, 63, 167, 172
Olivieri, Mary Olena, 142
open-admissions policies, 29–30, 32, 34, 37, 38, 145, 172–73
opportunity gaps, students of color, 14–15, 31
organization, writing studio programs, 125
other Englishes, 82
outcomes assessment (OA) model, 110, 112–16, 131–33
outsider status, 58

pandemic, 124–25, 172
Parsons, Jerry, 87–88
participation norms, 75
participatory inquiry, 108
part-time faculty. *See* adjunct faculty
pedagogical equity, 11, 12, 32, 85, 90–91, 136
peer colleagues, 6, 9, 10
Peirce, Bonny, 138
Pendakur, Vijay, 47–48
Penrose, Ann M., 49
performance measures, 113–16, 118

performance-based funding, 151, 152
Perryman-Clark, Staci, 83–85
persistence, students, 73
personal identity, 50, 51, 59, 65–66
persuasive writing, 97
Phelps, Louise Wetherbee, 6
Phillips, Cassandra, 103
placement tests, 36, 67, 121, 140–41, 145, 146, 149, 150, 171
Poe, Mya, 131, 133, 134, 140, 142
political context, writing instruction, 17
positionality in research and scholarship, 17, 67, 73
positive reinforcement, identity agents, 50, 55–56
prejudices, raciolinguistic marginalized students, 87–88
Prendergast, Catherine, 82
preparation, teaching, 102
proactivity, student learning, 172
professional activism, 146, 147
professional development, 112, 115. adjunct faculty, 120, 146; best practices, 114, 117; conferences, 10, 11; course committees, 114; curriculum design, 115; engagement, 164; first-year writing, 121; impact on student learning, 118–20; information literacy, 121; interactional inquiry, 123; mentoring programs, 146; organizations, 10, 20, 106, 123; publications, 19–20, 106, 123; support networks, 108, 122; two-year colleges, 10, 14; workgroups, 171–72
professionalization, 6–10, 164
program assessment practices. *See* assessments
programmatic listening, 136–37
publications, 19–20, 106, 123
purpose of higher education, 16, 29, 55, 117, 172

quantitative research, 49
queer students, 31, 52–53

racialized austerity, 33, 34
raciolinguistic writing: composition studies, 19, 82; critical race theory (CRT), 18, 81, 84; dominant social groups, 83, 84, 85, 97; identity, 47–48, 55–56; invisibility, 82; linguistic diversity, 61, 83, 84–85; marginalization, 36–37, 61, 83–85, 87–88; multiculturalism, 89, 92–93; positive teaching practices, 92–93; rhetorical traditions, 83, 94–96; self-image, 19, 85–86, 92; teaching solutions, 86; transformation, 87; writing studies, 18, 19, 36–37, 80–83, 85, 98, 167
racism: college institutions, 4, 5, 13, 16, 85; higher education, 13, 16, 27–28, 85; institutionalized, 12, 13, 16, 85; linguistic, 90, 91; research and scholarship, 9, 85, 172; systemic, 5; violence, 3, 90
Randall, Jennifer, 142
rates of student retention, 31, 33, 37, 149
reaccreditation, 110, 113, 115
reading-intensive writing courses, 56–58, 150
Reason, Peter, 106
recognition of faculty at two-year colleges, 163
reflection, academic identity, 51, 52, 55–58
reform. *See* education
refugee students: community identity, 72; second-language writing, 66, 88; symbolic capital, 70, 71, 72; trauma narrative, 72; writing assessments, 129. *See also* Generation 1 learners; immigrant students
regional conferences, 6
Reiff, Mary Jo, 122
relationality writing, 96
religious discrimination in higher education, 27
remote learning, 3, 169–70
research and scholarship: Black Language, 90; classism, 4, 5, 9, 85; classroom design, 48; code switching, 87, 89; collaborative research methods, 107; continuing-generation students, 49; controlled experiment approach, 107; critical race English education (CREE), 82; critical race theory (CRT), 18, 80, 133–34; data collection, 19, 67; disciplinary identity, 6; English departments, 163; English-language learners, 66; equity initiatives, 9, 38, 90–91, 136; ethnographic case study, 62; evidence-based storytelling, 19; feminist research, 108; first-generation students, 49; Generation 1 learners, 67; graduate seminars, 108; immigrants, 74; interactional/participatory inquiry, 108; positionality, 67, 73; racism, 4, 5, 9, 85; research/teaching binary, 9; second-language acquisition, 63–64; social justice, 133, 136; Students' Rights to Their Own Language (SRTOL), 87–89, 90, 92; two-year colleges, 6, 11–12, 35, 103; writing studies, 6, 7; writing-pedagogy research methodologies, 80

responsesiveness to diverse communities, 134
restructure of Wisconsin Colleges, University of, 152–53
retention rate initiatives, 33, 37, 47–48, 55–56, 103, 148–49, 152
Reynolds, Mark, 162
rhetoric and composition studies. *See* composition studies
rhetorical attunement assessment disposition, 135, 136, 140
rhetorical traditions, multicultural, 94–96
Richardson, Elaine, 94
role identity, 50, 51, 55–56
Roozen, Kevin, 98
Rosa, Jonathan, 92
Rose, Mike, 9, 16, 47, 63, 103, 172
Rowan, John, 106
Royster, Jacqueline Jones, 9
rubrics, first-year writing courses, 83
Rumbaut, Rubén, 66
rural students, 4, 150

SACS reaccreditation, 110, 113, 115
Sarfatti Larson, Magali, 7
Schacter, Elli P., 51
scholarship. *See* research and scholarship
Scott, Tony, 98
second-chance institutions, 103
second-language learning, 63–64, 71, 88–89, 90
secondspaces, 113, 124
self-awareness/self-image, students, 18, 19, 49, 53–56, 61, 76, 85–86, 92
self-determination, faculty, 152
self-placement, 171
Shapiro, Shawna, 65, 76
Shaughnessy, 16
Shuck, Gail, 76
signifyin', 94
Simnitt, Emily, 76
6/6 workload, 119
Slaughter, Joseph, 65–66
SLO. *See* student learning outcomes (SLO)
Slomp, David, 142
small-group writing studio sessions, 109
social assessment, 140
social capital, 18, 50, 68–70
social factors, critical race theory (CRT), 17, 18, 80
social identity, 50, 138
social justice teaching practices, 16, 29, 38, 88, 93–94, 131, 133, 136, 139, 140
social-rhetorical linguistic students, 61, 83
Soja, Edward, 106

Solórzano, Daniel, 141
Sommers, Nancy, 16
SOSL. *See* Statement on Second Language Writing and Multilingual Writers
space, writing studio programs, 102, 106–7
spending per student, 153–54
SPUJJ Collective, 106
SRTOL (Students' Right to Their Own Language), 36–37, 61, 85–88, 90, 92, 93
Standard Written English (SWE), 36, 91, 93
standardized testing, 121, 130, 141
state funding. *See* funding for higher education
state legislatures, 55, 104, 170–71
Statement on Second Language Writing and Multilingual Writers (SOSL), 88–89, 93
Stewart, Mary K., 142
storying, 96
structural inequalities, 9, 17, 31, 33–34, 37, 48–49, 56, 85, 136, 172
student writing: accelerated learning programs (ALPs), 109, 150; accountability, 131–32; assessment, 129; best practices, 134–35; creative thinking skills, 51; critical race theory (CRT), 133–34; critical thinking skills, 51, 132; first-year writing, 83, 84, 108; good-enough assessments, 133–34; grading equity, 36–37, 133, 134, 136; in-house writing placement tests, 121; institutional objectives, 129; literacy development, 146; performance measures, 118; rhetorical analysis, 57; self-image, 85–86, 92; Standard Written English (SWE), 36; socially just, 131; student learning outcomes (SLO), 110, 112–16, 118, 120; support, 38, 107, 133, 149; thirdspace experiences, 125; traditional constructs, 133; writing assignments, 117
student/teacher ratio, 119, 121
student-centered classrooms, 56–57
student-faculty interactions, 67
students: academic identity, 4, 17, 47–48, 50, 51, 53, 55–56, 74, 75; activism, 29; circumstantial barriers, 17, 37; community engagement, 14, 55, 56; culture, 55, 71, 75; diversity, 7, 8, 30, 31, 54–55, 83–84, 102, 137, 148; educational goals, 14; enrollment, 154; faculty-student interactions, 32; generational history, 49; identity agents, 55–56, 172; language backgrounds, 137; learning development, 146; linguistic diversity, 36–37, 61; marginalization, 4, 8, 36–38,

61, 82, 83, 84–85; mental health issues, 124; participation norms, 75; personal development, 65–66; retention rate initiatives, 3, 33, 37, 47–49, 103, 149; self-awareness/self-image, 18, 19, 53, 55–56, 61, 76, 92; social capital, 18, 50, 138; support networks, 16–18, 37, 38, 52, 73, 108–9, 155, 171; symbolic capital, 15, 18, 55, 57, 62–64, 73, 74, 125; traits, 54
students of color, 38; community identities, 55–56, 82; opportunity gaps, 31, 37; retention rates, 31, 33, 37, 149; self-image, 92; space, 102; support programming, 38, 149; transformative pedagogy, 57–58; writing assessments, 130, 131. *See also* Asian/Pacific Islander students; Black students; Latinx students; Native American students
Students' Right to Their Own Language (SRTOL), 36–37, 61, 85–88, 90, 92, 93
subtlety of language, 95
Suh, Emily K., 17, 18, 19, 167
Sullivan, Patrick, 14, 15, 16, 18, 63, 102, 103, 108, 111, 121, 122, 147, 157, 167, 172
support networks: accelerated learning programs (ALPs), 109, 150; adult English-language learners, 66; elimination, 155; first-year writing, 168; language-learning students, 69; professional development of faculty, 122; students, 16, 35, 37, 38, 52, 107–9, 149, 171; thirdspace, 107; two-year colleges, 70; writing studio programs, 150
survivance, 96
Sutton, Mark, 109
symbolic capital, 62–65, 67, 69–71, 74, 75
symbolic power, 64, 65, 73, 75–76
systemic rubrics, 83

Tassoni, John-Paul, 109
TCYA. *See* Two-Year College English Association (TYCA)
teacher/student ratio, 119, 121
teacher-scholar-activist, 156; accountability, 148; counternarratives, 162–63; disconnect, 164; inclusion, 11–12, 134; professional activism, 146, 147; writing instructors, 6–7
Teaching Composition at the Two-College, 102–3
teaching practices: accountability, 131–32; best practices, 117; bootcamp writing courses, 116; compassion, 51; contingent labor, 8; critical race theory (CRT), 18, 80, 133–34; curricular identity, 18, 19; deficit thinking, 17, 131, 132;

demographics, 30, 31; developmental education, 155; disciplinary identity, 6; equity initiatives, 9, 32, 38, 90–91, 136; faculty recruitment, 31–32; fast-track courses, 116; identity agents, 17, 47, 49, 51, 55–56, 74–76; language-diversity ideologies, 18, 80; political context, 17; preparation, 102, 104; professional identity, 9–10, 19, 123, 164; raciolinguistic positivity, 92–93; reading-intensive, 150; research participation, 9; rhetorical attunement, 136, 140; social context, 17, 139; student learning impact, 35, 73; sustainability, 163; symbolic capital, 74; teacher-scholar-activists, 6–7; teaching experience, 7–8; virtual teaching, 124; workload, 38, 110, 111, 146
tenure policies, 10, 123, 153, 156
testifying, 94
Thaiss, Chris, 97
The Politics of Writing in the Two-Year College, 162
The Profession of English in the Two-Year College, 162
thirdspaces, 19, 106, 108, 110, 125
"This Ain't Another Statement! This Is a DEMAND for Black Linguistic Justice," 93
Thompson, Nancy S., 106, 107, 108, 149
threshold concepts, 98
Tinberg, Howard, 121
Tinto, Vincent, 37, 48
tonal semantics/repetition, 94
Toth, Christine, 102, 103, 105–6, 108, 111, 122, 157
traditional assessment construct, 133
traits, students, 54
transfer of knowledge, 63
transfer to four-year colleges, 13, 14, 33
transformative pedagogy, 56–58, 87
transition, English as a Second Language (ESL) students to college credit courses, 62–63
translingual theory, 36, 134, 138, 141–42
trauma narrative, 72
travel funding for professional development, 10
tribal colleges, 38
TRiO programs, 48
Truman Commission Report (1947), 13, 15, 16, 27–29, 167
Trump, Donald, 13
tuition-free two-year colleges, 153, 170–72
Two-Year College English, 162
Two-Year College English Association (TYCA): advocacy initiatives, 156–58;

demographics, 165–66; professionalization, 9–11; recommendations, 171–72; surveys, 30, 32, 34–35
two-year colleges: access, 29, 102, 153, 170; accreditation, 104; administrative structures, 7–8, 104, 146, 148, 151, 152; admissions policies, 29–30, 32, 34, 37, 38; campus mergers/closures, 151, 153; community engagement, 14, 55, 56; diversity initiatives, 7, 102, 134, 148, 172; educational policies, 4, 7, 12, 146; enrollment/retention, 5, 15–16, 29, 31, 33, 37, 103, 148–49; faculty, 30, 31, 32, 33, 102, 104, 125, 154; funding/defunding, 7, 10, 13, 20, 33, 35, 39, 104, 110, 151, 153, 154; history and mission, 13–16, 28, 29, 34, 102, 103, 134, 146; institutionalized thinking, 105; professionalization, 6–7, 9; remote learning, 169–70; research and scholarship, 6, 11–12, 35; retention programs, 37, 47–48; rural/urban students, 4; SACS reaccreditation, 110, 113, 115; social justice, 16, 29, 38, 136; stereotypes, 103; student demographics, 30, 31; support centers, 70; systemic barriers, 105–6; tenure, 10; tuition, 13, 27–28, 153–54, 170–72
TYCA. *See* Two-Year College English Association (TYCA)

underemployment, 14
universal higher education, 16, 28–29
university systems, 55
unmarginalization 11, 85
urban students, 4, 58

value of two-year colleges, 103, 146
values-driven change, 75–76
Ventura, Jonathan J., 51
veterans, 8
Villanueva, Victor, 98
virtual teaching, 124

visa programs, 68
visual rhetoric, 95, 96

Walker, Scott, 146
Wardle, Elizabeth, 98
Warnke, Anthony, 20, 21, 103, 104, 157, 168, 172
Warwick, Nicole, 133
Washington, D.C., 3, 4
West, Andrea, 122
white linguistic supremacy, 83–85, 89, 91, 97
white students, 30, 31
wi-fi access, 4
Wilson-Nelson, Marie, 108
Wisconsin System, University of, 4, 21, 109, 145–47, 150, 152–56
Wong, Sau-Ling Cynthia, 73
workforce development, 5, 170
working-class students, 15, 57–58
workload, faculty, 33–36, 38, 110, 111, 118–21, 146, 155–56, 164–65
workplace readiness, 12
workshops for faculty professional development, 114
World War II, 28
writing assessments. *See* assessments
writing instructors. *See* teaching practices
writing studies. *See* composition studies
writing studios: accelerated learning programs (ALPs), 109, 149, 150; creating, 19; faculty support, 113; individualized support, 150; interactional inquiry, 108; organization, 109–10, 125, 168; small-group sessions, 109; space, 107
writing-intensive courses, 18, 80, 91–92, 133–34
writing-pedagogy research methodologies, 80

Yossa, Tara J., 141
Young, Vershawn Ashanti, 98

ABOUT THE AUTHORS

Joanne Baird Giordano is a professor of English at Salt Lake City Community College. She has published in many journals, including *CCC* and *TETYC*, as well as several anthologies on teaching and language practices in the classroom and in relation to institutional policies.

Jake Frye teaches developmental reading and writing. He helped create and continues to develop an accelerated precollege integrated reading and writing class that has shortened the developmental English sequence at Green River from twenty-five to ten credits. He continues to develop and implement more equitable placement practices in order to improve student placement into precollege and college-level coursework.

Rhonda Grego is a dean and English faculty member at Midlands Technical College in South Carolina. She has published articles in *CCC* and *Composition Studies*, among other places.

Brett Griffiths ("Griff") teaches reading, writing, and creative writing at Schoolcraft College. Her research focuses on college-level literacy and language instruction, faculty engagement and resilience, and the role of writing instruction in student success. Her scholarship has appeared in peer-reviewed scholarly journals, including *CCC*, *Pedagogy*, *TETYC*, *New Directions for Community Colleges*, *Community College Journal of Research and Practice*, and *WPA: Writing Program Administration*, as well as collected work, such as *Sixteen Teachers Teaching*.

Holly Hassel is a professor of English at North Dakota State University. She is the assistant chair of the Conference on College Composition and Communication and is past editor of *Teaching English in the Two-Year College*. She has published broadly.

Kirsten Higgins and **Anthony Warnke** teach basic writing and first-year composition at Green River College in Auburn, Washington. As cowriting program administrators, they designed an equity-focused accelerated learning program that helped revamp their department's developmental English sequence. Their scholarship has appeared in or is forthcoming from *Teaching English in the Two-Year College*, as well as edited collections on autoethnography and emotional labor in writing program administration.

Darin Jensen is an associate professor at Salt Lake Community College. His writing has appeared in a number of journals, including *New Directions for Community Colleges*, *Journal of Basic Writing Pedagogy*, *Composition Studies*, *College English*, *TETYC*, the *Journal of Developmental Education*, and *Writing on the Edge*. He coedited special issues of the *Basic Writing e-Journal* and the *WPA Journal*. He is the current editor of *Teaching English in the Two-Year College*. He is a coeditor of the *Teacher-Scholar-Activist* blog with Patrick Sullivan and Christie Toth, which won the 2018 John Lovas award from *Kairos* for best blog.

ABOUT THE AUTHORS

Jamila M. Kareem is a teacher-researcher who studies racialized social structures in academic communities and public social justice discourse. She is an assistant professor in the writing and rhetoric department at the University of Central Florida, where she teaches first-year writing and upper-division courses in rhetoric. Her essays have appeared in *Teaching English in the Two-Year College*, the *Journal of College Literacy and Learning*, *JAC: A Journal of Rhetoric, Culture, and Politics*, and the collection *The Good Life and the Greater Good in Global Context*.

Bernice Olivas is the winner of the 2021 CCCC Emergent Teacher award. She is an assistant professor at Salt Lake Community College in the Department of English, Linguistics, and Writing. Her work has appeared in *Teaching English in the Two-Year College*, *Assay*, and in the collection *Place-Conscious Citizenship*.

Mark Reynolds retired after thirty-seven years of teaching and administrative work at the community college now named Coastal Alabama in Brewton, Alabama. He is the author of several journal articles and essays on teaching writing and literature and on professional issues. He edited *Teaching English in the Two-Year College: Essays for a New Century* (NCTE 1994) and the collection *The Profession of English in the Two-Year College* (Heinemann 2005) with Sylvia Holliday. From 1994 to 2001, he edited *TETYC*. Over the course of his career, he served on multiple TYCA, NCTE, CCCC, and MLA committees. He continues to write professionally, mentor local writers, and advocate for those researching the history of two-year college English and appropriate graduate-level training for current and future two-year college faculty members.

Emily K. Suh is an assistant professor in the graduate program of developmental education at Texas State University. Emily taught developmental English and English as a Second Language at Southeast Community College in Nebraska for nine years. Her publications include articles in the *Journal of Basic Writing*, the *Journal of Developmental Education*, *Teaching English in the Two-Year College*, the *Journal of Developmental Education*, and the *Basic Writing e-Journal*, among others.

Patrick Sullivan teaches English at Manchester Community College in Manchester, Connecticut. His recent books include *Economic Inequality, Neoliberalism, and the American Community College* (Palgrave Macmillan 2017), *Democracy, Social Justice, and the American Community College* (Palgrave Macmillan 2021), and the edited collection *Sixteen Teachers Teaching: Two-Year College Perspectives* (Utah State University Press 2020).

www.ingramcontent.com/pod-product-compliance
Lightning Source LLC
Chambersburg PA
CBHW020530080526
44583CB00013B/805